Dear Jim—

Wishing you all the joys of a blessed Christmas.

Harold

1956

THE PHILOSOPHER AND MUSIC

The Philosopher and Music

A HISTORICAL OUTLINE

BY JULIUS PORTNOY

ASSISTANT PROFESSOR OF PHILOSOPHY
BROOKLYN COLLEGE

THE HUMANITIES PRESS

NEW YORK - 1954

TO ALFHILD

ACKNOWLEDGMENTS

I WISH to thank Professor Curt Sachs of New York University and Professor Thomas Munro, Editor of *The Journal of Aesthetics and Art Criticism,* for having read the manuscript. I shall always be grateful to both these scholars for their suggestions in the preparation of this work. To my wife, Alfhild Vold Portnoy, I owe a debt of gratitude for helping me in the organization and editing of this book.

I also wish to thank the following publishers for granting me permission to quote from their respective publications. George Allen and Unwin Ltd., *Nietzsche's Genealogy of Morals;* Basil Blackwell, *The Pre-Socratic Philosophers,* by Kathleen Freeman; The Catholic Education Press, *Motu Proprio;* The Clarendon Press, Oxford, *The Harmonics of Aristoxenus,* by H. S. Macran; Columbia University Press, *The Philosophy of Marsilio Ficino,* by Paul Oskar Kristeller; Faber and Faber Ltd., *Plotinus' Enneads,* translated by Stephen Mackenna; Hafner Publishing Co. Inc., *St. Augustine's City of God,* translated by Marcus Dods; *Art of Poetry,* Albert S. Cook edition; Harvard University Press, *Aristotle, On the Heavens; Poetics of Music,* by Igor Stravinsky; *The Journal of Aesthetics and Art Criticism, Nicholas of Cusa on the Meaning of Music,* by Kathi Meyer-Baer; *Similarities of Musical Concepts in Ancient and Medieval Philosophy,* by Julius Portnoy; *Platonic Echoes in Soviet Musical Criticism,* by Julius Portnoy; Loeb Classical Library, *Plutarch's Lives,* translated by Bernadotte Perrin; *De Oratore,* translated by H. Rackham; *Quintilian,* translated by H. E. Butler; *Longinus, On the Sublime,* translated by W. H. Fyfe; *St. Augustine, Confessions,* translated by William Watts; Macmillan and Co.

Ltd., *Kant's Critique of Judgement*, translated by J. H. Bernard; *The Musical Quarterly*, *Music in the Philosophy of Boethius*, by Leo S. Schrade; *Luther on Music*, by Walter Buszin; The Modern Library, *The Wisdom of Confucius*, translated by Lin Yutang; *The Philosophy of Schopenhauer*; *The Philosophy of Nietzsche*; W. W. Norton and Co. Inc., *The Rise of Music in the Ancient World East and West*, by Curt Sachs; *The Music of Israel*, by Peter Gradenwitz; *Source Readings in Music History*, by Oliver Strunk; *Music in the Baroque Era*, by Manfred F. Bukofzer; *Music in the Romantic Era*, by Alfred Einstein; Oxford University Press, *Oxford History of Music*; *Philosophies of Beauty*, by E. F. Carritt; Oxford University Press Inc. (New York), *The Basic Works of Aristotle*, edited by Richard McKeon; *The Dialogues of Plato*, translated by B. Jowett; Philosophical Library, *Style and Idea*, by Arnold Schönberg; William Reeves, *Historical Facts for the Arabian Musical Influence*, by Henry George Farmer; Charles Scribner's Sons, *Art and Scholasticism*, by Jacques Maritain.

INTRODUCTION

THE historical development of music in Western civilization has been influenced to a great extent by the writings of the philosophers. We shall find in the forthcoming pages of this book that although the philosophers were generally theoreticians who were not technically trained to evaluate the actual structure of music, they nevertheless had much to say about music and the effects which the art of music had upon human behavior. The extent to which the theories of the philosophers have influenced the course of music in Western civilization can be readily found in the social, cultural and religious life of Western man.

The ancient philosopher viewed music as something more than an expression of feeling. He was not content to accept music as an artistic form of communication through which the musical poet of antiquity conveyed his emotional moods and ideas to others. The Greek philosopher attempted instead to find out if music had its origin in some "higher source" which transcended human understanding. He believed that he detected moral overtones in melody and ethical significance in rhythms. He observed the effects of music upon human behavior and decided that music could improve or degrade character. Since he was ill equipped to understand the actual music itself, he attributed mystical qualities to the origin and powers of music. Because he mistrusted the emotions and exalted reason, he feared the effects which vivacious rhythms and sensuous tonalities could have on the body and mind. He deduced that rhythm and melody were an imitation of the movements of the celestial bodies which moved through the heavens emitting a divine music which was imperceptible to human ears. On the basis of this assumption, he concluded that the art of music was imitative of the laws of nature and since a moral order pervaded the universe, then music had moral value.

The fanciful imagery and moralistic tenets which the ancient philosopher ascribed to music were embellished in the writings of the Christians. The fathers of the Church, and the leaders of the Reformation after them, gave up the picturesque theory of the harmony of the spheres as the divine source of music for the belief that music was bestowed upon man by a benevolent Being for the purpose of enhancing the Word of God. In our own day, the utterances of the ancient philosophers have been modified and more empirically applied. The Greek doctrine of ethos is analyzed in terms of ideology and the Athenian use of music as a means of education has become a form of political edification.

This book does not purport to be a history of music or an outline of philosophy. Above all, it does not make any pretense of being a musicological study. The purpose of this book is to give a historical presentation of the origins and development of the aesthetics of music in Western civilization. It is the contention of the author that the aesthetics of Western music is rooted in the philosophy of Plato and that the writings of this Greek philosopher still exert a marked influence on music in our day.

It might be argued that there is little to be gained in pointing out similarities of musical concepts between the ancients and the moderns for the simple reason that the music of the Greeks and the highly complex music of the moderns are of a different emotional pitch. Nothing could be further from the truth than to suppose that the simple music of the Greek bard, by which he embellished his poetry with song, did not have the same kind of emotional appeal for his listeners as the highly complex music of the modern composer has for us.

The aesthetic principles by which we evaluate our music are based on the writings of the Greek philosophers. However these ancient philosophers may have impeded the development of music with their fanciful speculations, they have nevertheless given us criteria of values with which to formulate a judgment about music. But more than that, the Greek philosopher was concerned with the very problems pertaining to the music of his time that we in our own civilization are concerned with at present. The similarities of musical concepts in ancient, medieval and modern aesthetics are variations on the original theme which Plato included as a necessary prerequisite for the creation of an ideal society and the begetting of the ideal man.

The philosopher has mainly evaluated music, up until the eighteenth century, in terms of metaphysics, ethics and mathematics. He has thwarted the creative musician at every turn by his defence of traditional values and by his zealous retention of the status quo. The philosopher has been quick to question musical change and he has taken it upon himself to evaluate new music in the light of the old. He has left behind a legacy of intellectual arguments which the theologian and statesman have used effectively to combat new musical ideas which might threaten the stability of the liturgy or the political status quo. The few philosophic voices which have cried out against such prevailing aesthetic views on music have insisted that music signified nothing beyond itself; that it was not a subject for metaphysics, a matter of ethics, a means of educational discipline, or a political expedient.

The composer has stood up to authority throughout history even if he has, in the past, and must, in the present, compromise his aesthetic position to survive under the decrees of a Bull, the whims of a patron, or the resolutions of a political committee. The composer has been a slave to morality and religion, a lackey to a wealthy patron, a dispenser of ideology; but for all that, he has never been a fully obedient handmaid to any of these. He has by his very nature been consumed with the intense need for personal expression and has been imbued with a desire to vent his feelings. This conflict between thought and feeling, reason and judgment, between the philosopher and the composer has been an everlasting one throughout history.

It is possible to set up a system of values for an aesthetics of music which is not based on ancient doctrine but on humanistic values. Such a system of musical values can be achieved by discarding the outmoded myths which have shrouded the creation and appreciation of music and by guiding ourselves by the principle that music is fundamentally the expression of feeling in a stylized art form of rhythm and tone. Music is born of feeling to appeal to feeling. It is created out of emotion to move the emotions. Music is rooted in the soil of reality. It is the product of human experience even if it transcends experience by crystallizing feeling into sensuous tones and moving rhythms that can transport us to rarefied heights of momentary rapture. Music can give us relief from anxiety. Music is a medium of communication that is more emotionally effective and provocative than any other form of expression that has been devised by man with which to impart his feelings and ideas to others. Music embodies our hopes and aspirations, our anguish and despair. We can only get from music what we bring to it in sensitivity and understanding. However much the philosophers have written about music, they have nevertheless had less to say about it than any of the other arts for the very reason that the emotion which music evokes in us does not lend itself to rationalization as easily as the conceptualized arts of poetry or the drama.

The philosopher has given music a low status in the category of the arts for the very reason that music deals primarily with feeling, not reason; with emotion, not intellect; with imagination, not concepts. The philosopher has persistently believed throughout history, with few exceptions, that music without words is inferior to music with words. Pure instrumental music is vague and indefinite. It is the embodiment of emotion in tone and rhythm that awakens in us feelings that the composer felt to some degree when producing the music. But the philosopher is never sure that feeling can be trusted. He insists that words added to music conceptualize feeling, make the indefinite definite, and move the art of music from the lower level of emotion to the exalted plane of reason.

CONTENTS

THE PHILOSOPHER AND MUSIC

CHAPTER I

THE GREEKS

SECTION I—*The Pre-Socratics*

THERE is very little that we actually know about the music of that era in ancient history which corresponds to the time known as the pre-Socratic period in philosophy. What is known is fragmentary and can only be gleaned from the writings of the philosophers and the poets since the music itself is not extant. The study of pre-Socratic philosophy begins with Thales in the seventh century B.C. In the following century, Pythagoras established a school of systematic philosophy. This school was as much concerned with the ethical value of music and the empirical structure of musical tones as it was with the establishment of number as the true reality. The poets, as early as Homer in the ninth century B.C., have left us meager but precious fragments, more picturesque than real, pertaining to the music of the ancients. A history of the aesthetics of music can only begin by presenting this fragmentary material as gathered from these ancient writings and by arranging it in its proper historical order.

Our earliest knowledge of music in Western civilization stems from the writings of the Greek philosophers. What they had to say about music is not altogether original since views similar to theirs were held by the Egyptian priesthood and the wise men of the Orient long before the Golden Age of Greece. The contribution of the Greek philosophers lay in their systematization of the musical theories of their predecessors, thus leaving us a heritage of ancient musical philosophies. But when the Greek bard imaginatively altered these traditional musical values of the old world to fit Hellenic culture, the philosopher took it upon himself to become a protector of the past. He evaluated the new music on moral and metaphysical grounds and passed resounding judgments which still have their overtones in the music of our own day.

We must remember, when speaking of Greek music, that the Greek bard was both a poet and musician who did not separate the music from the poem. The poems of Homer, the odes of Pindar, were never recited except to music. The Greek poet and musician were one and his music was so completely dependent on the text that each single note was allied to each syllable of the spoken word.

The word music itself is of Greek origin and was in myth-like fashion originally considered an art which was directly inspired by and descended from a Muse. The early Greeks had three Muses to begin with: study, memory and song, but with the passing of time each art medium came to have a Mother Muse. Pre-Homeric legend has it that Orpheus the sweet singer and bard servant of Apollo, was himself the son of a Muse. The magic quality of his voice could heal the sick and engender religious devotion at the temple rites. In speaking of the sophist, Protagoras, Plato noted the entrancing effect which the rhetoric of Protagoras and similarly the songs of Orpheus had upon those who came within hearing.[1] Museus, the pupil of Orpheus, was described by Aristophanes as a physician of the soul who, we may assume, achieved his cures through the charm of the paeans which legend attributed to him. Aristotle had him say that "Song is to mortals of all things the sweetest",[2] and then went on to add, with reference to Museus, that music could serve as a means which could offer man relief from his toil.

---

[1] *Protagoras*, 315.
[2] *Politics*, 1339b.

Homer characterized the minstrels in the *Odyssey* as the favored mortals of the gods. The Muse endowed them with song not only to gladden the hearts of men but to watch over the morals of mankind.[3] Minstrels were the earthly intermediaries who made the will of the gods known to man. Through music, man, in turn, could implore the gods for deliverance from sickness and pestilence. Homer told, and Plutarch centuries later retold,[4] how the Grecians stopped the fury of a pestilence through the power and charm of music to appease the wrath of the gods "With sacred hymns and songs that sweetly please".

Hesiod, who lived about the 8th century B.C., retained the Homeric relation of the bard to his Muse. He told us that the Muses appeared to him while he fed his father's flock and commissioned him to be their prophet and poet. They gave him "the rhapsode's staff to betoken his mission as a singer" and before parting from him said "We know how to tell many falsehoods that sound like the truth; But we also know how to utter the truth when we choose." Little wonder that in the following century the philosopher Thales denounced Homeric legend as a distortion of reality which shied away from the truth. He accused Homer of not only creating mythical gods and inspiring muses but also of clothing them with divine attributes. Worse yet, to Thales, Homer believed that all mortals were subject to the caprice and whims of the gods and employed his artistic talents to admonish man to place his destiny in the hands of the gods. Hesiod took a more humanistic attitude towards the diviners of men but not enough so to please Thales, whom Aristotle called the father of ancient philosophy. Thales would have the Greek bard center his talents solely on the needs of man rather than to create hymns for non-existent deities.

In the same century, Xenophanes (c. 570 B.C.) of the Eleatic school of philosophy, like Thales, denounced the gods of Homer and Hesiod. Quite adroit at using the weapon of satire, he composed poetry that was vitriolic and revolutionary

---

[3] *Odyssey*, Bk. VIII, 64 (Translated by A. T. Murray); William Heinemann, London: 1931. ". . . whom the Muse loved above all other men, and gave him both good and evil; of his sight she deprived him, but gave him the gift of sweet song."

[4] *Concerning Music*, 42.

in its suggested social reform. He blamed all the human ills of his time on Homer and Hesiod who "have ascribed to the gods all things that are a shame and a disgrace among mortals, stealings and adultries, and deceivings of one another". All this lay in the fact that the earlier poets represented the gods in human form. "Men make gods in their own images; . . . If horses or oxen or lions had hands and could produce works of art, they too would represent the gods after their own fashion." These poetic illusions must be done away with, argued Xenophanes, "if social life is to be reformed." The statesman, Solon (638–558 B.C.), composed verse lamenting the inequality of man and his gods. Solon further applied his humanistic philosophy to Athenian music. He believed that it was possible to foster morality and citizenship through music which in turn would strengthen the State and make men less dependent on the whimsical gods. Alcaeus (600 B.C.), expressing the spirit of the century, composed hymns and political poems in which he abused the tyrants and his political enemies. With his famed contemporary, Sappho (c. 600 B.C.), he wrote love songs and drinking songs for the brilliant court of Lesbos. It was also in the 7th century that an outstanding musical figure and apostle of change, Archilochus by name, employed occasional musical dissonances and added new rhythmic meters to poetic verse.

Archilochus is credited with making a three-fold contribution to Greek music which is of great aesthetic significance. Through the use of a quickened tempo and the introduction of new rhythmic patterns Archilochus enhanced the music of his time with a mobility which it presumably lacked. Later writers credited him with introducing lively iambic meters and complicated changing rhythms, with the inclusion of speech like parts between melodic sections. History also attributes to Archilochus the advancement of the lyric song which was sung to the accompaniment of the lyre. The widespread nature of folk-art which prevailed in his time quite likely enabled him to draw much of his inspiration from the folk-lore and songs of the people. Archilochus also employed occasional dissonance by having the accompanying instrument play notes which were not in unison with the melody. This primitive form of polyphony was characterized as a degenerate cacophony by the traditionalists.

But in the following century, Pindar (c. 522–443 B.C.) refuted the irreligious views of the philosophers in his choral odes by imaginatively adding that the same mother nurtured both the gods and man, but the former were the privileged members of the earthly family who knew no death or human misery. Therefore warned Pindar, it is blasphemy to ape the gods and so "Seek not to become Zeus, mortal things befit a mortal." As an able music student of Apollodorus and the famed Lasus of Hermione, Pindar was well equipped by religious conviction and musical ability to praise the gods through song and verse. He told us that "near the vestibule of his home choruses of maidens used to dance and sing by night in praise of the mother of the gods."

The philosopher then asked the poet-musician "who is the mother of the gods?" Is it the primitive element, the one that precedes and from which all the others are generated? It seemed that the philosopher, in querying the beginning and nature of the universe, was actually altering the poetic terminology of Homer and Hesiod and calling the gods elements.

Pythagoras (c. 6th cent. B.C.) holds the enviable distinction of being the father of Greek musical science and the founder of an esoteric school of philosophy. There was a widespread belief in antiquity that in order not to divulge the secrets of his order, he left no writings. It is quite probable that Pythagoras was a well versed mathematician and scientist who formed his school as a religious brotherhood in which morality and politics were studied along with philosophy and the science of sound and motion. In his efforts to fathom the secrets of the universe, Pythagoras evolved the metaphysical belief that numbers were the true realities. His disciples became even more mystical and added that numbers were the very essences which constituted and governed all nature. Since man was part of nature, he was the embodiment of a combination of numbers and was numerically related to nature as a part is to the whole. He was what he was because of his numerical components. In nature, as in the arts which man created for his needs, proportion, symmetry, harmony and dissonance were born of mathematical relationships. Music was therefore a unity composed of numerical relationships and since numbers inherently possessed moral attributes, because nature was intrinsically good, music must be evaluated in moral terms. If the components of music had moral attributes, argued the Pythagoreans, then music itself had moral value. This moral conception of music tinged the Greek writings on the aesthetics of music with a doctrine of ethos which reached its fullest development and theoretical application in Plato. Aristotle said of the Pythagoreans: "they saw that the modifications and the ratios of the musical scales were expressible in numbers;—since, then, all other things seemed in their whole nature to be modelled on numbers, and numbers seemed to be the first things in the whole of nature, they supposed the elements of numbers to be the elements of all things, and the whole heaven to be a musical scale and a number."[5]

There is good reason to believe that Pythagoras travelled in Egypt studying the sciences and musical philosophy of the Pharaohs, just as the historian Herodotus did in the fifth century. Pythagoras probably came back to Greece with some elementary acoustical theories as well as definite ethical beliefs concerning music which he acquired from the Egyptian priesthood. He began to teach that mortal music was an earthly prototype of the celestial harmony of the spheres. The later Pythagoreans held that the heavens were a harmony which actually made music. As these heavenly bodies travelled through the skies the speed with which they moved caused them to give out blending sounds as though they were a celestial choir. These heavenly bodies emitted a series of sounds which were related to each other like the notes of the scale. The reason that we cannot hear them is because we have always been accustomed to them.[6]

---

[5] *Metaphysica, Bk.* I, Chap. V, p. 698; (translated by W. D. Ross), Random House, New York: 1941.

[6] "...the harmony of the spheres differs basically from the original theory of co-ordination. This latter had established that a certain planet was to another planet as a certain pitch was to another pitch; the harmony of the spheres meant something quite different: the planets, or rather their spheres, resounded in actual, though imperceptible, tones." Curt Sachs, *The Rise of Music in the*

Legend has it that Pythagoras discovered the octave and then deduced the intervals in the octave through a unique series of experiments in which he applied the knowledge he had gathered in his travels to fertile ideas of his own. Pythagoras found that in (1) stretching a taut string over a piece of wood; (2) placing his finger in the exact center of this monochord; (3) plucking it; each half of the string vibrated twice as fast as the whole

Ancient World East and West, p. 111; W. W. Norton and Co., Inc., New York: 1943.

"...the idea of a harmony of spheres took firm root in the minds of both the Greeks and the later Jewish philosophers, who could quote in support a passage in the Book of Job (38:7): '. . . the morning stars sang together, and all the sons of God shouted for joy.' Greek and Arab authors said that only Pythagoras had been able to hear the celestial harmonies, but a Jewish source (Philo Judaeus 2:299) ascribed the same capacity to Moses . . ." Peter Gradenwitz, The Music of Israel, p. 107; W. W. Norton and Co., Inc., New York: 1949.

Aristotle in the De caelo (290 b 12-29) refuted the Pythagorean theory of the harmony of the spheres which rests on the assumption that movement is necessarily accompanied by sound, and that sound emitted by the moving stars must be in relation to their size and speed. The Pythagoreans and Plato also held that the intervals between the planets and the spheres of fixed stars corresponded mathematically to the intervals between the notes of the octave. The sound which was produced was musical. "To the objection that we do not hear this music it is answered that we cannot expect to be aware of a sound which was going on when we were born and has continued without intermission ever since. It is only by contrast with intervals of silence that a sound becomes perceptible." Aristotle, On The Heavens, Bk. II, Chap. IX, p. 190; Harvard University Press, Cambridge: 1939.

The Renaissance came to Western civilization with the rebirth of Aristotelian realism and humanism over against the mysticism and authority of Platonism. In 1477 Tinctoris, churchman and musical theorist wrote: ". . . I cannot pass over in silence the opinion of numerous philosophers, among them Plato and Pythagoras and their successors Cicero, Macrobius, Boethius, and our Isidore, that the spheres of the stars revolve under the guidance of harmonic modulation, that is, by the consonance of various concords. But when, as Boethius relates, some declare that Saturn moves with the deepest sound and that, as we pass by stages through the remaining planets, the moon moves with the highest, while others, conversely, ascribe the deepest sound to the moon and the highest to the sphere of the fixed stars, I put faith in neither opinion. Rather I unshakeably credit Aristotle and his commentator, (St. Thomas Aquinas) along with our more recent philosophers, who most manifestly prove that in the heavens there is neither actual nor potential sound. For this reason it will never be possible to persuade me that musical concords, which cannot be produced without sound, can result from the motion of the heavenly bodies." Oliver Strunk, Source Readings in Music History, p. 198; W. W. Norton and Co., Inc., New York: 1950.

string, thus producing a tone which sounded like the original one emitted from the full string but on a higher level of pitch. He then applied this method to strings of the same thickness and tension and found that the lengths of the strings governed the tone but that the physical properties of the octave could be explained through the exact division of the string, be it of whatever length or thickness. But then how to fill in the upper and lower tones of the octave? Pythagoras further learned that if he held the string at a point representing the ratio of 3:4, he would get the interval of a musical fourth; and that through the ratio of 2:3 he would get the musical fifth. He regarded the octave, fourth and fifth as consonant tonalities and the third and sixth as dissonant tonalities.

Archytas of Tarentum who lived in the first half of the fourth century as a contemporary of Plato was said to have paid more attention to the physical study of music than did any of the Pythagoreans. His writings on music, which are much and varied, recorded not only his own findings and calculations, but those of other Pythagoreans who were experimenting arithmetically with the numerical ratios corresponding to the octave, fourth and fifth. Archytas first pointed out that no sound is produced without the impact or striking of one object on another. Secondly, he maintained, that "there are numerous sounds which are outside the range of our natural perception, because of the weakness of the impact producing them, or the distance of the subject from the source of the sound, or even because the sound is too loud." Thirdly, concluded Archytas, "Difference in pitch is due to the rate of motion communicated to the air by the blow: rapid motion gives high pitch, slower motion gives lower pitch." In support of these acoustical theories, he gave several illustrations: "the human voice, the note of the reed and the flute, the sound of the drum used in religious ceremonies." Although Archytas was deeply imbued with "the manifold wonders wrought by Number, there is no hint of any religious or magical" interpretation of numerical relationships in his writings as was the case among his fellow Pythagoreans. Acoustically, "he worked out the numerical ratios corresponding to the intervals between the notes of the tetrachord for three different types of scale: the enharmonic, the chromatic, and the diatonic." Aesthetically, he held that "The rational attributes of Number and Harmony are sufficiently wonderful in themselves;" and so he concluded, in contrast to the accepted view of his day, that in education, literature should be subordinated to music.[7]

Pericles, the builder of the Athenian empire, had gathered around him the outstanding philosophic, literary and artistic figures of his day. Phidias, the sculptor, the historians Herodotus and Thucydides, and the playwrights, Sophocles and Euripides, who championed the cause of the musical innovators, all adorned the life of Athens with their distinguished presence. In this atmosphere, the philosopher Anaxagoras maintained a profound contempt for official religion which he voiced under the guidance of his friend and enlightened protector, Pericles. Damon, whom Plato quoted in the *Republic* as a musical authority and practicing artist, shared in the cultural life of the Periclean court. In his capacity as teacher and close friend to Pericles, he assigned an important function to music in the training of character and the making of a good citizen. Damon believed that the penetrating effect of music "could not only arouse or allay different emotions, but also inculcate all the virtues— courage, self-restraint, and even justice." The quality of a musical composition would leave its mark on the soul, for good or evil both on the part of the performer and listener. Through appropriate harmonies, new characteristics could be created, or latent ones drawn out, not only in the young but also in adults.[8]

[7] Kathleen Freeman, *The Pre-Socratic Philosophers*, pp. 237-239; Basil Blackwell, Oxford: 1949.

[8] *Ibid.*, pp. 207-208.

"Music, therefore, is essential not only to a liberal education, but also to the common weal: he went so far as to say that no innovation in musical fashion is possible without a resulting change in the most important political institutions. Plato records this opinion in the *Republic*: Socrates is depicted as in full agreement with it, and Adeimantus is made to add that through music 'lawlessness creeps in unawares' in the guise of amusement, and after corrupting manners proceeds to undermine contracts, laws and constitutions until it overturns everything, public and private. These views doubtless represent the teaching of Damon and his pupils.

"A longer passage in the *Republic,* in which details are purposely left vague by Plato, hints at Damon's analysis of the components of music, such as

Damon considered music essential not only for a liberal education but also for the attainment of a sound state. In contrast to
the democratic spirit of the Periclean age, he paradoxically
taught that innovation in musical styles and rhythms carried a
warning of social change or even revolution. It was his contention, that if the Greek bard altered or varied artistic styles or
musical modes so as to alter or vary the traditional patterns of
musical expression, the emotional impact of these innovations
upon society would in turn influence cultural and social change.
Music, concluded Damon in agreement with the Pythagoreans,
had ethical value which should be utilized in the attainment of
a sound morality.

Democritus (b. c. 460 B.C.) held that the poet-musician was
blessed with divine reason. He praised Homer as a divinely
inspired poet whose creations expressed a beauty born of an
enraptured soul. Democritus described music as the youngest of
the arts which arose not from "necessity but from superfluity."
Like the statesman Solon he saw in music an educational and
social force which could enable man to strike a balance between
gymnastics and letters. Democritus believed with the Pythagoreans that the artist stood midway between the gods and man
and that it was the divined role of the inspired artist to help
man attune his soul to the universal soul through the rhythm
and grace of music.[9]

---

rhythm, foot, short and long syllable: to all these, both singly and in combination, he gave a moral value. A good education will banish those elements
which are akin to vice and excess, and will retain those akin to virtue and
order. Plato clearly approved of Damon's teaching; he makes the general
Laches commend Damon to Nicias as a teacher not only of music, but of
every other subject that is worthy of pursuit by young boys."

[9] Oliver Strunk, *Source Readings in Music History*, p. 83; W. W. Norton
and Co., Inc., New York: 1950.

The Roman philosopher Boethius who transmitted the musical aesthetics of
the Greeks to the Middle Ages wrote: ". . . the power of the art of music
became so evident through the studies of ancient philosophy that the Pythagoreans used to free themselves from the cares of the day by certain melodies,
which caused a gentle and quiet slumber to steal upon them. Similarly, upon
rising, they dispelled the stupor and confusion of sleep by certain other
melodies, knowing that the whole structure of soul and body is united by
musical harmony. For the impulses of the soul are stirred by emotions corresponding to the state of the body, as Democritus is said to have informed the
physician Hippocrates, . . ."

Socrates (469–399 B.C.), formerly a sculptor and the son of a sculptor, who turned to philosophy so that he could devote his life to educating the youth of Athens was depicted by Plato in the *Republic* as fully agreeing with the views of Damon on the ethical, political and educational value of music. A philosophy which made ordinary existence meaningful and purposeful, reasoned Socrates, was the most exalted of the philosophies. Music had the power to mould the souls of the young, to prepare them for such a life. Just as society could be fashioned after a "pattern in the heavens", Socrates believed, so music could attune the human soul to synchronize with this very pattern which permeated the behavior and activity of the heavenly bodies.

Although Socrates opposed the oratory of the Sophists he yet agreed with Protagoras that metaphysics could only lead one to scepticism and that mathematics was only barren speculation. He thereupon gave up the remainder of his life to the study of morality and education. Socrates came to believe that human salvation lay in creating such a cultural and enlightened intellectual life as to free man from superstition, false reasoning and prejudice. But such license, such freedom of thought was unknown even in free democratic Athens. In a short time, the conservative Athenian element turned against him. Aristophanes, who devoted a good part of his life to safeguarding tradition, looked upon Socrates as one more symbol of what he believed to be a chaotic culture which was settling upon Athens. Just as Aristophanes had ridiculed musical innovations in his poetry so he mocked Socratic philosophy in his derisive play the *Clouds*. Since Socrates questioned the role of the gods and queried the virtues of Greek democracy, he was charged with perverting the minds of Athenian youth and condemned to death.

During the closing hours of his life Socrates related a dream which came to him as he lay sleeping in his prison cell and which his pupil Plato recorded in the *Phaedo*.[10] "In the course of my life I have often had intimations in dreams 'that I should compose music.' The same dream came to me sometimes in one form, and sometimes in another, but always saying the same or

---

[10] 61; (Translated by Benjamin Jowett), Random House, New York: 1937.

nearly the same words: 'Cultivate and make music,' said the dream. And hitherto I had imagined that this was only intended to exhort and encourage me in the study of philosophy, which has been the pursuit of my life, and is the noblest and best of music." Socrates questioned a belief here, which had come to be accepted as an educational principle among the followers of Damon, that the study of music should only be utilized as a mathematical discipline in preparation for the noble study of philosophy. It was also implicit in this dream confession, Friedrich Nietzsche related in *The Birth of Tragedy From the Spirit of Greek Music*, that under the shadow of death, it became clear to him that dialectic, logic and reason had their limitations in the acquisition of knowledge and the pursuit of the good life. The power of music could bring us closer to ultimate truth than could science, for music helps us to achieve a harmonious union with nature.

SECTION II—*Plato*

THE writings of the Greek philosophers display conceptual similarities with the respective musical beliefs of the Egyptians, the Chinese and the Hebrews. Philosophies of music which may have had their origin in civilizations some 1500 years prior to the birth of Christ found their way into Greek thought.

Plato (427–347 B.C.) is the most notable of the Western philosophers to maintain that music, in both the classic and modern sense, should be used for the attainment of a sound morality. He was not altogether original in his views on the place of music in a well ordered society. Nor was he the first to consider the ethical implications that music presumably has upon character and human behavior. Yet, Plato remains an invaluable historical figure to whom we must turn for a starting point if we would develop an aesthetics of music in Western civilization. Not only do his writings contain a synthesis of the musical theories of the ancient East and West as well as those of his own day, but they bring together the musical practices of the Athenian generation which preceded his own.[11]

---

[11] *Protagoras*, 326.

We do not know whether Plato had any actual knowledge of the philosophy which Confucius had taught in the East. The similarity of their philosophies of music may be mere coincidence, but numerous passages which originally appeared in Confucius are all but restated by Plato. In a passage which has reference to ethics and religion Confucius wrote: "The music of Cheng is lewd and corrupting, the music of Sung is soft and makes one effeminate, the music of Wei is repetitious and annoying, and the music of Ch'i is harsh and makes one haughty. These four kinds of music are all sensual music and undermine people's character, and that is why they cannot be used at the sacrifices."[12] In the third book of the *Republic*, Plato stressed the ethical implications of music in a strikingly similar way.[13] He advocated that the Ionian and Lydian modes should be banished from the State since they were of an effeminate, soft, and relaxing character. The Dorian and Phrygian modes that were military in tone should be retained. Plato thereby began to construct his system of a musical aesthetics by attributing morality to the Greek modes. ". . . rhythms and music in general," he concluded in the *Laws*, in a manner similar to Confucius, "are imitations of good and evil characters in men".[14]

Plato held to the view that music should be one more educational means in the establishment of virtue and morality. He regarded music as being superior to the other arts on the premise that rhythm and melody more strongly affected the inner soul and emotional life of man than architecture, painting, or sculpture. A child thus exposed to the proper musical modes would unconsciously develop discriminating habits and abilities which would allow him to distinguish good from evil. After music had moulded the character of the child and made him emotionally stable, the study of philosophy would reveal to him in full consciousness the highest knowledge.

Music and gymnastics had a vital role in Platonic education. He reasoned that music should not follow gymnastics, rather,

---

[12] *The Wisdom of Confucius*, p. 264; (Translated by Lin Yutang), The Modern Library, New York: 1938.
[13] 399.
[14] *Bk.* VII, 798.

music should precede and dominate gymnastics because the body did not ennoble the soul. On the contrary, it was the function of the soul to mould the body. Furthermore, gymnastics could become coarse and lead to rowdiness and so it must be tempered with music. Music without gymnastics might produce effeminate aesthetes. Therefore, temperance and modulation of music and gymnastics would produce a well-balanced Athenian youth.

Many musical innovations had taken place during Plato's lifetime which he neither appreciated nor tolerated. He approved only of the traditional practice of writing lyric poetry which was to be recited or sung to a musical accompaniment. Poetry and music "blest pair of sirens" were inseparable sisters in Greek cultural life. The word "music" designated both the poetry and the melody. Plato considered the one more important than the other and maintained that since language was the direct expression of reason, the word or poetic line must be of a higher level than the melody. The poetic text is born of reason, while the melody is merely pleasing to the senses and is thus of a lower plane.

The Greeks did not possess a harmonic system as we know it. Melody was thoroughly dependent and followed the text closely. Greek music was so constructed that one note was normally set to each syllable and every syllable was conventionally treated as either 'long' or 'short', the long syllable being equal to two short ones. By the time Plato had begun to write, the growing practice of using the poem as a libretto and distorting the words to suit the music had already aroused protest.[15] Plato was the most vociferous of the protestors, but he was not alone in this view.

Plato retained the traditional Greek attitude that lyric and tune should not be separated from one another. To the Greek bard who faithfully followed in the traditional classic vein any such distinction would have been purely academic since poet and musician were one and the same person who composed and performed his ode as a musically rhythmic poetic legend or deed. Since Plato emphasized the superior value of the text by sub-

---

[15] Francis Macdonald Cornford, *The Republic of Plato*, p. 83; The Clarendon Press, Oxford: 1942.

ordinating the musical form to poetry, he was particularly displeased with those revolutionary musicians in his day who were actually creating music without words for the sheer sake of hearing pleasant sounds. "When there are no words", he wrote, "it is very difficult to recognize the meaning of the harmony and rhythm, or to see that any worthy object is imitated by them."[16]

Plato was most vitriolic in denouncing musical innovation. Although he was a creative artist in his own right, he yet retained a fanatical mistrust of the erratic artist whose restless cravings were constantly manifesting themselves by changing artistic forms. Plato feared that artistic license could only lead

[16] *Laws*, Bk. II, 669-670.

"Music is more celebrated than any other kind of imitation, and therefore requires the greatest care of them all. For if a man makes a mistake here, he may do himself the greatest injury by welcoming evil dispositions, and the mistake may be very difficult to discern, because the poets are artists very inferior in character to the Muses themselves, who would never fall into the monstrous error of assigning to the words of men the gestures and songs of women; nor after combining the melodies with the gestures of freemen would they add on the rhythms of slaves and men of the baser sort; nor, beginning with the rhythms and gestures of freemen, would they assign to them a melody or words which are of an opposite character; nor would they mix up the voices and sounds of animals and of men and instruments, and every other sort of noise, as if they were all one. But human poets are fond of introducing this sort of inconsistent mixture, and so make themselves ridiculous in the eyes of those who, as Orpheus says, 'are ripe for true pleasure.' The experienced see all this confusion, and yet the poets go on and make still further havoc by separating the rhythm and the figure of the dance from the melody, setting bare words to metre, and also separating the melody and the rhythm from the words, using the lyre or the flute alone. For when there are no words, it is very difficult to recognize the meaning of the harmony and rhythm, or to see that any worthy object is imitated by them. And we must acknowledge that all this sort of thing, which aims only at swiftness and smoothness and a brutish noise, and uses the flute and the lyre not as the mere accompaniments of the dance and song, is exceedingly coarse and tasteless. The use of either instrument, when unaccompanied, leads to every sort of irregularity and trickery. This is all rational enough. But we are considering not how our choristers, who are from thirty to fifty years of age, and may be over fifty, are not to use the Muses, but how they are to use them. And the considerations which we have urged seem to show in what way these fifty year-old choristers who are to sing, may be expected to be better trained. For they need to have a quick perception and knowledge of harmonies and rhythms; otherwise, how can they ever know whether a melody would be rightly sung to the Dorian mode, or to the rhythm which the poet has assigned to it?"

to anarchy in the State. It was on the basis of this conviction that he wrote in the fourth book of the *Republic*: "the attention of our rulers should be directed,—that music and gymnastic be preserved in their original form, and no innovation made. They must do their utmost to maintain them intact. And when anyone says that mankind most regard 'The newest song which the singers have,' they will be afraid that he may be praising, not new songs, but a new kind of song; and this ought not to be praised, or conceived to be the meaning of the poet; for any musical innovation is full of danger to the whole State, and ought to be prohibited. So Damon tells me, and I can quite believe him;—he says that when modes of music change, the fundamental laws of the State always change with them."[17]

Philosophic and religious censure of change had been as much in evidence in the East as it was in the West. Pythagoras had related that the High Priests of Pharaoh vehemently protested against the innovations of musical virtuosi. The priests argued that the artistic change was artificial and therefore dangerous to the spiritual and physical life of the nation.

Herodotus had also related that the Egyptians considered their religious melodies as being sacred in origin and for that reason would not allow any innovations or admit foreign tunes into their devotional services. Plato elaborated on this theme in the *Laws*[18] by adding that the Egyptians accredited their sacred melodies to the Goddess Isis". He then went on to praise the Egyptians for their ability to create melodies which had the power to subdue primitive passions in man and to purify the spirit. The implication is that only strictly tempered musical modes and tunes that were emotionally affective because of their direct simplicity were worthwhile.

Musical simplicity was not incongruous with natural law, argued Plato. His numerous comments on music imply that music could help man to rhythmically attune his finite soul with the infinite, through gracefully blending his thoughts and actions with the celestial bodies comprising the harmony of the spheres. Raucous cacophony was not only foreign to Greek culture,

[17] 424.
[18] *Bk.* II, 657.

concluded Plato,[19] but caused the human soul to clash with the ideal order of things.

Plato distrusted the power of music over human emotions, a power which he considered comparable to that of sorcery. He regarded the musical pipes (called flutes ordinarily in English translations) as particularly seductive and he wrote that the many-stringed instruments that were coming into vogue engendered confusion in the listener. He believed that only the traditional lyre, the simple harp and the shepherd's pipe were morally safe, particularly in the education of the young.

Instrumental and musical compositions alike were to be of a simple nature. Plato feared that the soft strains of music could lull the average citizen into a state of lethargy and thus leave Athens at the mercy of her enemies. He also took issue with the musicians' use of complicated rhythms and mixed musical forms.[20] If Timotheus (c. 446–357 B.C.), one of the well known musical innovators in the time of Plato, increased the number of strings in the lyre to eleven or twelve, that in itself constituted a potential danger to the existing State. Plato was impressed with the Spartan philosophy of music which censured any departure from the ancient canons of music. Plutarch related

---

[19] *Laws, Bk.* VII, 812.

[20] *Laws, Bk.* III, 700-701.

". . . as time went on, the poets themselves introduced the reign of vulgar and lawless innovation. They were men of genius, but they had no perception of what is just and lawful in music; raging like Bacchanals and possessed with inordinate delights—mingling lamentations with hymns, and paeans with dithyrambs; imitating the sounds of the flute on the lyre, and making one general confusion; ignorantly affirming that music has no truth, and, whether good or bad, can only be judged of rightly by the pleasure of the hearer. And by composing such licentious works, and adding to them words as licentious, they have inspired the multitude with lawlessness and boldness, and made them fancy that they can judge for themselves about melody and song. And in this way the theatres from being mute have become vocal, as though they had understanding of good and bad in music and poetry; and instead of an aristocracy, an evil sort of theatrocracy has grown up. For if the democracy which judged had only consisted of educated persons, no fatal harm would have been done; but in music there first arose the universal conceit of omniscience and general lawlessness;—freedom came following afterwards, and men fancying that they knew what they did not know, had no longer any fear, and the absence of fear begets shamelessness. For what is this shamelessness, which is so evil a thing, but the insolent refusal to regard the opinion of the better by reason of an over-daring sort of liberty?"

such instances of Spartan censure: "And indeed so great an esteem and veneration had they for the gravity and simplicity of their ancient music, that no one was allowed to recede in the least from the established rules and measures of it, insomuch as the Ephori, upon complaint made to them, laid a severe mulct upon Terpander (a musician of great note and eminency for his incomparable skill and excellency in playing upon the harp, and who, as he had ever professed a great veneration for antiquity, so ever testified by his eulogiums and commendations the esteem he always had of virtuous and heroic actions), depriving him of his harp, and (as a peculiar punishment) exposing it to the censure of the people, by fixing it upon a nail, because he had added one string more to his instrument than was the usual and stated number, though done with no other design and advantage than to vary the sound, and to make it more useful and pleasant. That music was ever accounted among them the best, which was most grave, simple, and natural. And for this reason too, when Timotheus in their Carnean feasts, which were instituted in honor of Apollo, contended for a preference in his art, one of the Ephori took a knife in his hand, and cut the strings of his harp, for having exceeded the number of seven in it. So severely tenacious were they of their ancient customs and practices, that they would not suffer the least innovation, though in things that were indifferent and of no great importance, lest an indulgence in one thing might have introduced another, till at length by gradual and insensible alterations the whole body of their laws might be disregarded and contemned, and so the main pillar which did support the fabric of their government be weakened and undermined."[21]

Timotheus exemplified the restless craving of the creative artist for artistic change. Poet-musicians were expressing their feelings through new techniques and mediums in defiance of traditional forms. "I do not sing of the past," Timotheus is quoted as saying, and then he followed with "In novelty is power. . . . To Hades with the old Muse." Rebellion in the arts was afoot. Aristophanes took up the challenge for the tradi-

[21] The Account of the Laws and Customs of the Lacedaemonians, Vol. I, 17; (Translated by John Pulleyn), Little, Brown, and Co., Boston: 1898.

tionalists and led a crusade against the new tendency in music. Pherekrates (5th cent. B.C.), a contemporary of Aristophanes, followed suit. But the innovators of the day kept altering music and instruments in their efforts to search out new avenues for expression. This trend alarmed Plato as he watched the traditional melodies and rhythmic patterns which had once distinguished Hellenic art pass out of popular favor. New styles, more ornate, became the fashion of the day. If we may take Plutarch's word for it, music in the time of Plato was gushing with emotion.

The term "music" to the Greek connoted a dual concept. In one respect, it embraced part of the educational curriculum such as reading, writing, mathematics, drawing and poetry. Secondly, it was employed in the manner in which we use it; that is, music in the strict sense of the word. So closely interwoven was music in the latter sense with reading, writing and mathematics, drawing and poetry, that any alteration in music was therefore to be carefully watched since it in turn affected the entire educational program of Greek youth.

The essence of Plato's philosophy of music is that music as an educational and cultural discipline should be used for the attainment of a sound morality. In the *Timaeus*, Plato propounded an ontology which envisioned the world as created out of geometric elements. While in the process of reducing nature to a mystical pattern of numerical relationships, he expressed the view that music was bestowed upon man for the purpose of helping him live a harmonious and judicious life.[22] Music thereby took on a teleological function which should help in the attainment of a sound morality.

Precisely what these ethical implications were may partly be

---

[22] *Timaeus*, 47.

"...music as is adapted to the sound of the voice and to the sense of hearing is granted to us for the sake of harmony; and harmony, which has motions akin to the revolutions of our souls, is not regarded by the intelligent votary of the Muses as given by them with a view to irrational pleasure, which is deemed to be the purpose of it in our day, but as meant to correct any discord which may have arisen in the courses of the soul, and to be our ally in bringing her into harmony and agreement with herself; and rhythm too was given by them for the same reason, on account of the irregular and graceless ways which prevail among mankind generally, and to help us against them."

found in passages of the *Republic* which expressed the conviction that the Ionian and Lydian modes should be banished from
the State since they were of an effeminate, soft and relaxing
character. The Dorian and Phrygian modes that were military
in tone should be retained. Once Plato had established a moral
basis for the Greek modes he further analyzed the attributes of
modes, namely rhythm and melody, and then asked in the *Laws*
whether rhythm and melody were in themselves "imitations of
good and evil characters in men?" With his musical doctrines
now rooted in moralistic principles he applied them in a
thoroughly practical manner to rebuke a primitive form of
polyphony that was coming into vogue in his day. Characterizing it as a cacophony which could only result in mental confusion Plato instructed the Greek bard to compose his musical ode
so that it could be rendered "note for note" and not with a
"complexity, and variation of notes" such as "when the strings
give one sound and the poet or composer of the melody gives
another," "concords and harmonies in which lesser and greater
intervals, slow and quick, or high and low notes, are combined,"
and complex variations when adapted to the notes of the lyre,
cautioned Plato, would surely create difficulties "for opposite
principles are confusing".[23] The conclusion followed that variety, complexity of rhythm and melody should be avoided for
they were apt to induce mental depression and confusion which
might lead men away from the natural order of things into the
realm of the irrational and folly.

Plato maintained that only strictly tempered musical modes
and tunes that were emotionally affective because of their direct
simplicity were beneficial. The proper kind of music could help
man to rhythmically attune his finite soul with the infinite. " . . .
rhythm and harmony find their way into the inward places of
the soul, on which they mightily fasten".[24] Raucous cacophony
might cause the human soul to clash with the ideal order of
things. Therefore bards who composed music incongruous with
the natural order must be cast out of society for they were
destroyers of souls and the forerunners of social doom.

---

[23] *Bk.* VII, 812-813.
[24] *Republic, Bk.* III, 401.

SECTION III—*Aristotle*

ARISTOTLE (384–322 B.C.) borrowed generously from Plato. He agreed with his teacher that music was an imitative art which was modelled after the cosmic harmonies. Aristotle further regarded music, as the Greeks did generally, to be the most personally imitative and representative of the arts since it was thought of as a direct image or copy of character. "Rhythm and melody supply imitations of anger and gentleness, and also of courage and temperance, and of all the qualities contrary to these, and of the other qualities of character, which hardly fall short of the actual affections, as we know from our own experience, for in listening to such strains our souls undergo a change. The habit of feeling pleasure or pain at mere representations is not far removed from the same feeling about realities; . . ."[25] In rhythm and melody we have the most realistic imitations of anger and calmness as well as of courage, temperance and all the 'opposites'. Not only states of feeling but ethical qualities and mental dispositions were reproduced by musical imitation. The music which a man made could mould the character of his listener for good or bad. Music was a reflection of its maker. It was not only that his character was depicted in what he created, but those who came in contact with his music were strongly influenced by it.

Aristotle may also have had Plato in mind when postulating the theory that tragedy should contain actions which excite pity and fear in order to accomplish an emotional katharsis.[26] Aristotle was certainly familiar with the passage in the *Laws* in which Plato observed that movement was good for the soul as well as

[25] *Politics, Bk.* VIII, Chap. V, 1340a, *The Basic Works of Aristotle;* (Translated by B. Jowett), Random House, New York: 1941.

[26] *Ibid.,* Chap. VII, 1342a.

"For feelings such as pity and fear, or again, enthusiasm, exist very strongly in some souls, and have more or less influence over all. Some persons fall into a religious frenzy, whom we see as a result of the sacred melodies— when they have used the melodies that excite the soul to mystic frenzy— restored as though they had found healing and purgation. Those who are influenced by pity or fear, and every emotional nature, must have a like experience, and others in so far as each is susceptible to such emotions, and all are in a manner purged and their souls lightened and delighted."

the body since rhythm could quiet fear and restore mental equilibrium. Plato wrote: "The affection both of the Bacchantes and of the children is an emotion of fear, which springs out of an evil habit of the soul. And when someone applies external agitation to affections of this sort, the motion coming from without gets the better of the terrible and violent internal one, and produces a peace and calm in the soul, and quiets the restless palpitation of the heart, which is a thing much to be desired, sending the children to sleep, and making the Bacchantes, although they remain awake, to dance to the pipe with the help of the Gods to whom they offer acceptable sacrifices, and producing in them a sound mind, which takes the place of their frenzy."[27]

Aristoxenus, the student of Aristotle, told us that the use of katharsis originated with the Pythagoreans. Actually, the practice of using music as a therapy for the mentally deranged was not Hellenistic in origin, but had been practiced in China and Egypt before the Greek priests came to use it. Aristotle probably broadened this theory after observing the effect which certain types of music had in inducing a mood or religious ecstasy, or as the Greeks called it "enthusiasmus", "such as is rarely seen in this country but whose proper home is in the East." Those subject to periods of mental disorientation were considered as being "Possessed" by the Gods and were treated by the Priesthood. The treatment was homeopathic in character in that it consisted of applying frenzied music to cure frenzied minds. The rhythmic motion of a wild and restless musical strain could so affect its emotionally unbalanced listener that mental equilibrium was restored. There are references in Greek literature where the Bacchic priests would assemble the women who were tormented and distracted of mind and bring them to the temple for treatment. The priests would then play wild pipe music and these women would be moved to dance and the more frantic the music became the more frenzied did the dance become. When the women were exhausted they would fall to the ground and sleep. Upon awakening, their irrational mental

---

[27] *Bk.* VII, 790-791.

states would have subsided and they would be either temporarily or lastingly cured.[28]

Aristotle also repeated the views of Plato on the ethical character of music. ". . . even in mere melodies there is an imitation of character," wrote Aristotle in the *Politics*, "for the musical modes differ essentially from one another, and those who hear them are differently affected by each. Some of them make men sad and grave, like the so-called Mixolydian, others enfeeble the mind, like the relaxed modes, another, again, produces a moderate and settled temper, which appears to be the peculiar effect of the Dorian; the Phrygian inspires enthusiasm. . . . The same principles apply to rhythms; some have a character of rest, others of motion, and of these latter again, some have a more vulgar, others a nobler movement. . . . music has a power of forming the character, and should therefore be introduced into the education of the young. . . . There seems to be in us a sort of affinity to musical modes and rhythms, which makes some philosophers say that the soul is a tuning, others, that it possesses tuning."[29]

But Aristotle did take issue with Plato on his ban of the pipes. "The Socrates of the *Republic*," wrote the founder of the Lyceum, "is wrong in retaining only the Phrygian mode along with the Dorian, and the more so because he rejects the flute; for the Phrygian is to the modes what the flute is to musical instruments—both of them are exciting and emotional. Poetry proves this, for Bacchic frenzy and all similar emotions are

---

[28] Paeans were originally charms against sickness and death. The word "paean" meant "healer". Originally, it was a medicine dance and later developed into a dance in honor of Apollo, the healing God.

"With sacred hymns and songs that sweetly please,
The Grecian youth all day the Gods appease.
Their lofty paeans bright Apollo hears,
And still the charming sounds delight his ears."
Plutarch, *Concerning Music*, 42.

Homer related in the *Iliad* that the paean was used to ban the plague. When Sparta fell victim to the plague several centuries later, the Cretan musician Thaletas was called by the governors to organize paeans which would induce the plague to subside.

[29] *Bk.* VIII, Chap. V, 1340b.

most suitably expressed by the flute, and are better set to the Phrygian than to any other mode."[30]

In further consideration of the musical modes, Aristotle went on to add that: "All men agree that the Dorian music is the gravest and manliest. And whereas we say that the extremes should be avoided and the mean followed, and whereas the Dorian is a mean between the other modes, it is evident that our youth should be taught the Dorian music."[31] Thus Aristotle formulated a doctrine of ethos based on the Golden Mean.

The judicious advice which Plato gave to the State Guardians in the *Republic* on musical education found its way into the *Politics* of Aristotle in somewhat modified form. Aristotle made it clear at the outset that those who judge music must first be performers with a fair degree of accomplishment themselves. Only those who had a knowledge of the various modes, rhythms and melodies and a technical appreciation of the music which was being performed could first, understand the music, and, secondly, evaluate it in order to form a rational judgment of its worth. The Athenian youth must therefore be made musically literate if he was to become an enlightened citizen. But how much musical education should the youth receive? Aristotle again prescribed according to the Golden Mean. "The right measure will be attained if students of music stop short of the arts which are practised in professional contests, and do not seek to acquire those fantastic marvels of execution which are now the fashion in such contests, and from these have passed into education."[32] Once the student had acquired a sound knowledge of music and had become proficient in the handling of instruments, he must be made to realize that over-indulgence in music for the sake of amusement could lead to vulgarity. But the dictates of the Golden Mean could still be followed if ". . . the young practise even such music as we have prescribed, only until they are able to feel delight in noble melodies and rhythms, and not merely in that common part of music in which every

[30] *Ibid.*, Chap. VII, 1342b.
[31] *Loc. cit.*
[32] *Ibid.*, 1341a.

slave or child and even some animals find pleasure."[33] What of instruments in the education of the young? "The flute, or any other instrument which requires great skill, as for example the harp, ought not to be admitted into education, . . . Besides, the flute is not an instrument which is expressive of moral character; it is too exciting. The proper time for using it is when the performance aims not at instruction, but at the relief of the passions. And there is a further objection; the impediment which the flute presents to the use of the voice detracts from its educational value."[34] "Thus then we reject the professional instruments and also the professional mode of education in music (and by professional we mean that which is adopted in contests), for in this the performer practises the art, not for the sake of his own improvement, but in order to give pleasure, and that of a vulgar sort, to his hearers. For this reason the execution of such music is not the part of a freeman but of a paid performer, and the result is that the performers are vulgarized, for the end at which they aim is bad. The vulgarity of the spectator tends to lower the character of the music and therefore of the performers; they look to him—he makes them what they are, and fashions even their bodies by the movements which he expects them to exhibit."[35]

When Philip of Macedon berated his son Alexander "Art not ashamed to pluck the strings so well?" he was actually expressing the philosophy of music which Aristotle, as the teacher of the young Alexander, tried to instill in his pupil. Plutarch related this story by way of reference to Antisthenes[36] the Cynic who said ". . . when he heard that Ismenias was an excellent piper: 'But he's a worthless man,' said he, 'otherwise he wouldn't be so good a piper.' And so Philip once said to his son, who, as the wine went round, plucked the strings charmingly and skill-

---

[33] *Loc. cit.*
[34] *Loc. cit.*
[35] *Ibid.*, 1341b.
[36] Antisthenes (444-365 B.C.) the student of Socrates and founder of the philosophic school of Cynics regarded music as an unnecessary and useless pastime. The Cynics maintained that "Good musicians often had souls out of tune" and as a consequence veered away from reality.

fully, 'Art not ashamed to pluck the strings so well?' It is enough, surely, if a king have leisure to hear others pluck the strings, and he pays great deference to the Muses if he be but a spectator of such contests."[37]

Aristotle's concern over the state of music in his day was also of Platonic origin. In the *Protagoras* Plato referred to a new phase of Greek music which began to take shape in the century before him and was beginning to gain wide approval among the populace of his own generation. The professional musicians who performed at contests were, to Plato's way of thinking, signs of a slowly but surely decaying Greek culture. Plato objected to the emphasis placed on subjective expression, free forms, elaborate melodies, rhythmic inventions and chromatic tonalities. The fifth century brought forth the professional musician in Greece in the guise of Timotheus, Euripides (480–406 B.C.), and Phrynis (5th cent. B.C.), a third progressive who "mixed hexameter and free lyric verse and made a lyre sound like a trumpet." It was an era in which musicians were altering modes and instruments according to their mood. They were experimenting with new rhythms and instrumental techniques for expressive purposes. It was an era of subjectivity which caused Plato and Aristotle to lament that Greek tradition was waning artistically.

Plutarch bore out the views of Plato and Aristotle by noting that in the time prior to Phrynis and the subjective trend "it was not permitted to musicians, as it now is, to introduce mutations in melody or rhythm at pleasure. The Nome, which they employed, having its appropriate pitch and measure, to these they were required to adhere without change."[38] Plutarch further supported his contention that, at the turn of the 5th century into the 4th century B.C., the innovations of Timotheus and Phrynis marred the dignified simplicity of the old music, by quoting from the comedies of Pherekrates and Aristophanes. He cited a fragment of a comedy by Pherekrates in which

---

[37] *Plutarch's Lives,* Vol. III, p. 5; (Translated by Bernadotte Perrin), William Heinemann, London: 1915.

[38] *On Music,* p. 17; (Translated by J. H. Bromby), Chiswick, London: 1822.

music was portrayed as a female character, covered with wounds
and complaining before Justice that:

> ". . . Phrynis, with the fury of a storm
> And eddying whirlpool, twisted all my form;
> And by a mischievous contrivance wrings
> Twelve harmonies from my five simple strings.
>
> .   .   .   .
>
> But, dearest Lady! would you truly know
> For whom my deepest wounds and miseries flow,
> It was Timotheus drove me from the Earth—
>
> .   .   .   .
>
> The most atrocious of my foes was he:
> Marks of his brutal violence you see
> I bear: for as alone I chanced to stray
> He met me in my solitary way,
> And rudely seized: my strength and spirits fly;
> And, in his twelve strings bound, I nerveless lie."[39]

Plutarch then quoted from Aristophanes who attacked Euripides and those who held artistic views similar to his as followers
of a decadent philosophy of art which had its roots in Periclean
liberality. "Of Philoxenus mention is made by Aristophanes,
the Comic Poet, from whom we learn that he was the first
who introduced songs into the Cyclian chorusses. Music is
represented as uttering her complaint thus:

> 'By him constrained am I compelled to bear
> The frantic drunkard's countenance and air.
> He makes me utter strange and impious sounds,
> Unknown to the harmonic scale; whose bounds
> They far excede; nor serve one useful cause
> Of harmony, contemning all her laws.
> My person, thus subjected to his will,
> He grasps, distorts, and loads with every ill;
> And I, resistless, am compelled to bend
> As the soft radish every way will tend.' "[40]

[39] *Ibid.*, p. 77.
[40] *Ibid.*, p. 77ff.

Aristotle was indebted to the Pythagoreans for his views on harmony and acoustics. The Pythagoreans maintained that the simpler the ratio of the two parts into which a vibrating string was divided, the more perfect was the consonance of the two sounds. Aristotle commented that this principle was also employed by the artisan in the making of reed-pipes. "In the reed-pipe an accord with the octave is obtained by doubling the length, and this is how flute-makers produce it. Similarly they obtain a fifth by means of a length in the ratio of 3 to 2, . . . and a fourth by means of a length in the ratio of 4 to 3."[41] Aristotle further noted that the "more frequent impacts upon the air are caused by the shriller note," and that "strings which are tightly stretched give a shriller note, for their movement is quicker."[42] Since Aristotle agreed with the Pythagoreans and Plato that proportion was order, which was naturally pleasant, he concluded that: "We enjoy different types of song for their moral character, but we enjoy rhythm because it has a recognized and orderly numerical arrangement and carries us along in an orderly fashion; for orderly movement is naturally more akin to us than one without order, so that such rhythm is more in accordance with nature."[43]

Aristotle, like Plato, believed that the ultimate end of music should be the good of man and society. But while Plato believed that music should imitate nature faithfully, Aristotle reasoned, independently of his teacher, that the function of music was not to imitate nature but to recreate the world of natural sounds into idealized musical tones. The composer of music came closer to fathoming the passions and behavior of man than any other type of creative artist, reasoned Aristotle, because tones were more expressive than colors. Music was a superior art to painting because of its temporal character.[44] Music not only portrayed the outward appearance of human feeling and action, concluded Aristotle, but represented the inner significance and emotional life of man's moods and activities more effectively than the other arts.

---

[41] *Problems*, XIX, 23, 919b.
[42] *Ibid.*, XIX, 35, 920b.
[43] *Ibid.*, XIX, 38, 920b.
[44] *Ibid.*, XIX, 27, 919b.

SECTION IV—*Aristoxenus and the Pythagoreans*

PLATO believed that music could mould character. He maintained that bad music could induce licentious moods which would encourage the moulding of bad character. He therefore insisted that the State Guardians must be well educated in music so that they could detect and discourage music with incongruous texts, or music that lent itself to obscene or inappropriate gestures, or music which tried to imitate sounds that were foreign to its nature, which could only result in poor imitations of the actual phenomena. Plato above all cautioned the elders that they must remain completely disdainful of the mere virtuosity and technique of instrumental music divorced from the significance of words. He had little faith that the average citizen could distinguish good from bad music, or that the populace could be trusted in matters of musical taste. The Guardians of the State must therefore be better schooled in music than the multitude, not in the proficiency of instrumental technique, but in understanding the nature of music and its effect upon behavior, for upon the elders fell the discerning task of deciding between good and bad music.

Aristotle, for the most part, restated the Platonic theories of music. Like Plato, he was interested in the numerical aspects of musical tones. The ideas which he presented on tonal construction and acoustics were more advanced than those of any other Greek with the exception of his pupil Aristoxenus.

Aristoxenus (b.c. 354 B.C.) shied away from the moral issues and purely mathematical interpretations of music to which both Plato and Aristotle held. Aristoxenus believed that sense and reason, the power to hear and the ability to discriminate should enable one to judge for himself whether music was good or bad. He did agree that certain musical modes bore an affinity to moral states,[45] but the affinity must not be taken too literally or be exaggerated.

---

[45] Theophrastus, another of Aristotle's pupils, who took over the Lyceum after the Master's death, also differed with his teacher on the ethical implications of music. Aristotle followed Plato in linking the Greek modes with total ethical character. Theophrastus connected the Greek musical modes with the passions only. Theophrastus attributed the origin and nature of

Aristoxenus was not altogether sympathetic with the musical innovations of his day either. He complained that much of the new music was no longer serene and simple. Embellishments were much too frequent so that the melody could not be discerned. The tonalities changed too rapidly and lacked continuity. The musical accompaniment went its own way, often noisily and even became raucous in quality. Like Plato and Aristotle, he labelled much of the new music degenerate.

In the Seventh Book of the *Republic* Plato distinguished between "the purely empirical approach to music of 'those good men who tease and torture the chords and rack them upon the pegs' and who are preoccupied with 'the blows given by the plectrum, and the peevishness, reserve and forwardness of the strings,' and the more scientific approach of the Pythagoreans who 'investigate the numerical relation subsisting between these *audible* concords.' He criticized the former for 'postponing their reason to their ears,' and for thus making themselves 'quite ridiculous'; but he was also critical of the Pythagoreans who are 'content to measure the notes and concords distinguished by the *ear*, one against another, and therefore toil without result.' They should rather, he believed, 'apply themselves to problems, with the object of examining what numbers are, and what numbers are not, consonant, and what is the reason of the difference.' "[46]

Aristoxenus also questioned the views of the Pythagoreans on the grounds that mere mathematics of itself could not explain the true nature of musical creation or appreciation. He also questioned the investigations of the empiricists who were more concerned with single musical tones than they were with the melodic relation of one tone to another.[47] Aristoxenus refused to rely on the ear alone to determine the aesthetic quality of

music to an emotional expression of grief, pleasure and enthusiasm. ". . . since love contains all the causes of music,—grief, pleasure, and enthusiasm,— . . . it should incline us more than any other passion to poetry and songs."
Plutarch's Symposiacs, Bk. I, Quest. V, 2, Vol. III, pp. 218-219; Little, Brown and Co., Boston: 1898.

[46] Theodore M. Greene, *The Arts and The Art of Criticism*, pp. 18-19; Princeton University Press, Princeton: 1947.

[47] Euclid (c. 300 B.C.), the outstanding mathematician and Pythagorean, wrote his treatise on Harmony under the Ptolemies in the scientific environs of Alexandria.

a musical work or to accept the view that aesthetic judgments in music were primarily an intellectual activity. He related that some of his predecessors "introduced extraneous reasoning, and rejecting the senses as inaccurate fabricated rational principles, asserting that height and depth of pitch consist in certain numerical ratios and relative rates of vibration—a theory utterly extraneous to the subject and quite at variance with the phenomena; while others, dispensing with reason and demonstration, confined themselves to isolated dogmatic statements, not being successful either in their enumeration of the mere phenomena . . . our method rests in the last resort on an appeal to the two faculties of hearing and intellect. By the former we judge the magnitudes of the intervals, by the latter we contemplate the function of the notes. We must therefore accustom ourselves to an accurate discrimination of particulars . . . for the student of musical science accuracy of sense-perception is a fundamental requirement . . . musical cognition implies the simultaneous cognition of a permanent and of a changeable element, and . . . this applies without limitation or qualification to every branch of music."[48]

"Until Aristoxenus appeared upon the scene," wrote Henry S. Macran in his introduction to the *Harmonics of Aristoxenus*, "the limits of Musical Science had been wholly misconceived. There existed, indeed, a flourishing school of Musical Art; there was conscious preference of this style of composition to that; of this method of performance to that; of this construction of instruments to that; and the habits formed by these preferences were transmitted by instruction. To facilitate this instruction, and as an aid to memory, recourse was had to diagrams and superficial generalizations; but with principles for their own sake the artist, empiricist as he was, did not concern himself. . . . Over against these empiricists there stood a school of mathematicians and physicists, professing to be students of music, and claiming Pythagoras as their master, who were busied in reducing sounds to air vibrations, and ascertaining the numerical relations which replace for the mathematical intellect the sense-

---

[48] *The Harmonics of Aristoxenus*, pp. 188-190; (Edited and Translated by Henry S. Macran), Oxford, The Clarendon Press, London: 1902.

distinctions of high and low pitch. Here we have a genuine school of science, the soundness of whose hypotheses and the accuracy of whose computations have been established by the light of modern discovery. Nevertheless, musical science was still to seek. For if the artists were musicians without science, the physicists and mathematicians were men of science without music. Under the microscope of their analysis all musical preferences are levelled, all musical worth is sacrificed; noble and beautiful sounds and melodies dissolve, equally with the ugly and base, into arithmetical relations and relations of relations, any one of which is precisely as valuable and as valueless as any other . . . So busy were the Pythagoreans in establishing the mere physical and mathematical antecedents of sounds in general, that they never saw that the essence of musical sounds lies in their dynamical relation to one another. Thus they missed the true formal notion of music, which is ever present to Aristoxenus, that of a system or organic whole of sounds, each member of which *is* essentially what it *does*, and in which a sound cannot become a member because merely there is room for it, but only if there is a function which it can discharge."[49]

Aristoxenus was perhaps the first of the musical humanists in Western civilization. His philosophy of music made man the sole judge of what is good and bad in music. He was fully appreciative of the contributions that the empiricists and Pythagoreans were making in their investigations of the physical and mathematical structure of tone. But he reasoned that isolated tones of themselves were not music and that knowing the numerical components of certain tones does not necessarily make for a more aesthetic musical attitude. A knowledge of the science of harmony was a prerequisite for understanding, but Aristoxenus believed that a true appreciation of music went beyond the understanding of the physics and acoustics of sound and culminated in feeling.

Aristoxenus brought us close historically to the end of Athenian culture and Greek musical creation. By his time, the introduction of pure instrumental music had outlived the cries of the philosophers and the role of the chorus in Greek tragedy

[49] pp. 87-89.

had undergone a momentous change. The Greek tragedy was a musical and dramatic work which employed both song and speech. The chorus sang or chanted throughout the play explaining the action going on and often created a mood for an impending disaster or climatic sequence. There were also songs for solo voices woven into the fabric of the plot which gave variation to the tonal continuity of the drama. About the time of Aristoxenus the passive rhythmic chanting of the chorus diminished as its members were given active parts in the tragedy.

Our knowledge of the actual Greek music which existed in the time of Plato, Aristotle and Aristoxenus is scanty and speculative. Many of the archeological musical findings which were first thought to be Greek, have been discovered to be of later origin. Most of the authentic melodies which we do possess exist only in part. Of these, the most important are the *Two Delphic Hymns to Apollo* which were unearthed and discovered on marble slabs in the ruins of the Treasury of the Athenians at Delphi. The first of these dates back to about 138 B.C. and is considered to be quite representative of Greek music. We also have a fragment from the *Orestes* of Euripides which is believed to be the oldest piece of Greek music in our possession. But our primary sources of historical and theoretical information are the writings of the Greek philosophers and theoreticians. What ideas we can gather about the music of this period came more from these writings than from the surviving specimens of music which are few and often fragmentary at best. It is a fair assumption that a good deal of the music was not recorded although the early Greeks possessed a system of notation. Since a good deal of the music was handed down orally, coupled with the fact that a poem and song would be composed for a particular event and then discarded, there is reason to believe that most of the Greek music was lost with the disintegration of Hellenic civilization.

SECTION V—*The Greco-Roman Era*

EPICURUS (342–270 B.C.), a contemporary of Aristoxenus, taught a way of life that was based on temperance and moderation. The noblest of all philosophies was the one which guided man toward the attainment of a practical approach and understanding of life which would make human existence more tranquil and peaceful. Epicurus agreed with the materialistic interpretation of nature which Democritus had originally given. He also held that the gods in their distant homes were unmoved by the miseries of humanity and even if they wanted to, they would be unable to exert any influence on the life of man. The human soul was material and shared the fate of the body. But Epicurus oddly followed Aristoxenus in the Pythagorean belief that the soul was a "harmony" of the body. Lucretius, (95–52 B.C.), the ablest exponent of Epicureanism, some two centuries later scoffed at this notion of applying musical terms, such as harmony, to the constitution and function of the human body. He wrote: "Since then the nature of the mind and that of the soul have been proved to be a part as it were of the man, surrender the name of harmony, whether brought down to musicians from high Helicon, or whether rather they have themselves taken it from something else and transferred it to that thing which then was in need of a distinctive name; whatever it be, let them keep it."[50]

Philodemus, a fellow Epicurean and contemporary of Lucretius, added "Music is irrational and cannot affect the soul or the emotions, and is no more an expressive art than cookery."[51] He carried out a polemic against those philosophers, namely Plato and Aristotle, for attributing ethical significance to the Greek modes. He refused to believe that music was imitative of natural phenomena or expressive of mental states. Only philosophers and critics, concluded Philodemus, who could neither sing nor play well attributed moral significance to music and so they "fall into ecstasies and compare tunes with natural phenomena."

Lucretius' *On the Nature of Things* contains the essence of

[50] *The Stoic and Epicurean Philosophers, On the Nature of Things*, Bk. III, 130-135, p. 117; (Translated by H. A. J. Munro), Random House, New York: 1940.

[51] Bernard Bosanquet, *A History of Aesthetic*, pp. 100-101; George Allen & Unwin Ltd., London: 1922.

Epicurean thought. It also offers a theory of the origin of vocal and instrumental music. Man first learned to sing by imitating the birds and then invented instruments to accompany his song and dance in leisure periods. "But imitating with the mouth the clear notes of birds was in use long before men were able to sing in tune smooth-running verses and give pleasure to the ear. And the whistlings of the zephyr through the hollows of reeds first taught peasants to blow into hollow stalks. Then step by step they learned sweet plaintive ditties, which the pipe pours forth pressed by the fingers of the players, heard through pathless woods and forests and lawns, through the unfrequented haunts of shepherds and abodes of unearthly calm. These things would soothe and gratify their minds when sated with food."[52]

During the reign of the Caesars, Epicureanism gathered into its fold an enlightened group who were as much opposed to the remnants of a lingering pagan polytheism as they were to Christian theology. The Stoic school of philosophy, founded by Zeno (c. 350–258 B.C.), represented an intellectual group during the early Roman period which sought to rejuvenate the remains of Greek religion. The Stoics rejected Plato's theory of Ideas and innate knowledge and concluded that sensation was the common source of all human knowledge. Virtue for virtue's sake was the noble motto of Stoic philosophy. The highest good was to be derived from doing one's duty out of sheer duty. The Stoics reasoned that the sage alone was free for he had acquired the secret of overcoming material gain and servitude to his passions. He had given himself to utter resignation for all things were determined by Nature and Fate. Reason led the wise man to accept these two forces as determinates which governed all thought and action. Therefore, it was proper that all men follow nature and give themselves wholly to her and the fate she keeps in store for each mortal. Since the harmony of music was modelled after the natural harmony, then man could be helped to live in accordance with nature by exposing himself to the proper musical modes and rhythms. On this point, the Stoics and Plato were in agreement.

[52] *Op. cit.*, Bk. V, 1379-1391, p. 190.

The Stoics, Cicero (106–43 B.C.) and Seneca (4 B.C.–65 A.D.), tell us that toward the end of the first century music flourished throughout the Roman world. Rhythm was particularly stressed and there was also evidence that the Romans employed a primitive type of polyphony. Wandering Greeks who acted as mimes, singers and instrumentalists were much in vogue and were accepted by the Roman upper classes as well as enjoyed by the plebians. Since the Romans pictured themselves as a great military power they furthered the use of brass instruments, reminding us of Aristoxenus who felt that the subtleties of the Greek musical system were wasted in a civilization where the colosseum took the place of the theatre and where the trumpets of the soldiers were more characteristic than the pipes of the shepherds.

The only complete treatise on music to come down to us from the Greco-Roman era is that of Aristides Quintilianus of the second century whose writings *Concerning Music* purport to summarize and concur with the musical views that were taught in the Academy and Lyceum of Plato and Aristotle. We actually have little information about the musical habits of Rome. Neither has their music been preserved. But there are numerous references of poetic satire levelled at the impropriety and nuisance value of music. Seneca lamented that orchestras and choruses grew to such gigantic proportions that there were often more singers and players in the theatre than spectators. Cicero added that music was no longer of "austere sweetness" which had prevailed in the older music of the Roman theatre. Somewhat philosophically, he concluded, music in its present state only offered childish pleasure, and was practically useless since it did not bring lasting happiness any closer.[53] In Rome, as in Greece, the moralist would have his say. He complained that the melodies were effeminate, and that music in general had become a degenerate art.

---

[53] *De Oratore*, III, 51; (Translated by H. Rackham), Wm. Heinemann Ltd., London: 1942.

"For as art started from nature, it would certainly be deemed to have failed if it had not a natural power of affecting us and giving us pleasure; but nothing is so akin to our own minds as rhythms and words—these rouse us up to excitement, and smooth and calm us down, and often lead us to mirth and to sorrow;"

The Romans contributed little to the growth of music. They adopted Greek theory and practices and modified them to their own use. Vitruvius, the Roman architect and man of letters, who lived in the time of Caesar and Augustus, inserted a chapter on musical harmony in his treatise on architecture which reflected the Roman dependence on Greek music. "Harmony is an obscure and difficult branch of musical literature especially for persons unacquainted with Greek", lamented Vitruvius. "If we wish to explain it we must use Greek words and some of these have no Latin renderings. Therefore," continued Vitruvius, "I shall translate (as well as I can) from the works of Aristoxenus. . . ."[54]

The Roman period was musically active but lacking in originality. The patrician families originally included music as part of a liberal education, with rhetoric, dialectic, geometry and mathematics. It was the fashion for ladies of the patrician class to be schooled in the playing of the cither and lyre. When these instruments became popular with the lower classes, the ladies of the upper classes decided to seek other forms of musical entertainment to set themselves off from plebian life. They engaged the wandering Greek musicians to sing and play for them and eventually gave up learning how to play the instruments altogether. The wandering mimes developed into a class of musical virtuosi, each in turn trying to outdo the other in technical display and sensational interpretations. Petty jealousies flared, professional claques were subsidized and contest judges were bribed to favor one singer over another. The women of Roman society took it upon themselves to further the interests of their respective prodigies. The wealthy brought talented musical slaves into their homes so that they might be entertained by song and instrument from morning till night.

The Romans, like the Greeks, looked to the theatre for a large part of their cultural life. In the Roman play, as in the late Greek, the chorus gave way to the solo parts, either spoken or sung, which were accompanied by an instrument called the tibia or pipes. The Greek poet and musician were originally one but the Roman dramatic and comic poet did not compose

[54] Vitruvius, *On Architecture, Bk.* V, Chap. IV, Vol. I; (Translated by Frank Granger), Wm. Heinemann Ltd., London: 1931.

his own music. He delegated creative composition to the professional musician. Music played a major role in the Greek theatre by sustaining the continuity of action and adding to the realism of the plot, but the Roman actor flaunted his artistry in individual scenes that often lacked continuity or realism. Music was given a minor role in the Roman theatre, merely to fill in the gaps between performers or at best to support a performer but never to detract from his egoistic recitation.

Quintilian (35 A.D.), a contemporary of Seneca's, bears him out on the Roman intellectual's concern over the music of his time. ". . . the music which I desire to see taught is not our modern music, which has been emasculated by the lascivious melodies of our effeminate stage and has to no small extent destroyed such manly vigour as we still possessed. No, I refer to the music of old which was employed to sing the praises of brave men and was sung by the brave themselves. I will have none of your psalteries and viols, that are unfit even for the use of a modest girl. Give me the knowledge of the principles of music, which have power to excite or assuage the emotions of mankind."[55]

Perhaps nowhere in ancient literature is the decline of Greek music so vividly presented as in Horace's *Ars Poetica*. His life synchronized with one of history's great epochs. At the time of his birth (65 B.C.) the final struggle between Pompey and Caesar as to which of the two was to become the master of the Roman empire had not yet begun. By the time Horace reached his twenty-first birthday the old order had already given way to the new. The Republic had become a Monarchy, in fact, if not in name. With the change in state came changes in the arts. The following excerpt from his *Art of Poetry* well describes the position of music during Caesar's reign.

---

[55] *Bk.* I. x. 31-32; (Translated by H. E. Butler), Wm. Heinemann, Ltd., London: 1921.

In the course of praising the Greeks' use of their musical system Quintilian writes: "Indeed nature itself seems to have given music as a boon to men to lighten the strain of labour: even the rower in the galleys is cheered to effort by song. Nor is this function of music confined to cases where the efforts of a number are given union by the sound of some sweet voice that sets the tune, but even solitary workers find solace at their toil in artless song." *Bk.* I. x. 16-17.

"When, on a day of revels, to begin
The feast from noontide was no more a sin,
A larger license and a scope less rude
Both to the music and the verse accrued.
For what should that mixed audience have of taste,
Clown grouped with cit, and boors by nobles placed?
Thus did the piper superadd erelong
The charms of gesture to the powers of song,
With pantomimic grace his sense expressed,
And trailed along the boards the floating vest.
Thus too, its tones increased, the lyre severe
Poured richer warblings on the ravished ear;
The muse in loftier numbers learned to soar,
Imped her bold plume for flights untried before,
And, fraught with fire prophetic, bade each line
Rival the raptures of the Delphian shrine.
    He that in tragic lay late strained his throat
To win the paltry prize—a shaggy goat,
Soon bared upon the stage a sylvan crew
And brought the wanton satyrs forth to view;
The solemn tone not wholly laid aside,
To humor and burlesque his hand applied;
And sought by grateful novelty of song
To rivet to their seats a boozy throng
From festive rites and revels just set free,
Ripe for loose pranks and full of tipsy glee.
Yet so to shift from grave to gay 'twere fit,
So temper the light satyrs' saucy wit,
That not each god, each hero, that of late
Stalked forth in purple robes and royal state,
Anon should all his pomp of speech let down
To the low slang and gabble of a clown,
Or, steering heavenwards his flight too fast,
Grasp empty clouds and soar into bombast.
The Tragic Muse, with bashfulness severe,
Disdaining the base gibe and trivial jeer, . . ."[56]

---

[56] 202-219, Albert S. Cook Edition, G. E. Stechert & Co., New York: 1926.

Plotinus (204–269 A.D.) referred to music in a thoroughly neo-Platonic strain. ". . . all music—since its thought is upon melody and rhythm—must be the earthly representation of the music there is in the rhythm of the Ideal Realm. The crafts such as building and carpentry which give us Matter in wrought forms, may be said, in that they draw on pattern, to take their principles from that realm and from the thinking There: but in that they bring these down into contact with the sense-order, they are not wholly in the Intellectual: they are founded in man."[57]

Like Plato and Aristotle he ascribed significance to the moral value of music, but, unlike them, not on a political basis but from a religious standpoint. With and through the Beautiful man could cleanse his soul and thus be led by degrees to a contemplation of the Good. If the rhythm in music was an earthly manifestation of the rhythm in the Ideal Realm, music was therefore the best capable of the arts to lift man to rarer and purer heights. But, like Plato, he also feared that by the same token this rhythmic pulse could lead one to Evil. Taking up where Plato left off, Plotinus attributed artistic creation to man's imitative ability to copy the Ideal. Inspiration came from above. The musician must be temperamentally equipped for his life's work. He must be "exceedingly quick to beauty, drawn in a very rapture to it: somewhat slow to stir of his own impulse, he answers at once to the outer stimulus." In addition, the musician must be sensitive to tone and color and repel harsh and unrhythmic harmonies. The musical soul longs for "measure and shapely pattern." "This natural tendency must be made the starting-point to such a man; he must be drawn by the tone, rhythm and design in things of sense: he must learn to distinguish the material forms from the Authentic-Existent which is the source of all these correspondences and of the entire reasoned scheme in the work of art: he must be led to the Beauty that manifests itself through these forms: he must be shown that what ravished him was no other than the Harmony of the Intellectual world and the Beauty in that sphere, not

[57] *Enneads*, V, 9, 11; (Translated by Stephen MacKenna), The Medici Society Limited, London: 1926.

some one shape of beauty but the All-Beauty, the Absolute Beauty; and the truths of philosophy must be implanted in him to lead him to faith in that which, unkowing it, he possesses within himself."[58] Once music was begotten, the composer's creation could so beguile the human soul that its hearer was hardly aware of the tantalizing influence of music upon it. The composer could evoke many moods and his listener could not help but submit.[59] Music was like a prayer to Plotinus, since music enabled the listener to become one with the composer. "The prayer is answered by the mere fact that part and other part are wrought to one tone like a musical string which, plucked at one end, vibrates at the other also. Often, too, the sounding of one string awakens what might pass for a perception in another, the result of their being in harmony and tuned to one musical scale; now, if the vibration in a lyre affects another by virtue of the sympathy existing between them, then certainly in the All—even though it is constituted in contraries—there must be one melodic system; for it contains its unisons as well, and its entire content, even to those contraries, is a kinship."[60] The doctrine of ethos in music which gained prominence with Plato, took on added zest in Plotinus, and then dominated the entire history of art in the Middle Ages.

Two years after the death of Plotinus, Constantine came into the world to make Christianity the state religion in his reign. Porphyry (233-305 A.D.), the student of Plotinus, who wrote a commentary on Ptolemy's *Harmonics,* indirectly contributed to Christian music. Plotinus did not mention the Christians in his writings and he may have shunned them as a people with queer beliefs which differed from his. Porphyry, however, was a staunch defender of paganism and a violent opponent of Christianity. As an ardent sponsor of asceticism he paradoxically

---

[58] *Ibid.,* I, 3, 1.

[59] Longinus, *On the Sublime,* xxxlx; (Translated by W. Hamilton Fyfe), Wm. Heinemann Ltd., London: 1932.

"Does not the flute, for instance, induce certain emotions in those who hear it? Does it not seem to carry them away and fill them with divine frenzy? It sets a particular rhythmic movement and forces them to move in rhythm. The hearer has to conform to the tune, though he may be utterly unmusical."

[60] *Op. cit.* IV, 4, 41.

furthered the Christian view by speaking out against the sensuous pleasure afforded by music. He likened the dramatic spectacles and dances with their music to that of horse racing. Porphyry, like Plotinus, reasoned that the creation of music had its origin in a higher sphere and did not emanate from the theatre. To desecrate music to a sensuous level or burden it with lewdness was to sin against the Ideal order. Music properly cultivated could bring man closer to this Ideal.

The Platonic theory that musical order was analogous to the moral order which prevailed in the universe and that music could better the soul of man if he would only expose himself to well-regulated music was questioned in the Greco-Roman era by some few empirically minded philosophers, as it was by Aristoxenus and Theophrastus in the Greek era. Sextus Empiricus, the philosophic Greek sceptic who taught about 200 A.D., brushed aside these Platonic analogies as the myths of speculative philosophers. He wrote that music was an art of tones and rhythms which was indicative of nothing beyond itself. Only the sensuous pleasure aroused by musical sounds could be the sole criterion by which music should be judged.

There were some other doubters of the Platonic theories on music in the following centuries, but very few indeed that we can find among the historical writings of the better known philosophers. Augustine and Boethius, two outstanding philosophers of the Middle Ages, transmitted the musical aesthetics of Plato to the Western world with religious and philosophical zeal. To disagree with the musical views of Augustine or question Boethius was tantamount to Christian heresy and philosophic ignorance.

CHAPTER 2

MEDIEVAL MUSIC

SECTION I—*The Patristics*

WE know more about the music of Western civilization in the twelve centuries that began with Christianity and extended to the rise of scholastic humanism in the 12th century than we know about the twelve centuries of Greek music that began with the Homeric age and ended with the decline of Greek civilization. But our knowledge of the actual music of the early Christian centuries is rather speculative for we possess little, if any, of the authentic sacred or secular music of the time. We are somewhat more fortunate in our library of music that has survived in modified form, both sacred and secular, from the latter half of the medieval period. We are, to be sure, decidedly richer in our accumulation of medieval manuscripts than we are in our records of Greek music of which we have in our possession only a few precious fragments. Yet, we must turn to the writings of the Church Fathers and medieval philosophers of pagan Rome, in the same manner that we did in our study of music through the writings of the Greek philosophers, for an account of the character and aesthetic significance of music in the medieval world. Scholars of medieval music have been known to devote a lifetime of research on some of the sections in this chapter. It would be foolish indeed therefore to hope that in this chapter which attempts to survey approximately twelve hundred years of musical thought, in some degree of chronological order, that we could do more than stress the historic trends and modestly peruse the musical beliefs of those theologians and philosophers who wrote on the nature and meaning of music in their time.

Early Christian music was of Hellenic and Hebraic origin. Since Christianity grew out of Judaism, it is not surprising that much of the music of the Synagogue found its way into the Church Service. St. Paul related that the first Christian hymns were borrowed from the Jewish Liturgy. The music of the Greeks and the Romans was also incorporated into the sacred music of the Christian faith, sometimes with, but more often than not, without the approval of the Church dignitaries. There was little that was actually creative in Christian music at the outset. It was a conglomeration of the East and the West, the Hebrew and the pagan.

The early fathers of the Church, the Patristics, also retained the philosophy of music which the Judaic hierarchy had toward its own music and the music of the Greek and Roman pagan. The fathers could see only hypocrisy and sensuality in the heathen's music. They were well aware that the pagan rites and licentious music which surrounded the Christian imposed a severe temptation on the average Believer to give up a vague assurance of happiness in the distant future for a blissful present. Christianity's position was anything but secure either as a religious or political force as yet. In addition, Christians were subject to abuse and often faced with intolerant hostility. The Roman scoffed at and mocked this new religion which assured all men of salvation in the hereafter. As though this were not enough to draw the Christian out of the fold, the fathers had not only to cope with but to overcome the destructive influence banal melodies could inflict on the moral life of the Christian.

The music of the pagan was representative of his cultural, social and religious beliefs. When the fathers termed it degenerate they spoke of a comparative difference between the daily philosophies of the Roman and Christian. The emphasis on the carnal in Roman religion naturally reproduced itself in their religious and amorous music. By contrast, their music lacked the sincere plaintive songs which the Christian sang in the adoration of his God. Roman music stressed sentiments alien to the theological concepts embracing Christian thought. Since pagan music characterized the society which bore it, the root of the evil lay first with the decayed Roman culture and secondly with the musical pagan who was depicting his society in a type of song which strongly appealed to the emotions. Heathen and Christian alike could be equally responsive to its charms. The fathers were helpless against Rome, but they could endeavor to protect their flock from the vile influence emanating from the Roman's music.

The Church Fathers regarded any inclination to develop instrumental music or instruments with disfavor. These fathers of the early centuries, who bore the burden of getting Christianity safely on its way, may have shunned instruments because they were reminiscent of pagan practices. Another possibility is that the early Christians were compelled to meet secretly and could not use instruments in their hushed prayer meetings for fear of being detected by their adversaries.[1]

[1] Peter Wagner, *Introduction to the Gregorian Melodies*, p. 12f., Part I; (Translated by Agnes Orme and E. G. P. Wyatt), The Plainsong and Mediaeval Music Society, London: 1901. ". . . it should be noted that Christians were long compelled by external circumstances to adopt a hostile attitude towards instruments, as everything depended on their not lifting for their enemies the veil of secrecy which hid their meetings. If Christianity had come into the world without the thousand difficulties which actually beset it; if instead of gradually conquering them it could have taken possession at once, church music would certainly have had an entirely different development, and, in particular, Christians would have made use of the whole apparatus of the instrumental music of their age, and would have purified it from the strains which defiled it, just as they did not reject on principle other intellectual acquisitions which antiquity had made. It is no mere chance that, as soon as external circumstances allowed, instrumental music was actually brought into the church, and it is very remarkable that even the organ, composed of flutes, was admitted. It was popular especially in ancient times at secular concerts, and was introduced into the church by the Byzantine Rulers, who endeavoured to adorn divine worship with all possible magnificence; thence it spread into the whole Christian Church. It immediately attained the rank of a liturgical instrument, and it has, not merely in modern times but ever since then, exerted a remarkable influence on the development of Church music."

During the first two centuries of Christianity, the Patristics displayed the same mistrust of musical instruments or musical accompaniments in religious ceremonies as the Rabbis had. Clement of Alexandria (c. 150-220) points out that even "The flute belongs to those superstitious men who run to idolatry." Plato had warned against the orgiastic nature of this instrument (pipes). Both the Greeks and Romans employed it in their frenzied Dionysian rites. Clement could only view such an instrument with misgiving since it lent itself to the excitement of the flesh rather than to spiritual contemplation. But there were some few instruments that Clement did not associate with heathen rites or consider morally damaging. He quoted the playing of the lyre in the *Old Testament* and the soothing effect it produced upon King David. He also recalled the allegory of the Jewish philosopher Philo (b. c. 20 B.C.) who likened "the human tongue to the God praising lyre". Philo had viewed the lyre as an instrument free from sensuality that soothed the feelings and brought surcease from strife and Clement concurred with him in this belief.

Clement was influenced by his fellow Alexandrian, Philo, whose philosophy was a mixture of Hellenistic and Hebraic theory. Philo attempted to reconcile the Bible with the views of Plato and like Plato regarded music not as an end in itself, but as a preparation in mental discipline for the study of philosophy. Clement similarly regarded music not as an end in itself but as a disciplined emotional means with which to propagate the Christian Faith.

We do have a commentary, in which St. John Chrysostom described the music of the late 4th or perhaps early 5th century. St. Chrysostom repeated the common ecclesiastical thesis that music is a peculiarly empowered force which if virtuously used is often helpful toward the cultivation of the Good. But he warned that the Church Fathers must be on guard to stamp out any type of music with pagan qualities which might arouse the baser impulses in man. Christ's most ardent disciple, according to Chrysostom, had known the worth of music in developing the religious fervor of youth. But times had changed since Paul and, lamented Chrysostom, "your children will utter songs and dances of Satan, like cooks, and caterers, and musicians; no one knoweth any psalms, but it seems a thing to be ashamed of even, and a mockery and a joke. There is the treasury house of all these evils."[2] Chrysostom observed that nurses lulled infants to sleep with song. Peasants sang while gathering and treading grapes. Sailors had their sea songs and women their weaving ditties. The mind endured hardships and difficulties more easily when it heard songs and chants.

"Inasmuch as this kind of pleasure is thoroughly innate to our mind," wrote Chrysostom, "and lest demons introducing lascivious songs should overthrow everything, God established the psalms, in order that singing might be both a pleasure and a help. From strange chants harm, ruin, and many grievous matters are brought in, for those things that are lascivious and vicious in all songs settle in parts of the mind, making it softer and weaker; from the spiritual psalms, however, proceeds much of value, much utility, much sanctity, and every inducement to philosophy, for the words purify the mind and the Holy Spirit descends swiftly upon the mind of the singer. For those who sing with understanding invoke the grace of the Spirit."[3]

St. Jerome (c. 340-420) whose Latin translation of the Scriptures came to be known as the Vulgate wrote: "Sing to God, not with the voice, but with the heart; not, after the fashion of tragedians, in smearing the throat with a sweet drug, so that theatrical melodies and songs are heard in the church, but in fear, in work, and in knowledge of the Scriptures. And although a man be *kakophonos*, to use a common expression, if he have good works, he is a sweet singer before God. And let the servant of Christ sing so that he pleases, not through his voice, but through the words which he pronounces, in order that the evil spirit which was upon Saul may depart from those who are similarly troubled and may not enter into those who would make of the house of God a popular theatre."[4]

The fathers' primary interest in music throughout the growth

---

[2] *Nicene and Post-Nicene Fathers*, Vol. XIII, p. 301; The Christian Literature Co., New York: 1889.

[3] Oliver Strunk, *Source Readings in Music History*, p. 68; W. W. Norton and Co., Inc., New York: 1950.

[4] *Ibid.*, p. 72.

of the Church was purely moralistic. They regarded music as a means with which to enrich the Service and, without any artistic basis for their decisions, checked musical tendencies for free expression. Consequently, as the Church grew in strength and decreased in tolerance, its musical precepts became absolute. Whatever reference the Church Fathers did make to music was invariably with the thought of how it could best be used to bring pagans into the fold or to heighten the religious fervor of those attending the Service. If the music to which the Psalms were sung attracted the populace, then music served a useful purpose indeed. St. Augustine (354-430 A.D.) candidly stated this much in the following passage taken from his *Confessions*. ". . . sometimes, in the desire of having the melody of all pleasant music, to which David's Psalter is so often sung, banished both from mine own ears, and out of the whole church too: . . . I call to mind the tears I shed at the hearing of thy church songs, in the beginning of my recovered faith, yea, and at this very time, whenas I am moved not with the singing, but with the thing sung (when namely they are set off with a clear voice and suitable modulation), I then acknowledge the great good use of this institution. Thus float I between peril of pleasure, and an approved profitable custom: inclined the more (though herein I pronounce no irrevocable opinion) to allow of the old usage of singing in the Church; that so by the delight taken in at the ears, the weaker minds be roused up into some feeling of devotion. And yet again, so oft as it befalls me to be more moved with the voice than with the ditty, I confess myself to have grievously offended: at which time I wish rather not to have heard the music."[5]

The Psalms, which had such fascination for King David, are in reality the oldest music of the Christians even though Chrysostom showed concern that they were not so well accepted and sung as he would have liked. St. Basil (330–379) also pointed out their popular use throughout the Christian world. He further defended Psalm singing, both antiphonal and responsory, as a colorful practice which gave added decorative contrasts to

[5] *Bk.* X, Chap. XXXIII, p. 167f., Vol. 2; (Translated by William Watts), Wm. Heinemann, London: 1925.

the solemn Liturgy. A passage in his writings aptly illustrates the value of Psalm singing in Christian life. "For when the Holy Spirit saw that mankind was ill-inclined toward virtue and that we were heedless of the righteous life because of our inclination to pleasure, what did He do? He blended the delight of melody with doctrines in order that through the pleasantness and softness of the sound we might unawares receive what was useful in the words, according to the practice of wise physicians, who, when they give the more bitter draughts to the sick, often smear the rim of the cup with honey. For this purpose these harmonious melodies of the Psalms have been designed for us, that those who are of boyish age or wholly youthful in their character, while in appearance they sing, may in reality be educating their souls. For hardly a single one of the many, and even of the indolent, has gone away retaining in his memory any precept of the apostles or of the prophets, but the oracles of the Psalms they both sing at home and disseminate in the market place. And if somewhere one who rages like a wild beast from excessive anger falls under the spell of the psalm, he straightway departs, with the fierceness of his soul calmed by the melody."[6]

Augustine, Basil and Chrysostom each looked to music as a means with which to propagate the faith. They also exhorted the youth of Christendom not to forsake the Psalms for pagan music. For these Fathers, as for the Greek philosophers, music constituted an ethical dilemma. It could degrade as effectively as it could elevate. Such, were its moving powers.

David's *Book of Psalms* has been a rich source of poetry for musical literature. The Psalms were not poetry alone but were originally standardized songs with instrumental accompaniment. In accepting the Psalms for Her own, the Church made this traditional Biblical poetry the textual core of Her music. The poetical nature of the Psalms enriched with a chanting strain, lent itself so well to the Liturgy that the early Church Service consised primarily of Psalm singing.

One manner in which the Psalms were chanted was the direct Psalmody which means that the entire Psalm was sung straight through without any "textual addition or modification". In the

---

[6] Oliver Strunk, *Op. cit.*, p. 65.

second type, the responsory Psalmody, the form of chanting was identical with the manner in which it was originally performed in the Synagogue where a cantor sang the Psalm and a choir responded with an Amen. The Hebraic cantor indulged in florid coloratura singing of the Psalms. When the Christians adopted the Psalmody for their own use they omitted the coloratura or melismatic singing which the Jewish cantor displayed and marked their own chanting with a simple humility becoming a newly founded religion based on penance and submission. It did not take very long, however, before the Christian soloists and choirs began to sing melismas which grew all the more complex with succeeding years. The last of the three types of chanting consisted of the antiphonal Psalmody. This style of chanting effectively employed two alternating half-choruses concerning which Philo has left us a colorful description.[7]

The melismatic Alleluia with which the congregation responded to the cantor bears an added point of interest. Alleluia or Hallelujah literally means praise the Lord. Its ornate use which is reputed to have been of as long as a quarter hour's duration varied in degrees in the Byzantine Church. The jubilus derived its use from the melismatic exultation which came on the last syllable of the Alleluia. Augustine defined the jubilus as a form of praise to the Lord which expressed human feeling that could not be conveyed by mere words or letters. "He who sings a *jubilus*, speaks no words, but it is a song of joy without

---

[7] Peter Wagner, *Op. cit.*, p. 19; Gustave Reese, *Music in the Middle Ages*, p. 60; W. W. Norton and Co., Inc., New York: 1940. Philo left us numerous references to music, but practically all of a purely ethical character. He observed that even in his time the chanting of the newly founded Christian congregations was similar to that of the Therapeutae, an ascetic and mystical brotherhood of Egyptian Jews. "All at once on both sides rise up . . . and form two choirs, the one of men, the other of women. Each choir chooses as its leader and cantor one who is distinguished as well by the dignity of his person as by his skill in music. Then they sing hymns to God, composed in different metres and melodies, sometimes all together, sometimes answering one another in a skilful manner. Next . . . they form the two choirs into a single one . . . as did the Jews when they went through the Red Sea. One is reminded of this company by the choir of pious men and women, as throughout the singing and the alternation of the melodies the deeper sound of the men's voices and the higher sound of the women's voices singing together compose a sweet and true musical symphony."

words; it is the voice of a heart dissolved in joy, which tries as far as possible to express the feeling, even if it does not understand the meaning. When a man rejoices in his jubilation, he passes from some sounds which do not belong to speech and have no particular meaning, to exulting without words; so that it seems that he rejoices indeed, but that his joy is too great to put into words." "And for whom is this *jubilatio* more fitting than for the ineffable God?" asked Augustine with reference to the 32nd Psalm. "He is ineffable, for speech is too poor for Him; and if speech cannot help thee there and thou darest not be silent, what remains but to exult so that thy heart may rejoice without singing words, and the immeasurable breadth of joy may not experience the restriction of syllables?" St. Jerome expressed a similar conception of the aesthetic and religious value of the jubilus. "By the term *jubilus* we understand that which neither in words nor syllables nor letters nor speech is it possible to express or comprehend how much man ought to praise God."[8] Perhaps the Fathers felt that they had to justify the use of this Oriental practice. Oriental literature is weighed down with illustrations of melismatic singing; so too, is Hebraic, but where or how it originated is something for the historian to ponder over.

"How abundantly did I weep to hear those hymns and canticles of thine," wrote St. Augustine into his *Confessions* while speaking of his baptism and the tremendous emotional force which the musical form, the hymn, had upon him. ". . . being touched to the very quick by the voices of . . . thy truth pleasingly distilled into my heart, which caused the affections of my devotion to overflow, and my tears to run over, and happy did I find myself therein."[9] The earliest mention of the hymn in the annals of Christian music is immediately after the Holy Eucharist in which Jesus and his Disciples joined in song. In Greek times, the hymn was a song of praise or adoration for some god. The two hymns to Apollo, mentioned in the previous chapter, are precisely that. Any act of praise or thanksgiving to a deity on the part of the Greek was considered a hymn, pro-

---

[8] Peter Wagner, *Op. cit.*, p. 32f.
[9] *Bk.* IX, Chap. VI, p. 29; Wm. Heinemann, London: 1925.

vided it was sung. When taken over by the Christians, it retained the same status of a song in praise of the Lord. Its texts were mainly poems not based on the Psalms.

St. Ambrose (c. 340–397) was one of the pioneers in developing the hymnal form. There is no certainty whether he composed all the hymns attributed to him or whether he was primarily interested in popularizing them. It is fairly certain that much of the hymn writing done in his time has been attributed to him as an example of that period rather than as an Ambrosian creation. Numerous other Church Fathers contributed to its development and to its acceptance as a form which, even in the fourth century, was regarded as superior to the Psalm. Again, there is no telling whether the same person wrote the music and the text. The simplicity of the hymn lent itself to congregational singing or perhaps it was written in simple style so that the congregation could easily take it up. The ease with which the hymn could be learned was undoubtedly a factor which fostered its popularity so that it was readily accepted throughout the Christian world. Some few among the diocese would not accept the hymn on the grounds that they would not relinquish the Biblical text of the Psalms for a secular poetic setting. These poems, in addition, were accompanied by pleasing melodies which were reminiscent of pagan melodic strains. It may have been for no other reason than this that the hymn was not accepted into the Liturgy in Rome until the ninth century.[10]

SECTION II—*Boethius*

IN Plato's Dialogue the *Timaeus* the creation of the world is described as having its inception in geometric forms, isosceles

---

[10] The Council of Laodicea, which was held in the middle of the fourth century, functioned as a stern censor of religious and artistic matters. This Council actively sought to exclude any remnants of Greek musical thought which had been retained in the Mass or which had found its way into the Church in one way or another.

The Council of Laodicea evoked a ruling that only Biblical texts should be admitted into the Service. Hymns were, therefore, looked upon unfavorably since their poetical texts were not taken from the Scriptures. Some ten centuries later, this same attitude was expressed by the reformed Protestant Churches of France and Switzerland. They, too, maintained that no text was worthy of inclusion in the Liturgy unless it had a Biblical source.

and scalene right-angled triangles. Earthly and stellar motions are explained by intricate mathematics. It was this dialogue which found its way into the intellectual thought of the Middle Ages. The magical efficacy of numbers held an alluring fascination for Augustine and the early fathers. Numbers could explain music, memory, and the movements of the soul. God even created the world by merely setting the proper numbers together. Since numbers symbolized all that man was cognizant of Augustine concluded, like the Pythagoreans and Plato, that music was based on mathematical law and good order. The attributes of order, measure, and beauty in the physical world had their roots in numbers. The entire universal structure was based on a harmonious numerical relationship. This Pythagorean and Platonic influence is found in Augustine's *De Musica* which is devoted mainly to meter, verse and theories pertaining to numbers. The first five of the six books in this treatise deal with rhythm and meter and in the sixth book, Augustine discussed music in its cosmological and theological aspects.

Like the Pythagoreans he regarded music as an earthly manifestation of the universal rhythm and with Plato he saw a moral significance in this phenomenon. He warned the Christians not to mistake the symbol of musical rhythm for what the symbol represented. Beauty and music, for him, were only artistic imitations of a higher order which God gratuitously bestowed upon mankind. He admonished the Christians to model their attitude toward music to that of David of Israel, for David was the man "skilled in songs, who dearly loved musical harmony, not with a vulgar delight, but with a believing disposition, and by it served his God, who is the true God, by the mystical representation of a great thing. For the rational and well-ordered concord of diverse sounds in harmonious variety suggests the compact unity of a well-ordered City."[11]

Plato's Dialogue the *Timaeus* also exerted a strong influence on the Roman philosopher Boethius (480–524). He shared the Platonic view expressed in this dialogue by stating in his own writings: "that the soul of the universe is united by musical

---

[11] *City of God, Bk.* XVII, Chap. XIV, Vol. II; (Translated by Marcus Dods), Hafner Publishing Co., New York: 1948.

concord. For when, by means of what in ourselves is well and fitly ordered, we apprehend what in sounds is well and fitly combined, . . . we recognize that we ourselves are united by this likeness." A mathematical relationship, he reasoned, binds the soul to the universal soul. Music, which was essentially mathematical, therefore took on moral significance, for the proper kind of music could keep the soul of man in harmony with the world soul. Improper music would disarrange this mathematical relationship, degrade the soul and destroy the body of man. The aesthetic thesis of the Greeks, which was begun by the Pythagoreans and developed by Plato, that music is related to us by nature and can ennoble or corrupt character, found its ablest exponent in the Roman world in Boethius.

The Roman philosopher Boethius began his work on music as a follower of Pythagorean and Platonic doctrine. He agreed with the doctrine of these two schools of philosophy, that music was essentially mathematical and should be used as a discipline in preparation for the study of philosophy. Boethius also concurred in the view that music had ethical value which could inspire men to higher learning and help bring them closer to the true reality by freeing them from this deceptive world of perpetual change. He, too, believed that music had the power to degrade the morals of men when it appealed to the passions. Boethius reasoned that man was endowed with innate musical qualities and that it was possible to escape from the sensuous qualities of this art, which often incited physical desire, by devoting oneself to the theoretical study of music which appealed to reason, for the intellect was superior to the senses.

It was at the early age of twenty that this precocious philosopher dedicated his book on music to those of his own age in the vain hope of stimulating a love of philosophy among them. Boethius did not complete his writings on music. He referred to music, in the years that were left him, solely in terms of an educational discipline for intellectual study and of its value for a sound moral way of life.

Toward the end of his life, as he lay in a dungeon awaiting an untimely end, he wrote of the Muse as a siren warily leading all those astray who came under her seductive charms. He called the Muse of poetry and song a "tragic harlot" who offered man "sugared poison" instead of giving him wholesome philosophical remedies with which to relieve life's taxing burdens. Philosophy alone, the mother of all the Muses, came to Boethius to offer him consolation as he lay waiting for death.[12]

The goal which Boethius originally set for himself was "To resolve, in some measure, the ideas of Aristotle and Plato into harmony—". The impact of his philosophy upon the medieval musician was both profound and lasting. "Boethius declared that for the sake of reaching the 'summit of perfection' granted by the philosophical discipline alone, it is necessary that man master preliminary fields of knowledge—that is, the mathematical disciplines, the *Quadrivium*, a term that Boethius himself seems to have introduced into the Latin world, . . . Boethius was convinced that whoever neglected such studies was totally and hopelessly ignorant of philosophy as a whole. Such neglect is without remedy: it forever withholds the reward from the student who aspires to the summit of perfection; unless he passes through the study of music within the scope of mathematics, he will be barred from the realm of philosophy. In other words: to acquire a knowledge of mathematics is a necessity of the first order. The goal of study, the end of education, is always philosophy; but the only path to it leads through mathematics."[13] Music as a part of mathematics thus contributed to the training of the intellect and was considered a discipline for philosophic study.

Boethius maintained that because of its inherent ethical value, the study of music surpassed any other discipline in the *Quadrivium* in shaping the mind and body. He echoed Plato in saying that music was capable of "improving or degrading the morals of men". He pointed out that lascivious minds took pleasure in lascivious melodies and stern minds derived their pleasure from more stirring modes, for people took to modes resembling their own character. But all men were subject to

[12] *Consolations of Philosophy*, I, I, pp. 131-133; Harvard University Press, Cambridge: 1946.
[13] Leo Schrade, *Music in the Philosophy of Boethius*, The Musical Quarterly, pp. 188-190; April, 1947.

corruption, concluded Boethius, the weaker wills were softened and corrupted and sometimes not even strong wills were able to resist. Boethius then continued that Plato was justified in warning against musical innovations for changing musical styles that were ethically questionable would surely degrade the minds of men. "Music was chaste and modest," reflected Boethius, "so long as it was played on simpler instruments, but since it has come to be played in a variety of manners and confusedly, it has lost the modes of gravity and virtue and fallen almost to baseness, preserving only a remnant of its ancient beauty."

Boethius not only transmitted the views of the ancients to the medievalists but was himself responsible for shaping the musical aesthetics of Western civilization for many centuries after his death. The Christian theologians were more than pleased with the Boethian conclusion that since music was essentially mathematical in structure and moral in value, it was necessary that the composition of music be as exacting as science so as not to mar the ethical nature of the music. The end result of this doctrine, as it was modified and elaborated on by the followers of Boethius, was that the moral value of music became dependent on science and the science of music eventually resulted in stereotyped forms. Any departure from traditional musical forms or accepted ecclesiastical church music, therefore reasoned the churchmen, was both unscientific and iconoclastic. The churchmen well knew that this was implicit in Plato, but to be able to recognize one more authority, even if a Roman pagan, who held views that they could use to their own advantage, only strengthened their position. The constitution of Pope John XXII (Pope from 1316–1334), written eight hundred years after the untimely death of Boethius, which included an attack against the new music of the time, thought so well of Boethius' musical aesthetics that the writers of this papal document saw fit to quote him in defence of sacred music in the Christian church. To the exponents of this new music, both creators and appreciators, the church hierarchy quoted from Boethius: "A person who is intrinsically sensuous will delight in hearing these indecent melodies, and one who listens to them frequently will be weakened thereby and lose his virility of soul."

Cassiodorus (485–580), the more fortunate contemporary of Boethius, who, with Boethius, helped make the musical philosophies of the Greeks known to medieval scholars, also treated music as a mathematical discipline and retained a Platonic strain in his moralistic views on music. "The Dorian mode," wrote Cassiodorus in a letter to Boethius, "effects chastity and pudicity." With Plato he agreed that the Phrygian mode "stirs to fighting and engenders wrath". The Aeolian mode "calms the tempests of the soul and lulls the calmed soul into sleep." The fourth of the ancient modes, the Iastic, "sharpens dull insight and directs the profane mind toward heavenly aspirations." The last of the modes, the Lydian, was not viewed by Cassiodorus in a wholly Platonic manner, but rather as a musical style which had therapeutic value since this very Lydian mode "soothes the heavy cares of the soul and expels vexation by pleasant entertainment." In the musical philosophy of Cassiodorus, music could be of spiritual value to carry men closer to God. Music could also engender varying moods. It was also a potent form of katharsis which, according to Cassiodorus, expelled vexation and soothed the emotions.

SECTION III—*The Gregorian Chant*

THE Christian Church from its very inception carried out a periodic campaign to suppress paganism. In order to suppress the pagan's religion it was necessary to destroy his temple and wipe out his art. A widespread destruction of pagan temples housing the unbelievers' decorative idols and amulets followed in full justification, in the minds of the zealous Christians, that the will of God was being carried out by such acts. But when it came to erasing the pagan's music, the zealots were helpless. There were no manuscripts to burn or composers to chastise. The music itself represented nothing tangible, but only ideas and expression. How does one kill ideas and expression?

As early as Augustine's time this religious hostility toward art was already well entrenched. There was a rising tide of opposition even to Christian art itself on the part of the clergy in the fourth century. By the time the sixth century came around, Gregory the Great, born 540 and Pope from 590–604, had already, while serving as Bishop of Marseilles, ordered the removal and destruction of all the sacred imagery within his diocese. His actions were based on the belief that there was a distinction between worshipping a picture itself and regarding it as a symbol. Gregory was fearful lest the common man should begin to worship the symbol rather than what the symbol represented. Music presented a similar problem. If the average churchgoer became so charmed by the sensuous appeal of religious music as to forget that the music was only meant to embellish the Holy Text, then music must be kept simple and the text emphasized.

Pope Gregory may well have recalled Augustine's warning to the Christians not to mistake the symbol of musical rhythm for what the symbol represented, for beauty and music were only artistic imitations of a higher order which God beneficently bestowed upon mankind. Gregory must have cherished the passage in Augustine which read: "Alas for those who love instead of you, your beckonings and stray among the traces." The views which St. Augustine expressed with reference to music in Christian life could not have found a more active champion than in Pope Gregory.

Gregory the Great is perhaps the most renowned of the pontifical figures. History has portrayed him as an art devotee and again as a powerful personality devoid of any artistic feeling or imagination. Various writers in the Middle Ages have eulogized him as a great and beneficent Churchman without bothering to distinguish between Pope Gregory's ecclesiastical genius for solidifying the Church and his disdain for art and learning. These writers have imputed liberal theories to him which were totally foreign to his philosophy. Succeeding generations came to know him, paradoxically, not for his masterful political and organizing ability, but for the music associated with his name.

To be certain that Christian principles and teachings were not questioned or heretically refuted, Gregory banned secular learning and gave to theological studies a prominence which it had never had before. Science and art were excluded from religious education. But since it was the common practice in the Middle Ages to regard music as a branch of mathematics, it was included in the educational quadrivium, composing arithmetic, geometry, astronomy and music.

Since Gregory had little use for secular learning it is no small wonder that profane musical tendencies, which needed constant suppression, did not particularly appeal to him. So zealous was he in religious administration that five years after ascending to the Papacy he is known to have censured certain church officiators who, following their vanity, cultivated their voices for the musical portion of the Service with time that should have been spent in more constructive ways. Gregory, thereupon, decreed that the deacons were to sing only the Gospel, and their subordinates were to sing the remainder of the musical part of the Service. He took the necessary steps to supply such subordinates by building additional seminaries and setting up a schola cantorum which furnished the Papal choirs with singers.

Following in the Augustinian path, Gregory looked upon music as only an aid in the officiation of the Service. He also adhered to Augustine's late beliefs by shunning everything and anything pagan that could possibly influence the Christian. Art and music, therefore, were erased as a cultural activity. Learning and research, however vague, were replaced by discipline, denial and penance. Yet, to this same Pope Gregory the Great was attributed the creative role of composing part of the antiphonal and the organization of the Liturgy. Musicologists, however, have reason to believe that this is more legendary than factual.[14]

The origin of the Gregorian Chant is a varied one. It was evolved out of Oriental, Hebrew and Greek music and the earlier simpler form of the Ambrosian Chant. One reason that is given for the creation of the Gregorian Chants is that they arose as a result of many complaints from the sectional clergy

[14] Paul H. Lang, *Music in Western Civilization,* pp. 62-65; W. W. Norton and Co., Inc., New York: 1941.

that church music was being performed improperly and much too sentimentally. Gregory is reputed to have gathered the varied ecclesiastical forms, sifted, altered, supposedly created new melodies, and then decreed in precisely what manner and in what place of the Service a particular bit of music belonged, thereby instituting a practice which led to a rigidly fixed and diversified Liturgy.

The Gregorian Chant is divided into three melodic categories: the syllabic, neumatic and melismatic. In the first group, each syllable of the text was set to fit just one note. On occasion, a syllable would be fitted to two or possibly three notes, but the tunes always remained of a simple character. In the neumatic form, some syllables were used with one note, but the usual practice was to have one syllable placed against a group of two or three notes. The third, the melismatic, was a florid style in which a lone syllable was sung quite ornately.

Gregorian melodies were constructed on a tonal system of four modes to begin with. Although these modes had their musical roots in Oriental and Hebraic tonalities, they are nevertheless called ecclesiastical modes since we associate their peculiar modal quality with the religious chant. The original four modes were called the Chief, but more commonly the Authentic modes. When four more were added, they were given the name of the Plagal modes. Composers employed them solely for men's voices.

Early Gregorian composers did not create original music. Their efforts were expended in adapting traditional tunes or parts of them and then revising them so as to fit some specific part of the varied Liturgy. The artistic efforts of these composers were centered on a formal revamping and rearranging of traditional tunes. So ingenious were they as arrangers that although the ecclesiastical music of the Middle Ages was based on a fairly limited number of melodies, they were nevertheless set to an abundant variety of forms. The ecclesiastical composer with monastic patience took infinite care to achieve a balance between the text and music, so that the text would not be sacrificed or the music become turgid. When a text was repeatedly used for a different part of the Liturgy, the composer would enhance it with a contrasting melody to suit its new function. These composers attained such artistry with monophonic writing that their contribution has remained a virile source of artistic stimulation for all who compose music.

A considerable amount of the Gregorian repertoire developed outside of Rome through the ensuing centuries. As the Church expanded, so spread its chant. England received it quite early through Papal missionaries. Many monastaries in Ireland untiringly added to its growth. Charlemagne saw to its acceptance in France and Germany. As a practical ruler he sought unity throughout his kingdom and wisely nurtured the ecclesiastical chant so that it might serve him as a unifying force. The Gauls, we are told, were unable to sense the aesthetic purity of the chants because of their native uncouthness and insisted on adding to this ecclesiastical music some refrains from their own none too welcome songs.

The Gregorian Chant employed a system of neumes as a means of notation. These neumes, which are to be found in Gregorian manuscripts preserved from as early as the 9th century, were able to give the singer only an approximate suggestion of the melodic course. The melodies and forms were conveyed from one generation to another, in a verbal tradition, since the neumes could only refresh the memory. Nevertheless, this system of neumes carried directly over into modern notation since it was able to denote a rise or fall of the melodic line to the singer. At some time in these past centuries a monk conceived the idea of musical notation and for some reason selected a horizontal line to mark off and divide one pitch from another. Shortly after, a second line must have been added so that by the 11th century the first known musical lines appear in manuscripts. A red line designated the tone F and a yellow line (sometimes green) stood for C. This led to the formation of the F and C clefs beginning with the 12th century, after which followed the G clef. Guido d'Arezzo, (995–1050) a Benedictine monk, improved on staff notation and is believed to have presented new theories on notation to Pope John XIX in the early part of the 11th century.

SECTION IV—*The Medieval Philosopher and Music*

MANY ecclesiastical musical forms owe their birth to secular and, not too infrequently, to profane texts with catchy tunes; in turn, church music directly influenced secular music. The clerical hierarchy kept a watchful eye on secular and what they considered profane music throughout the early development of the Church. Songs of the vernacular nevertheless found their way into the sanctuary. Those who worshipped and the priests who conducted the worship were similarly attracted by the secular music of the day and as a consequence the admonitions which came out of Rome were directed to both clergy and parishioners alike. The Church felt that it must give no quarter or dabble in alternatives if it was not only to hold its ground but to remain a stable and orderly bulwark against paganism and heretical influences.

In the development of musical forms we saw that the Psalms, which the Hebrews bequeathed to the Christians, were the oldest part of Church music. Jesus was so familiar with the Liturgy of the Synagogue that when taking leave of his Disciples he marked the religious tone of the Last Supper by the singing of Psalms. In later years, heathens and converts who curiously observed or zealously entered into the Church's activities became familiar with the Psalter. As the sects fled from their persecutors, they carried the Psalms wherever they found new homes. So widespread did the Psalmody subsequently become that it simultaneously fettered the Christian sects and also served as a rich musical source from which all the brethren could draw strength and spiritual comfort to see them through periods of trial.

St. Ambrose and his followers enhanced the status of the hymn in the ecclesiastical repertoire. It is not certain whether the melodies used for these hymns were solely of a folk origin or whether a good many of them were composed by the clerics. In either case, the melodic form of the early hymn was simple in character, which undoubtedly helped foster its acceptance and popularity. Each syllable of a text was set to one note of music to assure the greatest degree of simplicity.

The Gregorian Chant subordinated the melody to the text.

Since the chanting served as a melodic setting to a sacred text, the melody had to be unobtrusive and remain content to serve as a background. Many a Hebrew melody is ably disguised in the chant. Gregorian Chants also bear relics of the Greek musical system. The origin of the neumes used in the chant is somewhat of a mystery. We know that the Hebrews used vowel accents in singing their canticles. Whether this practice influenced the Christians, or how and when they arrived at their system of neumes, is unknown to us.

Isidore of Seville (570–636) stated that much of the music of his time had to be memorized and passed on by word of mouth to other generations, otherwise it would be lost forever. It was not until some four centuries later that Guido of Arezzo, who maintained that "no physical conclusion is of musical value which the ear does not endorse", invented notation and the beginnings of the scale as we know it today. Historians differ on precisely what his status was, but it is safe to assume that a major portion of the contribution granted him is historically sound. Guido devised a system which led to the solfeggio in which we use syllables to read notation. He took the hymn to St. John the Baptist and incorporated the first syllable of each line to indicate a different step of the scale.

> Ut queant laxis Resonare fibris
> Mira gestorum Famuli tuorum
> Solve polluti Labii reatum
> Sancte Joannes.

A whole tone separated ut to re, re to mi, fa to sol, sol to la and from mi to fa was a half note. The ut was later changed to do and the two initials of the last line in the poem were brought in after Guido as si to round out the full scale. Guido originally included an extra tone preceding ut, using the Greek character gamma, which added to ut, conceived the term gamut. In subsequent years, the word gamut came to denote the full scale structurally.

Guido was also concerned with the moral status of music in his time. He levelled the same charge against the attitude of many of the clergy toward music as Pope Gregory the Great had done more than four hundred years earlier. "And what is the most dangerous thing of all, many clerics and monks of the religious order neglect the Psalms, the sacred readings, the nocturnal vigils, . . . while they apply themselves with unceasing and most foolish effort to the science of singing. . . ."

The art of sequence, or the setting of a text to the final vowel of the Alleluia, is thought to have originated in Northern France in the 9th century. St. Augustine and St. Jerome, about 500 years before, had praised the extended vocalization of the Alleluia, or jubilus, as an exultation to God without words. The jubilus, however, did not lend itself easily to memorization and the idea of adding a text was begun to help the singers remember the extended melodies. To begin with, a syllable was applied to each note but eventually the sequences became so complex and overly popular that they posed a threat to the religious character of the Liturgy. The Church did not take kindly to this development of the sequence or to the art of troping either. The trope was an interpolation between the sung parts of the Mass.

The art of tropes and sequences was at the outset confined to the monasteries. Only later did they drift into the musical activities of the secular church parish, and then the art of troping in the vernacular was gradually inserted into the Liturgy by the clergy to elucidate the sung parts of the Latin Mass to the congregation. So popular did the trope and sequence become in the parishes that they developed into disturbing elements which threatened the traditional uniformity of the Liturgy. Since the trope and sequence were never recognized or accepted by the hierarchy as official parts of the Liturgy and because the Council of Trent (1545–1563) objected to their liturgical merit and poetic freedom, Pope Pius V, therefore, ruled that all but a few of the sequences be excluded from further use in the official Church Liturgy and that troping be completely eliminated from the Liturgy. The few sequences which were granted survival still retain their place in the Liturgy.

The extent to which the medieval philosophers directly or indirectly affected the course of music was considerable. St. Augustine zealously believed that it would be well to ban all pagan music and literature so that Christians would not be tempted to read the Roman poets or visit the Roman theatre. There was also a mystical side to this Saint's evaluation of music. He adhered to Pythagorean principles which reduced and attempted to explain the phenomenon, music, by proper number relations. Augustine reasoned that God had constructed the universe by assembling all the elements in exactly the right proportions so that each element was harmoniously balanced and equated with all the others according to Divine Will. If the element of rhythm in music was a copy of the universal pattern, then, Augustine concluded, music was a miniature representation of universal motion itself. This view was Platonic and had already been repeated by Plotinus. Boethius carried this argument one step further along the philosophical course of speculation by evaluating music in general according to Platonic theory. However theoretical the philosophers may have been in their evaluation of music, we need reflect only briefly to realize how greatly their metaphysical and ethical theories have influenced the course of musical growth.

The Catholic philosophers who lived in the several centuries following the first thousand years of Christianity were as uncompromising in their Platonic views on music as their predecessors were. Their philosophical positions may have been, in some instances, more humanistic than those of their predecessors, but their attitude toward music was equally as mystical. The underlying theme of humanism that we find in the philosophy of Abelard, the credo of St. Francis and the theology of St. Thomas, somehow is not carried over into their writings on music. The views which Abelard and St. Francis had on music as students were modified considerably after they had been admitted into the officialdom of the Church. The sensual pleasures which they originally received from music as young people took on an irreligious character in their estimation as Churchmen since the music of their former days suggested pleasure rather than repentance; it had appealed to the flesh and not to the spirit.

St. Augustine and Boethius both found an affinity between order in music and the moral order which prevailed throughout the universe. These two philosophers, Christian and Roman, maintained that well-regulated music was imitative of the order in the universe. Both men believed that music could improve or degrade the morals of man. Augustine and Boethius also fostered the Platonic theory that music was a form of mathematics which could help discipline the intellect and that by analogy mathematics instilled a harmonious order in the universe. To the followers of Boethius, this Platonic view was interpreted to mean that music was a science which was governed by the same mathematical laws that brought order to the universe and produced the harmony of the spheres. The science of music must therefore be as exacting as the mathematical laws which governed the universe. This Boethian view was to dominate the aesthetics of music for many centuries to come.

The youthful Abelard (1079–1142) distinguished himself as a musician whose accomplishments in composition and lute playing earned him a considerable reputation as a minstrel. We usually think of Abelard, Churchman and humanist, as a romantic writer of letters to Heloise and as a composer of vernacular songs which the Paris students sang. We often forget, however, that he composed or rearranged a number of hymns for the Church[15] and that he looked upon philosophy as a means with which to make Christian precepts intelligible.

St. Francis, like the rest of the dandies of his day, also composed songs and poems as a young man. But the older St. Francis, who felt that no suffering was too great to emulate the life of Christ, wrote the *Hymn to the Sun* as he lay close to death in a rat ridden cell. A hymn to the sun by a lesser Christian figure might have been regarded as pagan, but the pantheism of St. Francis which embraced a love for all God's creations was beyond question in faith and charity.

The eight centuries which separated St. Thomas (c. 1225–1274) from St. Augustine marked an approximate beginning and end of medieval philosophy. Indeed, medieval philosophy cannot be dissociated from theology since the scholastic thinkers

---

[15] Henry Osborn Taylor, *The Medieval Mind*, p. 51; MacMillan and Co., Ltd., London: 1927.

"At thy prayers, my sister Heloise, once dear to me in the world, now most dear in Christ, I have composed what in Greek are called hymns, and in Hebrew *tillim*."

exhausted their energies constructing systems of logical reasoning which would inductively and deductively prove the existence and divinity of God. Augustine and Thomas, the two intellectual giants of this period, held divergent philosophical positions on theory. But in their views on music there was no disagreement. St. Thomas shared the Augustinian view that the science of music was based on principles established by mathematics. "Hence, just as music accepts on authority the principles taught by the arithmetician, so sacred science accepts the principles revealed by God."[16]

Although the Catholic philosophers were aware that instrumental music as well as singing is described in the *Old Testament*, they tended to associate instruments with pagan rites and carnal pleasure. The more zealous Catholic philosophers even attributed symbolic significance to musical instruments. St. Augustine viewed the timbrel and psaltery as a reminder of the Saviour's taut body on the Cross. "On the timbrel leather is stretched, on the psaltery gut is stretched; on either instrument the flesh is crucified."[17] St. Augustine could not view these instruments with the same gaiety as the Hebrews in the *Old Testament*: "Let them sing a psalm unto Him with timbrel and psaltery."

The medieval philosophers of Christian faith whom we have considered were members of the Church in one official capacity or another. Their views on music have an inestimable importance for us in our day. The Patristics actually set up a criterion of values for religious music based on Greek philosophy and Hebrew theology which St. Augustine crystallized in his own writings. The Christian philosophers have contributed to our knowledge of music by leaving us descriptions and evaluations of the meaning and nature of music in their time. The Roman philosophers preserved the musical views of the Greeks in their more original form. They did not modify the Greek philosophies of music to religious needs as the early Church Fathers had

---

[16] *Basic Writings of St. Thomas Aquinas, The Summa Theologica*, Part I, Question 1, Article 2, Vol. I; Random House, New York: 1945.

[17] *Nicene and Post-Nicene Fathers*, Vol. VIII, p. 678; The Christian Literature Co., New York: 1888.

done. Aristides Quintilianus summarized the musical philosophies that were taught in the Academy and Lyceum and Boethius tried "To resolve in some measure, the ideas of Aristotle and Plato into harmony." Both the Christian and the Roman philosophers influenced the aesthetic course of music. They summarized the musical philosophies of the Hellenic culture which preceded their own. They evaluated this music and applied it to the needs of Western man. However we may agree or disagree with their evaluation and utilization of the music which they inherited from ancient Greece, the fact of the matter is that they have given us a set of aesthetic principles which are still used as a fundamental basis of judgment in our own day by church and state.

SECTION v—*The Liturgical Drama*

THE liturgical drama was a religious play that emerged from the art of medieval music. It started out as a simple means of explaining the Scriptures to the untutored parishioners and eventually degenerated into a pseudo-religious play that desecrated the holy church in which it was performed. The origin of the medieval liturgical drama has a vague historical parallel to the romanticized version which the philosopher Nietzsche gave of the beginnings of the Greek drama in his book, *The Birth of Tragedy From the Spirit of Greek Music*. The Greek drama was born from the spirit of Greek music, according to Nietzsche, and then degenerated into vaudeville-like sketches in the Roman playhouse. The liturgical drama arose out of the art of musical tropes and then fell into disrespectful presentations of Scriptural life and anecdotes.

The Patristics envisaged the theatre as a sensuous and bizarre form of art. Their prime spokesman, Augustine, lamented that the youth were entranced with the Homeric fables which the Roman playwrights unravelled before them.[18] In the second book of his *Confessions* he implied that the Christian received a sentimental joy in feeling more sorry for sinful lovers and spectacular villains in the theatre than they did for their own marred

18 *Confessions, Bk.* I, Chap. XVI.

souls and the wretched among them.[19] The overzealous puritan
Tertullian (c. 155–c. 222 A.D.), who left the Mother Church for
a weird heretical sect more in keeping with an ascetic Christianity, touched on the pagan theatre and religious music in his
writings. He pictured the Roman theatre as a heathen temple
which housed the two demons of drunkenness and lust, Bacchus
and Venus. Tertullian traced the origin of the theatre to the
pagan temple and the sacrificial altar on which the pagan, amid
the tune of pipes and blaring trumpets, spread incense and
offered up gifts to his unworthy gods.[20] Theatricals of such
beginnings could not possibly be the moral equal of the good
Christian music which the believers sang among themselves.
Psalms and hymns led men closer to God. The pagan theatre
drew men down to the Devil.

But the Church had a genius for overcoming obstacles hinder-
ing its religious growth and political ambitions. It was most
adroit in resolving philosophical antinomies to reconcile its
theology and it showed a similar ingenuity in its methods of
coaxing the heathen into the fold. To begin with, the Church
adopted the pagan's music whenever it was necessary and desirable to do so and converted his melodies to Its own use. Several
centuries passed and the Church began to look with favor upon
the educational virtues of symbolic painting. Only the theatre,
of the primary arts, was still to be brought into the artistic
trinity and this was achieved with the liturgical drama.

Religion, music, and text comprised the three elements of the
liturgical drama. In its beginning, the liturgical drama was a
mere dramatic dialogue which grew out of the tropes that were
inserted into the Liturgy to explain the sung parts of the Mass
to the congregation. The Liturgy had retained its traditional
Latin text despite the prevailing ignorance of the time which
denied the average Christian a knowledge of Classic Latin. Consequently, very few churchgoers understood the Liturgy. With
the advent of troping, the parishioners could at least follow the
literary phase of the Mass. This revolutionary turn came with
the explanatory interpolations which related the meaning of the

[19] *Ibid., Bk.* III, Chap. II.
[20] *De. Spectaculis, Bk.* X.

Service in the language of the people. This meant that no longer was the Mass to be comprehended by the few who were schooled, but the ordinary Christian could delight in his understanding of the troped portions of the Service. The popularity of the trope was so overwhelming that the interpolators, not being content to have it remain mere dialogue, added the third element, rhythm and rhyme.

The tropes were originally rendered in the form of a response. One member of the officiating clergy would either chant or read a passage from the Gospel or an Epistle in Latin and two or three other minor clergymen would respond by singing a paraphrase of the Scriptural passage or Epistle in the vernacular. After rhythm and rhyme were added to this dialogue a new dramatic form emerged which lent itself to more pretentious dramatic opportunities, such as relating religious history based on the miracles and mysteries of the Christian religion and the life and deeds of the Saints. The next advancement in the development of the liturgical drama was the inclusion of scenery to make the action appear more realistic.

The scope of dramatic action in the liturgical drama grew to such proportions that it exhausted the limited ranks of the clergy and there was no alternative but to bring in parishioners and university students to fill prescribed roles. It was at this time that the use of Latin in these religious plays began to wane since many of the lay actors could neither speak nor understand the language. Added to this difficulty, the lay actors as well as the clergy and choir boys participating in the drama began to improvise their parts and insert "profane" words and tunes so that numerous Church authorities decreed that lay actors were responsible for the degeneration of these holy plays and had to be excluded from participating in the liturgical drama. The Churchmen were also concerned over the fact that the liturgical drama, which originally began as troping in the monasteries and later became an aid in explaining the Service in the Parish Church, was now serving the purpose of encouraging the boy actors in these plays to bring secular music into the house of worship and to render this non-sacred music before the very altar. If the Church dignitaries needed assurance that they were not to relent in their vigil over music and morality, they found ample justification for their policy in reviewing the introduction of the lay actor into the liturgical drama.

The liturgical drama came into existence around the tenth century when the priests began to perform Christian plays for their parishioners in the church as part of important religious festivals. The performances were first given in Latin. In the eleventh century they were also given in the vernacular. With time, these religious plays grew into elaborate enterprises and the audiences which came to them became more numerous. The plays grew to such proportions and popularity, that they were given outside of the church, as well as inside the church, and in the "vulgar tongue".

The audiences came to these liturgical plays eventually for amusement more than for Christian enlightenment, and the performers were expected to provide the fun. The comic element in the liturgical drama increased and the plays grew "profane". As the texts in the liturgical drama became debased, so did the music. What had started out as a method of Christian education through the use of musical tropes degenerated into a play with music that emphasized the principle of entertainment more than religious enlightenment.

SECTION VI—*The Itinerant Musician*

THE eleventh century dispelled a prevalent superstitious fear, which was held in medieval times, that the world was to come to an end in anticipation of the return of Christ in the year one thousand. When this phenomenon failed to materialize, men started to build once more, to plan and to create. The world was to survive after all. God had heard the prayers and religious songs of the Christians and in His benevolence had postponed the day of Judgment. The Church then pointed out that the young must retain the faith and sacred music of their elders so that the omnibenevolent God who watched over Christendom would be pleased by their songs and responsive to their prayers in the same way that He had been to the religious music and supplications of their fathers.

This period of thanksgiving for man's survival had not yet subsided, in the beginning of the 11th century, when students and minor clergy began to migrate from one university town to another. They travelled through Europe until the early 13th century, presumably as budding theologians in search of knowledge and truth. But before giving themselves to asceticism or priestly garb, they entertained the desire to drink a full portion of worldly bliss which eventually hurried some to a full confession and turned others away from the Church altogether. These travelling students soon degenerated into a class of vagrantes or vagantes. They are ordinarily remembered by the name of goliards and are known to have been particularly active and influential in Germany and somewhat less so in France and England When not drinking or defrauding peasants, they took time to compose numberless parodies based on sacred texts or they used liturgical themes with a taunting text, pointed at morality and religion. While roaming about through much of Europe, on their way from one university to another, these wandering students and aspiring ecclesiastics were creating music, performing it and what is more, exchanging ideas. When their creativity failed them, they had no compunction about borrowing themes outrightly from hymns, litanies and the Mass. Sacred melodies and texts became subject to frivolous interpretation and ridicule. The entire repertoire of religious music became prey to the witticisms and irreligious parody of these students. The more depraved these students became as a group, the baser became their altered texts, the more mocking their borrowed and created melodies. The Church, irked by their satire and doubtful of their religious sincerity, denied them entry into her cloistered domains.

The French jongleurs, even more than the goliards, kept the art of music alive through the Middle Ages. Some of these itinerant musical poets were unschooled vagabonds who earned their way through life by the quick of the hand and sheer wit. They would just as soon furnish the music for a peasant wedding or perform acrobatic stunts at some noisy carnival as they would take the leading parts in religious plays. Their journeys carried them from province to province where they delighted the people with their stunts, gossip and song. To the people, the jongleur was their newspaper and theatre and bearer of song.[21] He brought laughter wherever he set foot and sometimes sad refrains. The people loved him for his roguishness, his music and witticisms. Yet, they feared him for his enticing charm and "supernatural powers" with which he could bewitch them.

There were also the tutored jongleurs, sometimes of noble birth, who found their way into feudal households and princely courts as singers, poets and reciters of ancient classical odes. Jongleurs of this status either remained as permanent members of a household or they would travel from court to court singing their songs and rendering poems to an invariably appreciative audience. Ecclesiastical dignitaries, nobles and rich burghers feted their guests and lavishly entertained to the music and poetry of this phenomenal personality, the jongleur.

The origin of the jongleurs is obscure although their presence on the Continent was quite in evidence in the 9th century. It is probable that they descended from the Latin mime who also played the part of a vagabond and often followed the Roman legions, entertaining Caesar's soldiers and the newly conquered peoples who were forcibly welcomed into the Empire. The jongleur followed the Crusaders, not because he had a religious urge to drive Islam from the Holy Land, but, because, like the mime, he took advantage of any adventurous expedition which gave him an outlet for his restlessness and an opportunity to sell his musical wares. The jongleur, like the mime, was an itinerant entertainer whom the chroniclers of Catholic literature shunned and ignored. The Church considered them particularly obnoxious since they were the most direct representatives of pagan culture who could infuse their "poisonous charm" into Christian morality through song.

The jongleur's role in the dark ages is not altogether consistent or clear. Jongleurs were poets and musicians of considerable originality. The Church officially regarded them as outcasts and yet it was not unusual to find an eminent jongleur listed as part of the household of some ecclesiastical dignitary.

[21] Pierre Aubry, *Trouvères and Troubadours*, p. 102; (Translated by Claude Aveling), G. Schirmer, New York: 1914.

Even monasteries occasionally beckoned the jongleur to their midst for special festivities. Quite obviously, churchmen in their private lives did not always adhere to the numerous decrees which various ecclesiastical councils voiced against the jongleur. The common man, for his part, enjoyed the antics of the jongleur at the religious carnivals and marvelled at his ability to heighten the colorful festivities in honor of some Saint. Still, he naively believed that this same jongleur was a bearer of the devil's brew and license.

Classed among the sorcerers and considered a sinful lot, the Church held the jongleurs to be a threat to religious authority and on occasion denied them Communion and the Sacraments. The Church regarded the jongleur from the 11th to the 13th centuries in the same manner as the early fathers envisaged the Latin mimes; as an insidious threat to Christian morality. The point of significance is that just as the mimes were the bearers of the secular music and poetry of their day so the jongleur kept music, poetry and perhaps literature, all of a semi and non-religious nature, alive through the latter part of the Middle Ages.

How did these musical-poets learn their art? Schools supposedly existed where budding jongleurs received instruction in the art of playing and singing. Jongleurs convened regularly during the Lenten season during which time they were forbidden to perform before the public. These meetings afforded them an opportunity to discuss matters in common and to exchange parts of their repertoire with each other.

The majority of knightly troubadours included a jongleur in their entourage.[22] It was the function of the jongleur to arrange his knight's music, replenish the repertoire with newly written tunes or poems and even furnish instrumental music. The jongleur did not actually accompany the knight when he sang, but he would probably fiddle his bowed instrument, perhaps a vielle (a parent of our present violin), playing introductions, interludes and postludes.[23] Jongleurs were also called upon

[22] *Ibid.*, p. 6ff.
[23] Gustave Reese, *Music in the Middle Ages*, p. 203; W. W. Norton and Co., Inc., New York: 1940.

to perform the newly composed songs of their masters whenever the occasion called for it. The jongleur also was expected to compensate for his knight's artistic deficiencies. A knightly troubadour who wrote graceful verses but mediocre tunes would acquire the services of a jongleur adept at composing melodies, or the other way around. A troubadour who could compose poetry and song, sing and play, would be less dependent on the jongleur. A stringent ethical code reduced the most eminent troubadour to the rank of a jongleur were he to allow his art to become mercenary or a means of livelihood. It was also possible for an exceptionally gifted jongleur, such as Colin Muset, to promote himself to the class of troubadour.

The jongleurs have been referred to as the "genuine Bohemian" of the medieval art world. They consisted of an unorganized group of colorful individuals for the greater part of their existence. A social distinction was originally made between the roving illiterate jongleur and his more cultured brother who frequented court circles or lived in the castle of some nobleman where his status was at best that of a favored servant. His picturesque garb and cosmopolitan air gave him entrée to the highest and lowest social functions. By either the end of the 13th or early 14th century the jongleurs had achieved social status and recognition. It was about this time that the name minstrel was commonly used for all jongleurs.

The home of the troubadour was in southern France. By the second half of the 12th century his poetry and songs found their way from the southern into the northern provinces. This was partly due to the Crusade of 1147 which brought parties of pilgrims together from the north and south, and partly through royal marriages that united families from both sectors. The troubadour of the north assumed the name of trouvère to distinguish himself from his southern cousin.

Some of the poems of the troubadours and trouvères dealing with love, religion and politics were set to several melodies, but the troubadours and trouvères did not permit the use of the same melody for any two different texts. A slight variation of the original melody would be accepted as something new, but repetition of an existing melody would mar the reputation of the singer and the song. The most musically gifted of the known trouvères was Adam del la Halle who composed *Robin et Marion*, the oldest preserved play we have of French medieval society which is a secular subject set to music.

The musical aesthetics of the troubadour was based on simplicity. Poetic text and musical line were treated with equal consideration. The troubadour regarded his poetry and song as a unified art form. He did not, as a rule, separate one from the other. Dante briefly summed up their philosophy in the *Divine Comedy* with the aphorism of the troubadour, Folquert of Marseilles, that "A verse without music is a mill without water."

The troubadour and minstrel carried their art across the Channel into England somewhat after the Norman conquest of 1066. Eleanor of Aquitaine originally introduced the art of the troubadour into northern France when she married Louis VII while he was yet a prince. Eleanor possessed a strong affection for music and was regarded by the troubadours of Aquitaine as their muse and guardian of song. When she came to northern France for her marriage she brought the famous troubadour, Bernard de Ventadorn, with her to introduce the music of the southern province to the northern one.[24] In the year 1152 her marriage to Louis VII was annulled after which she became the wife of Henry of Anjou, the first of the Angevin line to assume the rule of England. Again, she reputedly brought Bernard de Ventadorn to her court to have him introduce the art of the troubadour into England. So great was the impact of Norman court life upon the Anglicans that French became the state language and French literature and music became the vogue among the intellectuals and nobility.

French art spread its influence in yet another direction, Germany. Once more, a woman's love for music influenced the cultural life of an entire nation. When Beatrix of Burgundy married Frederick Barbarossa she brought the trouvère, Guiot de Provins, with her to Germany. Through their joint efforts French music and literature colored Germanic art and thought. The vagantes had already left their musical mark upon the German people and the importation of French artistic ideas

---

[24] Walter Pater, *The Renaissance*, pp. 31-33; Jonathan Cape, London: 1928.

blended with goliard poetry and songs created a rich musical background for the minnesinger. The music and poetry of the German minnesinger, like that of the French trouvère, dealt with love, religion, politics and intrigue.

The minnesinger became, through his songs and poems, Germany's prophet. There was something astir in the political atmosphere which the sensitive imagination of the minnesinger interpreted as impending change. No doubt, he had the support of the Hohenstaufen dynasty. The minnesinger questioned the divine role and social powers of the papacy. He would have torn Christianity asunder in Germany were it not that Pope Innocent III recovered the power for the Church which it originally held and became master of the political situation. But the artist had already set the spark to the fiery imagination of the thinking element throughout Germany and Austria. Even though Papal authority became supreme once more in the Germanic provinces, the momentum of change had only come to rest until another artist, more fanatic and zealous than Plato, broke with Rome completely.

The minnesinger, Walther von der Vogelweide, was born into the nobility so that his place in the intrigue filled Hohenstaufen court was not socially precarious or dependent on his genius as a lyric poet and composer. He has been described as a knightly poet-musician and there is also a belief that he wandered through the Germanic provinces in the guise of a minstrel. A romantic thinker as much as he was a virulent poet and composer, he fostered through his art an already present anti-papal movement which Frederick I had set in motion. German poets and musicians took it upon themselves to separate the German Empire from Rome. The Pope was called Anti-Christ. Christianity and Papal rule were being theoretically dissociated for the first time in twelve hundred years. Walther became the artist's able champion and spiritual guide. But Frederick suffered military defeat and to recoup what prestige he could walked barefooted through the snow and knelt before Pope Alexander III in contrition. Rome had the upper hand once more. Walther von der Vogelweide witnessed this cataclysmic turn of events and all he could do was stand by and watch the following Pope,

Innocent III, pave the way for the decline of the German Empire.

The troubadours broke down geographical barriers to spread a new type of art wholly free from clerical supervision or jurisdiction in all the countries surrounding medieval France. Yet, the poetry and music of the troubadour was a nobleman's art which was not necessarily shared by all Frenchmen or those of a lowly class throughout Europe. This music contained a recurring theme of social strife attributed to a bitter struggle for supremacy between Pope and King. The troubadours had taken the folk-tunes of the people and although appropriating them to their own use, they nevertheless circulated and preserved them. The Church throughout the centuries acted otherwise by banning folk-music and ignoring it so that these folk-tunes were not recorded and there is no telling how many of them became lost. Had they been notated with the same care that Church music was, our knowledge of medieval music would have been rich indeed. But the Church considered folk-music vulgar and unworthy of being recorded.

The troubadours and minnesingers, as well as the jongleurs and goliards, have actually left us little of their musical output. Quite probably, they did not always take the pains to write their music down. The tunes were short and repetitious and since they could be easily committed to memory, medieval singers most likely did not bother to notate their tunes all the time, or they may not have known how to do so. This may be the reason why we have more of the actual poems than the music itself. Some melodic themes of these medieval musicians have been arranged in modern notation which, however noble a venture, is incapable of fully suggesting the original spirit in which they were rendered.

CHAPTER 3

THE PHILOSOPHER AND MUSIC IN THE GOTHIC AND RENAISSANCE

SECTION 1—*The Philosopher, the Church and Medieval Polyphony*

THE late medieval ages were centuries of great philosophical struggles between systems of thought in the Church. The early Middle Ages knew Plato as the author of the *Timaeus* in which he allegorically described the origin of the world with the mysticism of a Pythagorean. These same centuries knew Aristotle as a logician. Only a very few of the Platonic and Aristotelian writings were known to the Western scholar at that time and their knowledge of these ancients was therefore limited to the handful of Latin translations which had been made from the Greek. But in the 12th and 13th centuries the Latin West came into contact with the writings of Jewish and Arabian philosophers who had preserved the works of the Greeks during the centuries when Christianity was combatting the rational and aesthetic heresies of the pagan. Before then, the Christian scholars had known the Greeks, namely Plato and Aristotle, as the Patristics had interpreted them, usually in sympathy with Christian dogma. The Christian scholar also knew the ancient philosophies of music as they had been interpreted and incorporated into the writings of Augustine and Boethius.

In the 12th century, the writings of the Arabian philosopher Al-Farabi (d. 950) were translated into Latin. His exposition of Aristotelian philosophy familiarized the Christian world with the Peripatetic system of thought which included the aesthetics of Greek music. Abelard also made a plea in the 12th century for greater humanism in Christian endeavor and weighed the roles which faith and reason should respectively play in a religious life. In the 13th century, the more empirically minded Roger Bacon came to the side of Aristotelian science versus Platonic myth and in the same century the synthesis of Plato and Aristotle, faith and reason, myth and science, was made compatible with Christianity in the philosophy of Thomas Aquinas.

Aristotle had ridiculed the Platonic acceptance of the Pythagorean harmony of the spheres theory, but the medievalists were reluctant to give up this picturesque relationship between music and celestial choirs. So, too, were their successors for the next seven hundred years. The role which the philosopher played in the history of music from the 12th to the 14th century was that of a theoretical defender of the revered names of Plato and Boethius. The distinction between Platonic idealism and Aristotelian naturalism may have divided the Christian intellectuals in their theology but since Aristotle had appropriated Plato's views on music and reiterated them with some minor variations, this, to the minds of the medieval humanists, gave all the more credence to the aesthetic validity of the Greek musical values. Even so eloquent a humanist as Abelard, whose secular songs as a youth were sung by the Paris students, agreed, in his role as a Churchman, with Augustine that a good Christian should not read the heathen poets or partake of their music. As sound an Aristotelian as Bacon, whose views on music in the role of education were decidedly progressive, evaluated the musical innovations in religious music with Platonic fervor.

The centuries which we refer to as the dark ages in the Western world have left us very little actual music. In this phase of Christian civilization as in that of Greek civilization we are dependent on the scholarly treatises which have survived. The span from the 12th to the 15th century is somewhat better in supplying us with actual music, but the modern student of history still must look to the medieval treatises of the philosopher and theologian, who were actually one, for the status of music.

Our knowledge of ancient philosophy and music would be much the poorer if the Islamic and Hebraic scholars had not preserved the writings of the Greeks. The Byzantine Christian in the Near East was better versed in the philosophy of the Greeks than the Western Christian. He also thought of himself as a more cultured and intellectually superior individual than his Western cousin. But ecclesiastical decrees on music affected all of Christianity. The Church considered music as a form of religious edification and just as there was one unswerving faith to be held in all Christendom so too the music of the Catholic Church must be made uniform.

The philosophy of the Greeks may not have prospered during these centuries of Christian supremacy, but the development of music was decidedly more fortunate. The art of part singing was introduced into the religious Service by improvising a simple melody to be sung counter to the solemn chanting of a Gregorian tune. From this humble beginning of two voices singing counter to each other grew the art of polyphony, which was as significant a development in the historical evolution of music as was the invention of musical notation by Guido of Arezzo. The medieval musician had first given music a specific system of note values which primarily indicated the direction of the melody. His second contribution was the introduction of part singing. This may well have been appropriated from other cultures but was developed by the ecclesiastical composer; not always, however, in a manner that pleased the more zealous guardians of the Faith.

Polyphony is music written as a combination of two or more simultaneous melodies either for voice or instruments or both together. The origin of polyphonic music is not known. Our historians of music can only speculate, at best, as to when and in what part of the world it originated. We know that Greek music was monophonic, a single voiced melody which accompanied the lyric; and yet, there is a reference in Plato to an innovating type of music in which the singer sings one note and produces another on his instrument. Plato unfortunately did not elaborate on this ancient musical practice and there is no other known reference in the writings of the Greek philosophers which refers to this two part style, which is suggestive of a primitive form of polyphony. It was with reference to the teaching of the lyre that Plato admonished the educators to avoid the complexities of notes and rhythms which were marring the simple beauty of Greek music. "And with this view," he wrote, "the teacher and the learner ought to use the sounds of the lyre, because its notes are pure, the player who teaches and his pupil rendering note for note in unison; but complexity, and variation of notes, when the strings give one sound and the poet or composer of the melody gives another,—also when they make concords and harmonies in which lesser and greater intervals, slow and quick, or high and low notes, are combined,—or, again, when they make complex variations of rhythms, which they adapt to the notes of the lyre,—all that sort of thing is not suited to those who have to acquire a speedy and useful knowledge of music in three years; for opposite principles are confusing, and create a difficulty in learning, . . ."[1]

In the works of the medieval philosophers there is a highly mystical passage on elementary polyphony by the Irish philosopher John Scotus Erigena (800–877) in which he draws an analogy between a melody composed of diverse parts and the dissimilar elements that produce a harmonious universe. Writing in his *Divisione Naturae*, he goes on to say, "the beauty of the whole universe of similar and dissimilar things has been built up in a wonderful harmony from diverse *genera* and various forms in different arrangements of substances and accidents, compacted into an ineffable unity. For an organized melody composed of diverse qualities and quantities of voices is discerned, note by note individually, to be separated by different proportions of high and low, yet they are mutually co-adapted in accordance

---

[1] *Laws*, Bk. VII, 812-813; (Translated by B. Jowett), Random House, New York: 1937.

with established and rational rules of the art of music . . . rendering a natural sweetness, . . ."[2]

The earliest type of polyphonic music of which we have any record in the West was the medieval form of organum which went through several stages of development, from a simple two part composition to a complex several voiced one, during the ninth to the thirteenth century. The most highly developed form of polyphonic music in the late medieval period, the Gothic, and in the Renaissance, is to be found in the motet. In the 16th century, polyphony marked the grandeur of the Palestrina Mass and two hundred years later polyphony was brought to its aesthetic fulfillment in Bach's art of the fugue.

There are several references to polyphony from the 9th to the 13th century which are of practical significance in tracing the historical evolution of polyphonic music in Western civilization. An unknown author of the 9th century left us a treatise on polyphony called *Musica Enchiriadis* in which he described the kinds of organum that were being used in his day. Three centuries later, an Englishman by the name of John Cotton wrote that polyphonic music in the 12th century was being practiced in many ways, "but the most easily comprehensible manner," he wrote, "is when contrary motion be especially considered— in which the organizing part descends while the Cantus Firmus ascends, and vice-versa."[3] Giraldus Cambrensis (c. 1147–1220) also furnished us with a description of the advanced part singing which he found the people of Wales performing with remarkable facility. "In their musical concerts they do not sing in unison like the inhabitants of other countries, but in many different parts; so that in a company of singers, which one very frequently meets with in Wales, you will hear as many different parts and voices as there are performers, who all at length unite, with organic melody, in one consonance and the soft sweetness of B flat. In the northern district of Britain, beyond the Humber,

2 Henry George Farmer, *Historical Facts for the Arabian Musical Influence*, pp. 350-351; William Reeves, London: 1930.

3 Gustave Reese, *Music in the Middle Ages*, p. 261; W. W. Norton and Co., Inc., New York: 1940.

and on the borders of Yorkshire, the inhabitants make use of the same kind of symphonious harmony, but with less variety; singing only in two parts, one murmuring in the bass, the other warbling in the acute or treble."[4]

The art of polyphony did not fare too well either in the papal documents or in the writings of the theologians on the sacred music of the late medieval and Renaissance periods. The Church authorities registered the same complaint against polyphony as Plato had done in the Laws against two part music. The theologians did so for different reasons, to be sure, but the grounds for their opposition were similar. Plato was distressed that the musical innovations of the Greek bard were being carried over into the education of Athenian youth. He believed that two different musical parts played simultaneously or in a staccato-like fashion expressed opposite principles which induced confusion and eventual moral degeneration. A youth exposed to such musical training would not only experience difficulty in mastering the elements of music but would run the risk of becoming confused by such a cacophonous art that could seep into the innermost parts of the soul and affect the body. The Guardians of the State must therefore supervise the education of the young to see that only the traditional modes and rhythms were taught for their very nature of simplicity and unity would instill order and discipline in the student.

The Catholic Church became concerned over polyphonic music because of the belief among many Christian leaders that it disturbed devotion, obscured the text, and engendered confusion rather than inculcating into the congregation a feeling of peace and calmness during worship. We do not know precisely when polyphony was first introduced into the Church but we do know that throughout the centuries the Church has voiced its displeasure at the more complex music that found its way into the house of worship. The Church was fearful lest this new secular music replace the traditional solemn plain-chants which by association called up a devotional mood in the wor-

---

[4] *The Historical Works of Giraldus Cambrensis, The Description of Wales*, Bk. I, Chap. XIII, p. 498; (Translated by Sir Richard Colt Hoare), George Bell and Sons, London: 1887.

shipper. This new style of complex music which had no religious association for the Christian brought only confusion to those in the congregation who tried to follow the intricate polyphony and furthermore desecrated the sacred character of the Service. Plato had pointed out that license in musical practices was a foreboding sign of impending change in the laws of the State. The Church, by analogy, argued that secular music, which was not in keeping with tradition, but which was permitted to be performed in the Church, might well encourage additional innovations which would eventually threaten not only the religious Service and sacred doctrine, but the very authority of the Church itself.

The Catholic philosophy of music was not promulgated by a few zealots in the Church only. It was a widespread feeling among the dignitaries of the Faith that polyphony distracted the congregation from pious devotion with its part singing and truncated melodic line instead of a sustained melodic line.

The Scholastic philosopher and Bishop of Chartres, John of Salisbury, (c. 1115–1180) complained: "Music defiles the service of religion. For the admiring simple souls of the congregation are of necessity depraved—in the very presence of the Lord, in the sacred recesses themselves of the sanctuary—by the riot of the wantoning voice, by its eager ostentation, and by its womanish affectations in the mincing of notes and sentences." "Could you but hear one of these enervating performances executed with all the devices of the art, you might think it a chorus of Sirens, but not of men, and you would be astonished at the singers' facility, with which indeed neither that of the nightingale or parrot, nor of whatever else there may be that is more remarkable in this kind, can compare. For this facility is displayed in long ascents and descents, in the dividing or in the redoubling of notes, in the repetition of phrases, and the clashing of the voices, while, in all this, the high or even the highest notes of the scale are so mingled with the lower and lowest, that the ears are almost deprived of their power to distinguish."[5]

The theologians of the 13th century were no less critical of

[5] *The Oxford History of Music*, Vol. I, p. 290; Oxford University Press, London: 1929.

polyphony than their predecessors in the 12th century. The leaders of the Church varied in their degree of opposition to polyphony. Many of them did not object to the art of part singing in the Service, but they agreed officially that polyphony could be more appropriately tuned to Christian worship. Even the humanistic members of the hierarchy were adamant that certain polyphonic abuses would have to be corrected. We have such evidence in the writings of Roger Bacon (c. 1214–1294), Churchman, philosopher and scientist. This Franciscan monk had a realistic awareness of the value of music in worship and education. He recommended to the clergy that they acquire a fundamental knowledge of music so that they would not be in ignorance of the use and value of ecclesiastical music. He also referred to the educational value of music in secular learning and pointed out "that children learn mathematical truths better and more quickly, as is manifest in singing, . . ."[6] Bacon was one of the most enlightened Churchmen of the 13th century and his views on the psychological merit of music in worship and education must have been those of his superiors as well as his own. Bacon also believed that the solemn tradition of the religious service was being defiled by the disturbing influence of polyphonic music. He must have had the approval of his superiors on this objection too.

In 1274 the second Council of Lyons issued several canons to curb this new music of which John of Salisbury wrote so disparagingly. Then in 1324–1325, Pope John XXII issued a Bull from Avignon which decried the use of new musical forms and techniques which were replacing traditional tunes and practices. This document repeated the unchanging law of the Church that music brought into the Service of worship must preserve the integrity of the text by using modest melodies. "But certain exponents of a new school," reads this Papal document on sacred music, "who think only of the laws of strictly measured time, are composing new melodies of their own creation with a new system of notes, and these they prefer to the ancient, traditional music; the melodies of the Church are sung in 'semibreves' and

---

[6] *Selections from Medieval Philosophers, The Opus Majus*, p. 49; (Translated by Richard McKeon), Charles Scribner's Sons, New York: 1930.

'*minimas*' and with gracenotes of repercussion. By some the melodies are broken up by '*hochetis*', or robbed of their virility by '*discanti*' (2 parts), '*triplis*' (3 parts), '*motectis*', with a dangerous element produced by certain parts sung on texts in the vernacular; all these abuses have brought into disrepute the basic melodies of the Antiphonal and Gradual; these composers, knowing nothing of the true foundation upon which they must build, are ignorant of the Modes, incapable of distinguishing between them, and cause great confusion. The mere number of the notes, in these compositions, conceal from us the plain-chant melody, with its simple, well-regulated rises and falls which indicate the character of the Mode. These musicians run without pausing, they intoxicate the ear without satisfying it, they dramatize the text with gestures and, instead of promoting devotion, they prevent it by creating a sensuous and indecent atmosphere."[7]

The theologians of the late medieval period and the Renaissance were as much concerned about a new type of music which, to their minds, was a menace to the Church, as the Patristics had been in the early centuries; and as the Greek philosophers in antiquity had been concerning music and the State. The several canons which the 13th century Churchmen issued to curb the new music, and the Papal Bull which Pope John issued in the 14th century against the new music which "conceal from us the plain-chant melody, with its simple, well-regulated rises and falls", were not of lasting effect, for in the 16th century, the Council of Trent once more took under consideration the question of polyphony. Evidently, it was easier for the Church authorities to supervise learning and scholarship than to carry out sanctions effectively against secular musical innovations that were being brought into the religious Service.

SECTION II—*The Musician, the Church*
and Medieval Polyphony

THERE were several types of instruments in the Middle Ages which were so constructed as to produce musical sounds simul-

---

[7] *Papal Documents on Sacred Music*, Society of St. Gregory of America, New York: 1951.

taneously. The hydraulic organ, which was known to the Romans and the Byzantines, was capable of producing two distinct sounds or voices at the same time. The Scottish bagpipe has quite an ancestry and it can be traced back, under a variety of names, to early times in the history of Western music. In the bagpipe the simple deflation of the bladder produces vibration for the drone which supports the theme and the pipe which supplies the wind. Even the jongleur "who accompanied his chanson de geste on the vielle underpinned his melody with a succession of crude chords."

We owe our knowledge of medieval instruments, in a large measure, to those Gothic artisans who portrayed the musical instruments of their time in painting and sculpture and described them in rhymes and verse. Gothic paintings and sculpture have left us a clear picture of these instruments, and poetry has outlined their use and significance in late medieval society. We also know that the medieval instruments were used independently, and as accompaniments, and also to fill in parts of a manuscript when required to do so. The organ was the most highly developed instrument of the Middle Ages and Renaissance and had the distinction of being the prime instrument of the Church. Those theologians who complained about the desecration of sacred music usually included the novel uses to which the organ had been put in the Service as part of the disturbing influence.

Part music and musical notation both passed through several stages of development. Notation passed through three distinct stages. In the notation systems of the Greek, Roman, as well as early Christian music, note symbols did not indicate time values since the melody was subordinated to the text. Poetic meter set the pace and the musical line only followed the rise and fall of the text. In a later, or second stage, the values were hinted at indirectly by the system of neumes which are found in the Gregorian Chants of as early as the 9th century. In the third stage, time values were indicated by corresponding symbols so that only at this point can we say that a mensural system which contained notes signifying definite time values had been achieved.

Music of necessity was bound to become measured if part music was to progress. Solo music often abetted free musical reign but when several voices joined in song, as in polyphony, then it became essential to regulate the course and action of each singer in order to blend his voice with the others. Part music, therefore, progressed as the composer instilled more order and control into his score through the various symbolic values which he had at hand.

A treatise of an anonymous English scholar studying in France close to the 13th century, who was given the name of Anonymous IV, left us a history of some famous polyphonic composers and of the development of the art of part music at the School of Notre Dame. Two of the outstanding musical contributors to the art of polyphony in the Notre Dame School, Anonymous IV tells us, were Leonin and Perotin. According to this English scholar, Magister Leoninus of the 12th century composed an entire cycle of organa in a work called *Magnus Liber Organi*. Leonin's music so impressed this Englishman that the latter referred to this composer and choirmaster of the Notre Dame Cathedral as optimus organista, the greatest composer of organa. Little is known of Perotin other than that he was the guiding spirit of the Notre Dame School between 1180 to 1236.

Toward the end of the 13th century, Jacobus of Liege, the author of *Speculum Musicae*, wrote that in his own generation "the moderns use only motets and cantilenae." This motet of which Jacobus wrote was the most highly developed polyphonic form and consequently, of the many voiced musical art forms, was the most criticized by the ecclesiastical authorities. There were other 13th century polyphonic forms, such as the conductus. The more highly complex character of the motet however only brought annoyance to the theologians, even if the moderns of the late medieval ages were charmed by its aesthetic qualities. There is little wonder, nevertheless, that the theologians became concerned over musical matters when they were treated to a rendition of one type of motet, that was quite the vogue, in which three different melodies, with varying texts, were sung simultaneously in independent rhythms against a Gregorian tune. It is questionable whether the Gregorian Chant was heard above the music produced by the other three voices singing in different languages. John of Salisbury and Pope John XXII were specifically grieved that this type of music obscured the liturgical chant or chopped it beyond recognition in hocketting, as they called it, and so destroyed the sacred character of the religious music.

Of the secular motets, the French were the most interesting. The composer of this polyphonic form related the social problems of the day, censured the clergy and twitted the nobility, all in motet form. Some of these motets were in praise of love, others exalted the joys of drink and still others sentimentally proclaimed the glorious acts of some saint or king.

It is somewhat amusing upon reflection to note that the clergy censured the composer's music and the composer, in turn, censured the clergy through music. The clergy objected to the polyphonic abuses of such composers as Pierre de la Croix (end of 13th century), for one, who added a third and then a fourth voice to the motet, each voice having a melodic and rhythmic independence and a different text. Nor did the clergy relish the knowledge that many of these tunes that were sung counter to the liturgical chant in the motet were of a trouvère origin that might well be associated with an amorous escapade. The secular motets in which the composers and poets ridiculed the lavish estates and courtly living of the high medieval and Renaissance Church dignitaries were particularly irksome. But the Church was no more effective in combatting these secular musical signs of disrespect than it was in impeding the musical tendencies that were threatening the sanctity of the religious Service.

Philippe de Vitry (1291–1361) was a scholar and statesman whom history remembers as a talented polyphonic musician and able Bishop of the Church. He retained the ancient concept that music was a branch of mathematics. Roger Bacon had already pointed out, in the previous century, that mathematical truths were unfolded to the young in the art of music. De Vitry also held the traditional Platonic view that music was a copy of the Ideal Order which was revealed to the scholar in the study of philosophy. He concurred with Pope John XXII that the musical abuses of the 14th century could be eliminated if the composer would regulate his music instead of creating with complete disregard for tradition. De Vitry therefore composed motets in which all the voices were melodically independent but retained a similarity of note values and identical meter throughout.

Guillaume de Machaut (1300–1377) was the outstanding composer of his century. His personal life adds up to that of a trouvère, a worldly ecclesiastic and a humanist. He composed motets in the same regulated style that de Vitry had introduced and then went on to develop the polyphonic possibilities of the trouvère ballad. Some of these ballads dealt with the trouvère's preoccupation with love; others had a social ring and suggested to the clergy that they give up some of their land with honor rather than have it taken away. Machaut also composed a polyphonic Mass which is supposed to be the first complete Mass written by a single composer.

The theoretical writings on music in the Middle Ages usually bore the mark of Boethian influence. Boethius had transmitted the musical philosophy of the Greeks to the medieval world by drawing an analogy between music and mathematics and had then included music in the educational *Quadrivium* as a mental discipline for higher learning. The writings of Roger Bacon bear out just how marked this Boethian influence was in the educational philosophy of his own time.

The late medieval ages also retained the metaphysical dualism, that music was imitative of the Divine Order. The philosopher Erigena drew such an analogy with reference to polyphony and the musician de Vitry echoed this simile four centuries later. There were also theorists and composers who paid little heed to ancient doctrines or to the invariable cries of the Church that music was being debased because the composer was departing from tradition. The fact that the art of polyphony, which probably began in religious music as the improvisation of a simple counterpoint to a liturgical chant, or plain-song, had developed into a highly complex and aesthetically satisfying form was evidence that creative initiative does not easily succumb to a philosophical system or an ecclesiastical format. The composer of the medieval ages wrote music for Christian edification. Much of this music rhythmically and melodically was secular in origin and was brought into the Church by ecclesiastical composers who were influenced by these secular sources.

The doctrines of Boethius were passed over by the medieval

composer but only the rare scholar questioned his authority. One of these, Johannes de Grocheo (c. 1300), rejected the Pythagorean number theory and Boethian philosophy by refusing to believe that the creation of music was a numerical and rhythmic duplication of the cosmic order. He questioned whether Boethius was justified in calling music a mathematical science. He disagreed with Boethius, or his followers who elaborated on his musical philosophy, that the laws of music must be as exacting as the very laws which brought order and design to nature. Grocheo stressed the ethnic and cultural value of music in his own writings. He anticipated the writings of such future scholars as Montaigne, Rousseau and Herder, by pointing out that music differed according to the different habits and languages of people.

There were at least three instances of Church antagonism to musical innovations during the 13th and 14th centuries. First, it will be recalled that the Greek bard did not employ a system of rhythmic and note values because his music was wedded to poetry so that he rendered his song in declamatory style. Medieval religious song was similarly dependent upon the text, with smooth flowing rhythms which called for little variation in note values. When Pope John XXII complained in his Bull that "ecclesiastical music is now performed with semibreves and minimas, and pestered with these short notes," the Pope was not only outlawing counter rhythmic music with varying texts but he was also condemning the breaking up of long sustained notes into shorter and even syncopated note values, as in hocketting. Second, during the ars nova period, a name for the music of the 14th century in contrast to the music of the 13th century, ars antiqua, there was a growing tendency among composers to alter traditional rhythms. Binary rhythm or duple time was originally prohibited in religious music on the moralistic grounds that the number three had a sacred connotation. Any desire or attempt by the 14th century composer to use binary rather than tertiary rhythm was frowned on by the Church. Third, Greek, and then medieval music, was originally based on the octave, fourth and fifth. During the 13th century French composers began to follow the English in using the interval of a third. The

French Clergy paradoxically objected to the use of this pleasing new interval even though it was based on the number three, simply because it altered the musical traditions of the past.

SECTION III—*The Florentine Academy*

THE Greek-Byzantine Christians, like the Arabians, kept up an active interest in classical civilization and literature. Byzantine scholars included Plato and Aristotle among their studies during those years when Greek was only a dead language to Western intellectuals. Some of the Crusaders who came in contact with Byzantine culture were so impressed with it that they took back some of this classical learning to the West. Rome, however, looked upon this development with disfavor since the ecclesiastics saw nothing but heresy in these classical trends in education and culture. The Roman Church decided that it would be necessary to counteract this infiltration of heretical Greek-Byzantine thought into their theology by taking definite measures. The Pope sent the theologian and philosopher Nicholas of Cusa (1401–1464) to Constantinople to lay the basis for a possible union of the Eastern and Western Churches. The Eastern Church was asked whether it would not be well for the sake of Christianity to reconcile their respective differences and actually achieve one catholic and universal church. But the Greek Church would not give up its sovereignty to the extent asked of Her even though She anticipated a Turkish invasion of Constantinople and was aware that She would have to call upon Rome to help stave off the Infidel.

Byzantine scholars, however, did go to the West, particularly Florence. Ostensibly, many of them were sent by the Eastern Church, in turn, to see if the two Churches could unite on a common ground. Although this merger between Greek and Roman Catholicism did not materialize, the classical learning the Byzantine scholars and diplomats carried with them spread infectiously wherever they set foot.

After the Turks captured Constantinople and put an end to the Byzantium Empire in 1453, her remaining Greek scholars fled to Italy to seek refuge at the Florentine Academy. This

Academy was founded, through the benevolence of Cosimo de' Medici, by Gemisthus Pletho, a Greek-Byzantine delegate who some thirteen years before the fall of Constantinople served as an ambassador to the Council at Florence which had been convoked in a futile effort to unite the Greek with the Roman Church. The aim of this newly founded Academy was to reintroduce Platonic philosophy to the Western world and combat the pseudo-Aristotelian philosophy which had come to pervade Catholic doctrine and thought. Nicholas of Cusa, for one, now a Cardinal, became so intrigued with the teachings of Plato, that he asked the Roman scholars to re-value Plato's relation to Christianity in the light of the original writings of the founder of the Academy so that the Western world would not be misled by the distorted dogmas which the Churchmen had arbitrarily developed from his philosophy.

The philosopher Marsilio Ficino (1433–1499), a student of the Florentine Academy, affirmed the stand taken by the Cardinal and maintained that only a real understanding of Plato could recapture the spirit of Christianity which had long passed out of the Church. The views of Nicholas of Cusa and of Ficino not only found favor with many ecclesiastical dignitaries but had a marked influence upon the thought and art of Renaissance life.

Pythagorean and Platonic mysticism is well preserved in the musical philosophy of Cardinal Cusa. He compared the art of polyphony to the harmony of the spheres. "For the eternal mind creates as does the musician who wishes to express and represent his inner images; for he takes the variety of musical parts and imposes on them rules of measurement which result in harmony, so that the harmony resounds in sweetness and perfection."[8] He repeated the Greek theme that earthly music was a prototype of heavenly music but added that the Church fathers used music as a symbol only to compare the music of men to God's handiwork. Beyond the symbol itself was a transcendent order or as Nicholas said "The very spiritual things which we cannot comprehend directly are investigated through

[8] Kathi Meyer-Baer, *The Journal of Aesthetics and Art Criticism*, p. 306; June: 1947:

the bridge of the symbol, . . ." When musical symbols were employed as similies to interpret the heavenly orbits of celestial choirs "those signs of joy derived from musical harmony . . . which came down to us from the writings of the Church Fathers as known signs to measure the eternal bliss, are only remote material signs, which differ infinitely from those spiritual joys that are not accessible to our imagination."[9]

The aim of 15th century aesthetics was to discover the magic formulas of the Greeks, the exact mathematical formulas that would reproduce Phidian forms. Symmetry, proportion, perspective, mathematically deduced, permeated the activity of artistic life. Nicholas, in keeping with the spirit of the times, agreed with Plato that mathematics was the basis of music, mathematics was a mental discipline.

Nicholas told us that when listening to music "we perceive with our senses the concordant parts; we measure the intervals and concordances with our reason and with the help of our musical training. This faculty (of reason and the power to profit by education) we do not find in animals. . . . They therefore cannot learn music though they perceive sounds (through the senses) as we do and take pleasure in sounds that agree together. On this account we are entitled to call our soul reasonable: viz., because it is a measuring and numbering power which grasps whatever requires precise distinction. Our ears are favorably inclined upon hearing beautiful musical concords. Thus reason, seeing that concord is based on number and proportion, invented the rational theory of musical chords, based on the theory of numbers."[10]

Nicholas harked back to the Greek theory of affections or passions and pointed out as a Churchman that passions "pass away, and sensuous impressions are beautiful only insofar as they mirror spiritual ideas or beauties."[11] The Platonic doctrine of ethos was also present in the writings of Nicholas for he was concerned with the effects of musical rhythms and modes upon the soul. But as a product of humanism, he threw off the ancient

[9] *Ibid.*, pp. 305-306.
[10] *Ibid.*, p. 304.
[11] *Ibid.*, p. 307.

belief that the composer was a mediator between God and man
who made the Divine Will known on earth. He decried the
Platonic notion that the artist was a Muse inspired, often crazed
individual, who created solely with guidance from above, and
expressed the Renaissance conviction that the artist was a
creator in his own right.

Whereas Nicholas of Cusa was less well versed in music than
the other arts, Marsilio Ficino had a deeper interest in music
than in the other arts. We are told that he played an instrument
and gave frequent performances before large circles of his
friends. He also spoke with great conviction about the effects
of music upon the soul and further echoed Plato in the belief
that the essence of the beauty of sounds consisted in consonance
which he related to the concept of proportion. This music had
its origin in the soul of the musician and could therefore act
on the soul of the listener. He agreed with Plato that music
could penetrate into the innermost parts of the human soul and
affect the course of bodily action. " 'Since song and sound come
from the thought of the mind, from the impulse of the imagination, and from the passion of the heart and, together with the
broken and formed air, move the air-like spirit of the listener,
which is the bond of Soul and body, it easily moves the imagination, affects the heart, and penetrates the innermost sanctuary
of the mind.' "[12] " 'Serious music preserves and restores the consonance of the parts of the Soul, as Plato and Aristotle say and
as we have experienced frequently.' "[13]

Ficino stated that music had a therapeutic effect which could
expel vexation. Music could also induce a contemplative mood
to bring one closer to God. " '. . . I frequently dedicate myself
to the more serious strings and songs after the study of theology
or medicine, in order to neglect the other pleasures of the senses,
to expel the troubles of Soul and body, and to elevate the mind
as much as possible to sublime things and God.' "[14]

"To emphasize the metaphysical meaning and origin of music, Ficino sometime reverted to the Pythagorean doctrine of

---

[12] Paul Oskar Kristeller, *The Philosophy of Marsilio Ficino*, p. 307; (Translated by Virginia Conant) Columbia University Press, New York: 1943.
[13] *Loc. cit.*
[14] *Ibid.*, p. 308.

the harmony of the spheres. The celestial spheres, attuned to each other according to the rules of consonance, produce a divine music imperceptible to us; and human music, being an earthly imitation of the celestial sounds, through its admirable effect induces the Soul to elevate itself into the realm of celestial harmony. 'Through the ears the Soul perceives certain sweet harmonies and rhythms, and through these images it is exhorted and excited to consider the divine music with a more ardent and intimate sense of the mind.' "[15]

Ficino evaluated poetry in close connection with music, "since poetry also appeals to the ear and, in addition to using words, often incorporates melody and always has rhythm. But poetry is superior to music, since through the words it speaks not only to the ear but also directly to the mind. Therefore its origin is not in the harmony of the spheres, but rather in the music of the divine mind itself, and through its effect it can lead the listener directly to God Himself."[16] Ficino differed from Nicholas of Cusa and agreed with Plato that the poet did not follow the arbitrary impulse of his human thought but was inspired by God. He referred to the Platonic theory of divine madness of the *Ion* and *Phaedrus* to account for the composer's inspired creativity.

Ficino's theories on music were essentially traditional in the Platonic and Augustinian vein. As a practicing musician, however, Ficino considered the interval of a musical third as a consonant tone. The ancients, as well as the musical theoreticians of his own time, regarded the octave, the fifth and the fourth as the only consonant musical intervals. He "asserts that the Platonists could not have understood music so well as the moderns, as they were insensible to the pleasure arising from thirds, which they regarded as discords . . . the most grateful of our concords, and so necessary that without them our music would be destitute of its greatest ornament, and counterpoint monotonous and insipid."[17]

Ficino's Italy was not to be the center of musical life for

---

[15] *Loc. cit.*
[16] *Loc. cit.*
[17] Warren D. Allen, *Philosophies of Music History*, p. 40; American Book Co., New York: 1939.

another century, but the fact that he spoke of the third as a consonant tone means that the use of this interval had found its way into the music of the Italian Renaissance. But, for the development of 15th century music, we must look to the low countries, not Italy. Albrecht Durer wrote in his travel diary on his trip to the Netherlands, as late as August 5, 1520, "The Church of our Lady at Antwerp is so very large that many masses are sung in it at one time without interfering with each other. They have wealthy endowments there, so the best musicians are employed that can be had." The fortunes of war help to explain why Paris which reigned supreme as a musical center during the 12th, 13th and 14th centuries should have sunk in significance artistically toward the 15th century.

SECTION IV—*The Aesthetics of Renaissance Music*

THE art of polyphony, which had been developed by the French school, attained fuller aesthetic importance in the school of Cambrai. Out of this school, which was to dominate the musical tastes of Europe for a century, came such names as Binchois and Dufay. The town of Cambrai in Burgundy became the center of 15th century music. It was here, at the Burgundian court, that the liberal protector of artists, and able musician in his own right, Charles the Bold, held the most brilliant and luxurious court in all Europe. It was to the school of Cambrai Cathedral that pope and king turned for talented musicians.

Guillaume Dufay (c. 1400-1474) was the master of the Burgundian school. After receiving his training in the cathedral choir at Cambrai he joined the papal choir. His travels to other important musical European centers made him familiar with the varying musical trends of the different court and ecclesiastical composers, all of which influenced his own music and that of Burgundian aesthetics. Under his guidance the Burgundian school became infused with the intellectual liberalism and formal sensitivity that marked the Renaissance life of Italy. Here too, at Burgundy, the composer created in an atmosphere which encouraged a definite division between church and secular music.

Burgundian music differed in a number of ways from Gothic.

The Burgundian school had its roots in the Gothic school, which preceded it, but the Burgundian composer wrote music along stricter lines, shying away from the 14th century aesthetic notion of improvisation. The Burgundian composed his music in a conventional form which required from the performer strict adherence to the score. The Renaissance search for Greek artistic forms had a direct influence upon the musician so that he also wished to emulate the spirit of the times. The veneration of formal design became as much in evidence in music as in painting and sculpture.

The Burgundian composer turned away from what he considered harsh, antiquated Gothic tonalities. The Gothic composer had about exhausted the use of the traditional octave, fourth and fifth. The Burgundian composer employed thirds freely and even sixths thus giving his music a fuller tonality. The contrast between the musical aesthetics of the Gothic and Burgundian schools is further marked by the austerity and stolidness of the former to the smooth flowing and lyrical character of the latter's music. This lyrical quality in Burgundian music allowed the composer to exploit the musical possibilities of vocal music.

The music which the Burgundian composer wrote enriched the text while the Gothic composer often disregarded the relationship of music to the text. The Gothic composer was prone to show more interest in displaying his virtuosity through technical ability than in developing a sensitivity to formal design which characterized the work of the Burgundian composer. The Gothic practice of contrasting several conflicting tunes to a number of varying texts was as musically audacious as it was bombastic, but such musical exhibitions of contrast and bombast were furthermost from the Burgundian's ideas of musical aesthetics. Yet, the subdued character of the Burgundian's music limited its emotional possibilities. By its very nature it was unable to deal with the epic or majestic. It reflected Renaissance philosophy by giving itself to the contemplative spirit of the times. The Burgundian composer was unwittingly Platonic in his musical aesthetics for, aside from his worship of form and marriage of text and music, he unknowingly practiced Ficino's tenet that artistic activity, like other manifestations of a spiritual life, is based on restraint and contemplation.

Jan van Ockeghem (1430–1495) was an outstanding musician who dominated the second half of the 15th century. He studied under Dufay and was himself the teacher of the greatest musician of the Renaissance, Josquin des Prés (1450–1521) whom Martin Luther referred to with deep reverence and spoke of his art as the containment of all that is good in music.

England also contributed to Renaissance music. The English composer freely experimented with musical intervals and melody. In the writings of Dunstable (d. 1453) there is even a vague feeling of harmonic relationship between one chord and another rather than the traditional method of each chord merely functioning as a support for the melody. Only Byrd (1542/3–1623), loomed greater than Dunstable as a composer of the English Renaissance.

In Italy, the Platonists were still holding forth philosophically and artistically, fully delighted with the new literary vistas which the study of Greek had opened up to them. Even their Aristotelian adversaries took heart and rebelled against the dogmatic interpretation which the Church imposed on the founder of the Lyceum. By the 16th century, the Church would no longer tolerate these iconoclasts and brought a number of them before the Inquisition to retract or face death for their beliefs. But the Church could not stem this trend in humanism either intellectually or artistically. The composer, also influenced by this version of Platonic philosophy, began to emphasize the text and sacrifice counterpoint and melody, not because the Church favored such a musical philosophy but because the humanistic ideal, to imitate the Greek, was based on the premise that music should enrich the poetic text. The Renaissance composer became completely Platonic. He developed the notion that the function of music was to embellish the written word, to bring out its full emotional possibilities within its literary context so that the poetic line would have its greatest effect upon the listener. Herein was the aesthetic basis of Renaissance a cappella art.

In 1552, a student of Josquin, Adrian Petit Coclicus (c. 1500–

1563), published a work called *Musica Reservata,* music in the new style, which he attributed to his distinguished Flemish teacher. The *Musica Reservata* was rooted in a system of aesthetics which emphasized the doctrine of affections, the enhanced interpretation of the written word through music. This concept of affections, which stems from the writings of Plato and Aristotle, and was dealt with in the works of Nicholas of Cusa in the early Renaissance, was to continue to permeate the philosophic treatises of the following centuries, although the term "affections" was not always used in precisely the same way by the ancient and Renaissance philosophers.

Rome became the center of religious music in the 16th century. The Holy See attracted the most illustrious musical talents of Europe at the same time that it was combating the secular paganism of Renaissance liberalism and the Protestant Reformation. The Netherlander, Orlando di Lasso (c. 1532–1594), and his devoutly religious Italian colleague, Palestrina (1525–1594), came under the influence of the Counter Reformation. It was a period of general house cleaning within the Catholic Church, philosophically and artistically. Just as the Council of Laodicea in the early years of Christianity had played a very important role in Byzantine church music by abolishing the use of instruments and the participation of the congregation in the singing of the chant, so the Council of Trent (1545–1563) and a special papal congregation (1564) moulded the future course of Roman Catholic church music in the 16th century. The churchmen charged that polyphony neglected the text and emphasized the secular music. They echoed the Council of Laodicea and added that the Church employed an overabundance of instruments in the Service. They repeated the complaints of earlier churchmen that the singers irreverently sacrificed proper enunciation of the words so that they could, with vanity, display their vocal skill.

Precisely what conclusions the Cardinals arrived at are not altogether clear, but we do know that they considered the view that all music that was inconsistent with the dignity and tradition of the Service should be abolished. Tropes and sequences, with the exception of a favorite few, were cast out of the liturgical repertoire. Polyphony as a whole was viewed with serious mis-

givings on the grounds that it had been a corrupting and sec-
ularizing influence of the solemnity and simplicity of church
music from its very beginning. The Cardinals considered, and
then fortunately gave up the notion, whether it would not be
more in keeping with Christian worship to eliminate from the
Service all music other than religious chants.

While the Church was combating secular influences that were
believed to be corrupting the Service of worship, the infectious
desire for intellectual and artistic expression spread beyond the
theorist and artisan to the lay people. The philosopher Montaigne (1533–1592) wrote that in his travels through Italy he
was astounded to see the peasants in Tuscany "with a lute in
their hands, and at their side the shepherds reciting Ariosto by
heart; but this is what one may see in all of Italy." Instrumental
and singing groups blossomed throughout all of Europe in the
16th century. Musical instruments became a delightful addition
to the average household. Improvised musical gatherings flourished. It was an era in which even the laity was versed in music.
In this atmosphere of Renaissance enlightenment and culture
the art of the madrigal was created and developed into an advanced form of vocal polyphony.

Renaissance scholars actually knew little about Greek music
itself. They had sought to recapture the spirit of classic Greece
but, without a knowledge of actual Greek music to guide them,
they based their aesthetic theories on the writings of the Greek
and Greco-Roman philosophers. Those philosophical tracts
which had been preserved from antiquity stressed the mathematical and moralistic aspects of music and repeated the metaphysical doctrine of the harmony of the spheres in which the
Pythagoreans related music to the cosmic harmonies.

The Renaissance composer tried to emulate the Greek bard.
Plato wrote that during the Golden Age of Greece the Greek
bard composed his melody to the rhythm and meter of the
poetic text and the Renaissance musician did likewise in his zeal
to create an ideal balance between text and music. Hermann
Fink declared in his *Practica Musica* (1556) that "if the old
composers were eminent in the treatment of difficult mensural
procedures, the newer composers are superior to them in the

matter of euphony and are especially eager to fit the notes to the words of the text in order to render their meaning and mood with the greatest clarity."[18]

Pietro Aron (c. 1490–1545) succinctly contrasted the Renaissance concept of creative composition to the aesthetic practices of the Gothic composers. He wrote (1523) that the music of the "moderns" is better than that of the old composers "because they consider all parts together and do not compose their voices one after the other."[19] The music of Dunstable showed an unconscious effort in the direction of chordal writing but it took the later Renaissance composer to consciously veer away from the horizontal fashion of successive part writing to that of perpendicular chordal composition. In the earlier forms of music, the composer created his music in the traditional linear style of voice leading in which he dealt with single parts or voices. The Renaissance composer began to think and hear music not as isolated voices or separate parts but as clusters of tones arranged in chords which were harmonically related to what preceded and what was to follow.

The Renaissance men of letters devoted their arts and talents to glorifying the past, spurred on by the apprehension that if the great traditions of antiquity were neglected, they might pass into obscurity for another thousand years. The scholar Heinrich Loris (1488–1563), or Glareanus, praised Josquin des Prés, as the embodiment of the humanistic spirit and warned that any altering of his style would be deviating from the true spirit of classicism. The Venetian composer and theorist Gioseffo Zarlino (1517–1590) "paints an ideal picture of the music of the Ancient World, takes pride in what his own time has done to create it anew, and flatly rejects the music of the Middle Ages, which seems to him a species of artistic sophistry . . . he looks on music as an imitation of nature and endeavors to derive his teachings from natural law. . . . He was . . . the first to deal with harmony in terms of the triad rather than of the interval, the first to recognize the importance of the fundamental antithesis

---

[18] Paul H. Lang, *Music in Western Civilization*, p. 198; W. W. Norton and Co., Inc., New York: 1941.
[19] *Ibid.*, p. 293.

of major and minor, the first to attempt a rational explanation of the old rule forbidding the use of parallel fifths and octaves, . . . it was at his suggestion that the first printed edition of the *Harmonics of Aristoxenus* (in Latin translation) was undertaken."[20]

His pupil, Nicola Vicentino (1511–1572), was even more ardent than his teacher in attempting to construct an aesthetics of music which would relate Renaissance practices with the musical philosophies of the Greeks. He distinguished between sacred and secular music. Religious music, he maintained, should be based on a religious text. The music itself must be conducive to worship. It should have a solemn beginning to engender reverence, a sonorous polyphonic structure to sound majestic, and possess a serenity that will soothe the perplexed. The influence of Plato and Augustine dominated his aesthetic doctrines. He found in the ancients the solution of the perfect marriage of words and music. Plato, the pagan, and Augustine, the Christian, believed that the melody should be dependent on the text, that music should be the handmaid of the composer with which to embellish a poetic line or religious text. Vicentino, a child of humanism, followed the ancients in maintaining that the word, the concept, should dominate the melody. Music should serve to enrich the text, to animate the written word.

---

[20] Oliver Strunk, *Source Readings in Music History*, p. 228; W. W. Norton and Co., Inc., New York: 1950.

CHAPTER 4

PROTESTANT MUSIC

SECTION I—*Luther*

MARTIN Luther (1483–1546) was originally a scholar who became a monk and then turned reformer by rebelling against the corrupt practices of the Catholic hierarchy. He divided the Christian religion of Western Civilization in two on the very day that he nailed his famous Ninety-five theses, on October 31, 1517, to the Church door in Wittenberg. By this act of defiance to the established authority of Rome, Luther exposed the abuses of the Catholic hierarchy to the German laity. Martin Luther thus became the first and greatest leader of the Protestant Reformation, theologically as well as artistically. His original journey to Rome, which was taken in matters concerning his order, left marked theological and musical impressions upon him. It was in Rome that the worldliness of the Papacy fully came to grate on his monastic principles. It was also in the Papal city that he came in contact with the renowned musicians whom the Pope had beckoned to Rome and with the music of Josquin des Prés of whom he later said: "That God preaches the gospel through music is proved by Josquin, whose compositions flow along happily, easily, spontaneously, gently, and, like the song of the finches, are not forced or strained by rules."

Luther wrote in his *Euology of Music*: "Music is a beautiful, gracious gift of God. It has often been the inspiration of my sermons. Music rouses all the emotions of the human heart; nothing on earth is so well suited to make the sad merry, the merry sad, to give courage to the despairing, to make the proud humble, to lessen envy and hate, as music."[1] Elsewhere in a letter he continues: "There are, without doubt, seeds of precious virtues in the hearts of those who are moved by music; whereas those with whom this is not the case must be called blocks and stones. We know that the devil hates and fears music, but I do not hesitate to say that, after theology, there is no art to be placed beside music. Music and theology alone are capable of giving peace and happiness to troubled souls. This plainly proves that the devil, the source of all unhappiness and worries, flees music as much as he does theology. This is why the prophets practiced music as they did no other art. They did not link their theology to geometry, nor to arithmetic, nor to astronomy— but to music, and through music they preached the truth with songs and psalms."[2] Luther reflects that "St. Augustine was afflicted with scruples of conscience whenever he discovered that he had derived pleasure from music and had been made happy thereby; he was of the opinion that such joy is unrighteous and sinful. He was a fine pious man; however, if he were living today, he would hold with us. . . ."[3]

Luther played the lute and flute and took a delight in singing Gregorian Chants, masses, motets and contrapuntal song arrangements. The art of polyphony fascinated him. "How strange and wonderful it is," he said, "that one voice sings a simple unpretentious tune (or tenor, as the musicians call it) while three, four, or five other voices are also sung; these voices play and sway in joyful exuberance around the tune and with ever-varying art and tuneful sound wondrously adorn and beautify it, and in a celestial roundelay meet in friendly caress and lovely embrace; so that anyone, having a little understanding, must be moved and greatly wonder, and come to the conclusion that

[1] Paul Nettl, *Luther and Music*, p. 12; Muhlenberg Press, Philadelphia: 1948.
[2] *Ibid.*, p. 24.
[3] Walter E. Buszin, *Luther on Music*, the Musical Quarterly, p. 89, January, 1946.

there is nothing rarer in the whole world than a song adorned by so many voices. He must be a coarse clod and not worthy of hearing such charming music, who does not delight in this, and is not moved by such a marvel. He should rather listen to the donkey braying of the (Gregorian) chorale, or the barking of dogs and pigs, than to such music."[4]

Luther, like his Catholic predecessors, did not object to changing secular songs into religious ones to fit Protestant needs. He also adapted the Catholic Service and introduced simple congregational hymns in the vernacular to give each member of the congregation the opportunity to take an active part in the Service. "We have planned," he wrote to George Spalatin in 1524, "to follow the example of the prophets and the church fathers and to compose German songs for the German people so that God's Word may resound in the singing of the people. We are seeking poets and musicians everywhere for this purpose. . . . I request you to work with us in this matter and try to translate and adapt some of the psalms for singing. Enclosed you will find a copy of my *Aus tiefer Not schrei ich zu Dir* (*Out of the depths I cry to Thee*). I would ask you, however, to avoid new words and the expressions of the court, so that the people may easily understand. Let the words be as simple as possible but at the same time pure and suitable; and see that the meaning be clear and as close as possible to that of the psalms. We must therefore use our own judgment, determine the original meaning, and translate it freely."[5]

A year later Luther added in his writing *Against the Heavenly Prophets*: "Although I am willing to permit the translating of Latin texts of choral and vocal music into the vernacular with the retention of the original notes and musical settings, I am nevertheless of the opinion that the result sounds neither proper nor correct; the text, the notes, the accents, the tune, and likewise the entire outward expression must be genuine outgrowths of the original text and its spirit; otherwise everything is nothing more than an apish imitation."[6]

Luther not only retained a love for the music of the Mother

---

[4] Paul Nettl, *Op. cit.* pp. 15-16.
[5] *Ibid.*, pp. 38-39.
[6] Walter E. Buszin, *Op. cit.* p. 95.

Church but he borrowed from the Catholic repertoire liberally
to enrich the Protestant faith artistically. He candidly professed,
in commenting on a collection of burial hymns which appeared
in 1542: "To set a good example, we have made some selections
from the beautiful music and hymns used in the papacy, in
vigils, masses for the dead, and at burials, and have published
some in this volume. . . . However, we have changed the texts
and have not retained those used in the papacy. . . . The songs
and the music are precious; it would be a pity, indeed, should
they perish."[7]

Luther frequently joined his youthful comrades in singing
collegiate airs when he was a student. His love for music was
always discerning. With his fine tenor voice and favorite instrument, the lute, from student days on, he often sang and played
the works of the Flemish and German masters with friends. He
enjoyed good secular music even as a monk, but he had retained
more of the Augustinian philosophy in his musical outlook than
he dared to admit in his numerous denunciations of what he
considered to be the carnal and corrupt secular songs of his day.
As the leader of the Reformation he traced the historical significance which music held in the furtherance of Christianity and
outlined the role which he felt music should play in the propagation of Protestant doctrine.

"Every Christian knows," wrote Luther, "that the practice
of singing spiritual songs is wholesome and well-pleasing unto
God, for everybody knows that not only the prophets and kings
of Israel (who praised God with vocal and instrumental music,
with songs and stringed instruments), but also the early Christians, who sang especially psalms, used music already in the
early stages of the Church's history. Indeed, St. Paul encouraged
the use of music 1. Cor. 14, and in his Epistle to the Colossians
he insists that Christians appear before God with psalms and
spiritual songs which emanate from the heart, in order that
through these the Word of God and Christian doctrine may
be preached, taught, and put into practice." "Bearing all this
in mind, I, together with several others, have collected a number
of spiritual songs in order that a beginning might be made to
prepare and gather such material and also that others, whose

---

[7] *Ibid.*, p. 90.

ability is greater than ours, be induced to do such work." "The music is arranged in four parts. I desire this particularly in the interest of the young people, who should and must receive an education in music as well as in the other arts if we are to wean them away from carnal and lascivious songs and interest them in what is good and wholesome. Only thus will they learn, as they should, to love and appreciate what is intrinsically good. I am not of the opinion that because of the Gospel all arts should be rejected violently and vanish, as is desired by the heterodox, but I desire that all arts, particularly music, be employed in the service of Him who has given and created them."[8]

Luther would have every Protestant child given a musical education. "I say for myself;" he writes, "If I had children and would be able to carry it out, I would insist that they study not only the languages and history, but also singing, (instrumental) music and all of mathematics. Is this not all child's-play, through which the Greeks in former times trained their children, who developed into men and women of remarkable ability, fit for every eventuality of life?"[9]

The ethical importance which Luther gave to music, one of the liberal arts, is again in keeping with the Greek doctrine of ethos. Luther also regarded music as a mental discipline. Music remained for Luther as it was for Augustine "a disciplinarian and moral trainer" which to Luther made men "more gentle and refined, more conscientious and sensible."[10] To those preparing for teaching and the ministry Luther stated: "A schoolmaster must be able to sing, or I will not look at him; nor should one admit young men to the ministry unless they have practiced and studied music at school."[11] Luther also refers back to the Greek unity of song, dance and gesture which the Franciscan monk Roger Bacon had suggested in the training of Catholic children for a liberal education. "When maidens and youths indulge in folk dancing with suitable music and gesture", wrote Luther, "it is an *officium humanitatis* and pleases me greatly."[12]

The moral symbolism which Luther applied to various modes

---

[8] *Ibid.*, pp. 87-88.
[9] *Ibid.*, p. 92.
[10] Paul Nettl, *Op. cit.* p. 34.
[11] *Loc. cit.*
[12] *Ibid.*, p. 17.

is again reminiscent of the Platonic and Augustinian overtones in his musical aesthetics. In discussing the Gregorian Chants and the nature of the eight modes, he concluded that since "Christ is a kind Lord, and His Words are sweet; therefore we want to take the sixth mode for the Gospel; and because Paul is a serious apostle we want to arrange the eighth mode for the Epistle."[13] Elsewhere he added: "In music, the leading tone is the Gospel, the other notes the law, and as the law is softened by the Gospel, so the Gospel dominates the other tones and is the sweetest of voices."[14]

Luther also repeated an early Christian practice of applying allegorical interpretations to musical instruments. He did not ally musical instruments with the body and suffering of Christ as St. Augustine had done, but associated various instruments with Christian endeavor. Luther encouraged the use of instrumental music in the religious Service, but he insisted that it should be simple and aesthetically appropriate to the Protestant Service.

SECTION II—*Calvin*

A PURITANIC reaction to Luther's musical aesthetics began with the Swiss reformer Ulrich Zwingli (1484–1531). Zwingli was a poet and musician as well who had not only set two of his own songs to four part music, but played almost every instrument. His poetic nature and musical virtuosity did not deter his reforming religious spirit from cold-bloodedly allowing the organ in Zurich to be hacked to pieces, while the organist stood by helpless and weeping. This negativistic attitude toward music became even more pronounced with Calvin who deliberately set out to purify Luther's musical theories on the function of music in the church and home. Both Zwingli and Calvin feared that music would distract the faithful from the true purpose of religion.

John Calvin's (1509–1564) philosophy of music is summed up in the statement that "properly practiced it affords a recreation

---

13 *Ibid.*, pp. 75-76.
14 *Ibid.*, p. 95.

but it also leads to voluptuousness . . . and we should take good care that it does not furnish the occasion for dropping the reins to dissoluteness or for causing us to become effeminate in disorderly delights." Luther never fully discarded the musical liturgy of the Roman Church but the Calvinists would not admit any religious music into their Service except congregational singing. French, Italian and German folk-songs which were often of a lascivious nature had made their way into the Masses of the Catholic Church until well into the 17th century. Not only did the Calvinists hold that such music, however adapted to liturgical needs, was in no way suitable to arouse religious thoughts and feelings, but they also held that it was evil to begin with since it stressed the carnal and worldly rather than the spiritual and sacred.

Religious fanatics and anti-papists in Switzerland stormed churches and monasteries to cleanse them of the last vestiges of "Romanism". They destroyed organs so that they could never be played again. They erased altar paintings and murals so that the religious would not mistake the pictorial symbol for what the symbol actually represented. They chopped down statues so that the believers would not worship graven images. They even imprisoned the composer, Louis Bourgeois, because he altered the tunes of several Psalms without permission.

Luther's rebellion against the Catholic Church was based on theological differences and practices. But it was not long before political and social contrasts between Catholic and Protestant divided Christianity even more into two hostile groups. The strictness with which the Protestant ministers sought to enforce rigid laws of morality and regulate the dress and habits of their parishioners was also applied to music.

The Calvinists developed a growing antagonism to the Mass and organ, which eventually influenced the Lutherans. The Calvinists at best tolerated music and as time went on they came to regard it as a papist horror and abomination. Whereas the hymn alone with its secular text remained the unquestioned requisite of the Lutheran Service, the Calvinists rejected even that and began to create their own hymns on the sole basis of the psalter.

In his articles for the Reformed Church in 1537 Calvin recommended congregational singing of the Psalms in public worship. After he was expelled from Geneva in 1538 he took up residence in Strassburg where he tried to emulate Luther by compiling a Psalter for use in his church. Calvin deemed that the Reformed Church Service should be centered around the sermon so that through the sermon the Bible could be taught and explained. Since the Psalms are part of the Scriptures, Calvin found a place for them in the Service for he was well aware that Holy Writ could be made even more appealing to man through song than through sermon. Calvin fanatically guarded the Reformed Church from falling victim to the theatrical ceremonies of the Catholic Church. He insisted that the Service be devoid of all artistic adornment and that it be confined musically to the singing of the metrical versions of the Psalms and other Scriptural passages. Calvin remained adamant in the view that the Service should be conducted in the vernacular so that it would be understood by all who came to pray and learn.

Although Calvin refused to admit any type of music other than simple congregational singing into the religious Service he did permit some polyphonic settings of the Scriptures. These could be sung only in the home, in the family and with friends; not for mere artistic pleasure, but for the edification and praise of the Lord. Calvin called upon all Protestant composers to give of their talents to further the work of the Lord by setting the Psalms to music. But the austere liturgic-aesthetic demands which Calvin imposed upon the composers for the most part limited their creativity to simple harmonization of the Psalms.

Calvin insisted that the Psalms be sung in unison and without accompaniment. He abolished the choir so that the Service would be more democratic and the entire congregation could sing the Lord's praise with their own lips. When the Huguenot composer Goudimel (c. 1505–1572), who was one of the most prominent musicians of his day, wrote his four part setting of the Psalms, Calvin looked upon them with disfavor. "They were too complicated for congregational singing, and the very beauty of their harmonic text would attract attention to itself." In a tone reminiscent of Augustine he wrote: "Certainly if singing be attempted to that gravity which becomes the presence of God and Angels, it adds a dignity and grace to sacred actions, and is very efficacious in exciting the mind to a true concern and ardour of devotion. Yet great caution is necessary, that the ears be not more attentive to the modulation of the notes, than the mind to the spiritual import of the words. . . . Whatever music is composed only to please and delight the ear, is unbecoming the majesty of the church, and cannot but be highly displeasing to God."

Calvin believed that all art worthy of the name was a gratuity which God had bestowed upon man. Those arts which carried out God's Will on Earth were good and those arts which only offered sensuous enjoyment and did not further a Christian way of life were the demonic devices which the devil employed to debase man. Calvin would not permit instrumental music in his Service. He ruled out the use of the organ in the Church Service lest organ music detract from the the significance of the simple hymn. A vain organist might be more apt to display his virtuosity and embellish the simple music, which would be contrary to Calvin's idea of liturgical music. Calvin insisted that the Holy Word and not the melody or arrangement was important in the Service; there must be no obstacle set in the way of the congregation for devout worship.

Calvin's philosophy of music influenced all Protestantism so that composers wrote music which would not detract from piety and devotion. Stylistically, they lifted the chorale tune from the traditional tenor part and placed it in the treble or soprano voice. They stressed the vernacular, emphasized simplicity, and omitted any form of artistic embellishment. And yet, the rich polyphonic contributions which Claude Le Jeune (c. 1528–1600) made to Protestantism were indeed a contrast to Calvinistic austerity. In Protestantism as in Catholicism, and as we shall shortly see in Judaism as well, the composer, however rare, gave vent to his feelings and refused to be shackled to aesthetic doctrines which were devised by religious men who took it upon themselves to determine God's Will in musical matters. Calvin's theological and musical beliefs nevertheless exerted a powerful pressure on the Lutheran world and eventually had a puritanic effect on the worship and music of the Lutherans themselves.

The fiery spirit of John Calvin directed the course of Huguenot music in France. The Huguenot Psalter, of which there were over a hundred French editions in the 16th century, exerted a tremendous influence on all of Protestant Europe and the American colonies. In England, many of the leaders of the Protestant movement were equally opposed to the arts in religious worship. Monasteries and convents were suppressed, their instruments and music ruthlessly destroyed. Henry VIII (1491–1547) himself tried to preserve the Catholic ritual after he broke away from the Mother Church, but the more zealous brethren who supported his break with Rome would not be deterred from their mission to rid England of Papal influence. They maintained that Catholic music favored musical virtuosity and did not emphasize the word of God. Catholic music was complex and in a foreign tongue. Their demands were artistically summed up in a letter which Archbishop Cranmer (1489–1556) wrote to Henry with reference to church music. "The song should not be full of notes, but, as near as may be, for every syllable a note so that it may be sung distinctly and devoutly." The leaders of Protestantism, like the early church fathers, were of a common mind in the kind of music which was necessary for prayer and worship.

The English Puritans disbanded the Cathedral choirs and much to the regret of Oliver Cromwell (1599–1658) destroyed church organs and choir books wherever they could find them as an expression of their fanatical hatred for the "popish" musical practices which had been retained in the Service. Cromwell, and many of his followers, publicly displayed their love for music and were well aware of the need for artistic expression and appreciation in the life of man. But Cromwell and his lieutenants fully agreed with their more fanatical followers that music, if not eliminated from the Service, should at least not be emphasized at the expense of scriptural enlightenment. The Puritans closed the theatres because the music on the stage was profane and sinful. They objected both to playing and listening

to secular music on the Sabbath, and to elaborate music in the
Church Service. They approved of music in the home provided
it was not offensive to Christian virtue.

Edward Winslow (1595–1655), one of the founders of New
England, described the departure of the Pilgrims from Leyden
in 1620, saying that the congregation, much moved, sang
Psalms, "there being many of our congregation very expert in
music." But moral demands and physical hardships had their
effect on the artistic life of the settlers and their families. The
Pilgrim Fathers brought with them a musical knowledge of the
Psalms and once these separatists from the English Church found
a religious haven in a new world they reacted to the "popish"
elements which they objected to in English Protestantism. The
more zealous leaders of the Puritan settlers were determined to
eradicate any Roman influence from their church. Many of
them believed that the Psalms ought not to be sung because they
were not divinely inspired and believed that their prohibition
would be an act pleasing to God. The Puritans outlawed the
organ and practically ruled out both secular and religious music,
vocal and instrumental.

The hardships of pioneer life which compelled the early settlers to utilize every ounce of energy in their struggle for
self-preservation, did not allow time for secular amusements.
The Puritans gave their full energies to cutting down the forests,
tilling the soil and guarding themselves from hostile Indians who
would destroy them. Work and caution became the gospel
which must be adhered to if they were to build a church in the
New World. Idleness and time taken from work for amusement
was sinful. Puritans associated music with leisure and time spent
in playing or singing could be better put to use in furthering the
security of the Puritan to do God's Will on Earth.

Although the more ardent Puritans disavowed all forms of
music, there is little doubt that music was still played and sung
in the home. Even the antagonism which certain Puritans developed toward Psalm singing did not keep congregations from
using them in their Services. Toward the middle of the 17th
century a simple manner of congregational singing developed.

Music became an integral part of Protestant worship among

practically all of its denominations in the years that were to follow. The Calvinistic hostility to music was originally part of an artistic reaction to the religious pomp of the Catholic Church. Luther was more sympathetic with Catholic ritual and music than either Zwingli or Calvin. He regarded music as a Heavenly gift through which man could offer up prayer and praise to the Lord. But the Calvinists did not relinquish the musical heritage of the past altogether. They looked with favor on the Catholic, Orlando di Lasso, and used his music where they could. The Jesuits, in turn, who guided the Counter-Reformation in the Catholic Church thought it would be well to emulate the democratic spirit of the Protestant Service, even if it meant compromising some of Loyola's scornful decrees concerning music. The followers of Loyola recognized that the Protestant use of the vernacular had tremendous psychological value and so they decided that it would be equally as advantageous to Catholicism to provide the followers of their faith with religious songbooks. Music was an effective expedient for both Catholics and Protestants.

SECTION III—*Aesthetic Similarities in Protestant, Catholic and Jewish Music**

THERE is a decided similarity of aesthetic concepts in Protestant, Catholic and Jewish music. Protestant and Catholic music is aesthetically rooted in Platonic philosophy and Hebrew theology. The Protestants retained the basic musical concepts of the Catholics and the Catholics themselves never gave up the musical legacy which they inherited from their Hebraic forefathers. The Rabbis' admonitions against immoral songs and the advice which Plato gave to the State Guardians are of the same spirit ethically and aesthetically.

What appeared as mere aesthetic theory in the Platonic dialogues became an artistic actuality in the Middle Ages. This transition from Greek aesthetic theory to medieval musical

---

* The content of this section is based on my paper *Similarities of Musical Concepts in Ancient and Medieval Philosophy* in the Journal of Aesthetics and Art Criticism, March, 1949.

practice was made when some of the Patristics introduced Plato
to early Christianity as an infallible authority whose views on
music should be used as a criterion of judgment in the realm of
the sacred as well as the secular. The church fathers stressed
certain of the characteristic Platonic views: (1) that music has
strong ethical implications; (2) that music is a highly effective
means to attain a desired emotional state; (3) the traditional
relationship of text to tune; (4) distrust towards musical innovation. These four aesthetic theories of music did not remain
exclusively Catholic. The aesthetic influence which Plato exerted
on Plotinus in the Greco-Roman period and later on St. Augustine, also had its overtones in the musical aesthetics of Luther
and Calvin.

Plato's own interest in music was primarily moralistic. The
impress which his philosophy of music left upon generations
that came after him was indeed great. There is no evidence
whether Hebraic music was affected by him directly, but
Catholic and Protestant liturgical music still bear the Platonic
stamp on their pages. This sustaining Platonic influence can be
traced to those four musical concepts already mentioned that
the founder of the Academy espoused in his writings.

Greek music penetrated into Palestine and became the fashion
among the intellectuals there, much to the dismay of the
spiritual leaders. It must have affected the cultural life of the
Jews in Palestine severely, for, prior to the destruction of the
Temple, the religious guardians of Judea took up the cry that
the secular strains of the Greek pagan were having a bad moral
effect upon the Jewish populace. The spiritual leaders of Judea
admonished their people, even under threat of divine punishment, to give up "immoral" Greek songs of lustful implications
and return to their own sacred tunes even on festive occasions.[15]

The Patristics who nurtured Christianity through her unstable
infancy were as seriously concerned with the moral aspects of
music as the Hebrews. St. Augustine was particularly Platonic
in warning the early Christians to guard against the licentious
tunes emanating from the Roman theatre that might draw them

---

[15] A. Z. Idelsohn, *Jewish Music, In Its Historical Development*, pp. 22, 92;
Henry Holt and Co., New York: 1929.

from a righteous or moral life. This zealous convert came to believe that the infectious melodies of the street and the theatre were promptings of the evil spirit and were therefore sinful. The only good music, for him, was the religious music which brought men closer to God in a communion of song and worship. The spirit of St. Augustine manifested itself more than a thousand years later in the musical philosophy of John Calvin.

The second point is the role music has played as a phychological means for the attainment of a desired emotional, religious and social end in ancient and medieval philosophy. Plato maintained that music should be one more instrumental force in the establishment of virtue and morality.

The Hebrew Prophets also looked upon music as a tool for the conveyance of ideas. They told their people "that profane songs of love and lust are sufficient cause to destroy the world, and that Israel's religious songs save it." Therefore, "If you have a sweet voice, glorify God with the gift He bestowed upon you, chant the *Shema*, and lead the people in prayer."[16] Religious music alone could bridge the existing gap between God and man. Numerous references in the *Old Testament* touch upon the secular nature of music, but it is usually distinguished from the sacred. When Judea was taken into captivity in later years the religious and secular music of the Israelite became inseparable. Music offered the Hebrew a means of emotional relief through which he could express his longing and grief. It was not an expression of a freely creative people but a means of imploring Jehovah for deliverance from bondage.

Augustine's prime interest in music lay in its effectiveness in bringing the pagan into the fold and in how music, as a psychological device, could be instrumental in heightening the religious enthusiasm of the average churchgoer. If music to which the *Psalms of David* were sung attracted the populace and brought them to church, then according to Augustine, music served a useful purpose.

Luther regarded music as a rhythmic language which could more effectively than mere prose educate men and bring them closer to an understanding of God. However creative a musician

---

[16] *Ibid.*, p. 92.

Luther may have been, his aesthetic theories are saturated with a theology that is altogether reminiscent of Augustine. Early Protestant musical thought had an artistic creed, to be sure, but it was based on religious and organizational needs closely patterned on the methods of the Mother Church. The leaders of the Reform, like their Catholic predecessors, had to make use of every means possible to win over the emotional and psychological forces in man, and the intrinsic qualities of music suggested themselves to Luther as one important means of helping the Protestant movement in Germany succeed.

The third point is the relationship of the melody to the text in the music of antiquity and the Middle Ages. Plato never relinquished the traditional Greek attitude that lyric and tune should not be separated from one another. He emphasized the moral value of the text by subordinating the musical form to poetry.

The Jewish philosophers generally considered melody to be subordinate to textual needs. In Jewish music the text was primary. Instrumental music was used mainly to accompany and embellish. The Rabbis even regarded instruments with misgiving since they enabled Jewish singers and dancers to emulate pagan forms of worship within the Temple. The Rabbis further maintained that the Holy Scriptures were more important in worship than vain melodic invention and tuneful accompaniment.

St. Augustine stressed the desirability of using only Biblical texts for religious music. Although he did not formally sanction the use of Biblical texts adapted to the popular folk-tunes used in his day, he was well aware of the infectious character that a catchy tune could have on the masses. The saving grace for a street song or folk-tune lay in its aesthetic marriage with a Scriptural passage that would allow the ordinary Christian to become more familiar with the sacred text. The Patristics considered the text superior to the melody and the Scholastics in later centuries retained this view.

The musical precepts which Calvin imposed upon a puritanic and self-denying French Protestantism stand out as a glaring travesty on the cultural history of France. It was in France that the earliest forms of organum were expanded into highly developed polyphonic writing. The motet was perhaps the outstanding contrapuntal development of the Notre Dame School in the late 12th and 13th centuries. Yet, some three hundred years after France reigned supreme musically in Europe, Huguenot music was relegated to a missionary function for the propagation of the new faith. Calvin demanded that the Protestant composers confine their creative activity to simple harmonization of the Psalms. He allowed only the simplest forms of congregational singing for devotional Services. Rather begrudgingly, he permitted some polyphonic settings of the Scriptures, but this more complex type of music was to be sung in the home and among friends. Even in the home or among friends, cautioned Calvin, the performers were to remember that they were singing Holy Writ.

The last of the four concepts deals with the element of change in ancient and medieval music. Thales' classic denunciation of Homeric legend as a distortion of reality is the earliest instance of philosophic censure of artistic license and innovation in pre-Socratic philosophy. The father of ancient philosophy presumed that the philosopher could distinguish the true nature of reality from illusion more readily than the artist could. The philosopher and the priest have, on the contrary, hampered artistic trends more often than not through the centuries. Time has proven them to be the false prophets while the artist they so "judiciously" censured not only intuited the reality of his own era but anticipated the needs of the future.

The Judaic hierarchy was equally suspicious of heretical influences that might affect Jewish law and ritual. New ideas, artistic, philosophic, or theologic, were immediately brought under surveillance. But the spiritual leaders of Jerusalem were not altogether successful in stifling new trends either in the era prior to Christianity or after the Jews were compelled to wander through foreign lands. Alien cultures always had a strong effect upon these Jewish wanderers, and the Jews, in turn, influenced the countries which befriended them. The Rabbis, nevertheless, kept exhorting their people not to ape the ways of the respective countries in which they found themselves. Alien Western music is as foreign to Jewish life, warned the Rabbis, as Christian theology is to the *Old Testament*. What displeased the Rabbis all the more during these years of endless wandering were unorthodox secular strains that would on occasion make their way into the Jewish Service. The introduction of new songs into the Synagogue invariably aroused protest against innovation and disregard of tradition. As late as the 16th century in Germany, the Rabbis complained bitterly against those cantors who were abandoning the old sanctified tunes inherited from their fathers.

Augustine expressed grave concern that popular changes in liturgical music would eventually alter the sanctity of the liturgy itself. He believed that since popular strains, folk-tunes and innovating musical tendencies stemmed from pagan sources and the illiterate populace, the introduction of such worldly tunes into the religious ritual would only enhance pagan art rather than Christian virtue. Therefore, concluded Augustine, liturgical composers must confine their creative talents to pure ecclesiastical forms if they would foster Christian needs. Pope Gregory I thought so well of this Augustinian bit of logic that he initiated a campaign to preserve the traditional Church music by shielding it against all outside influences that might be of an unreligious or carnal tone.

Luther was not opposed to musical change, but the change had to be in keeping with Protestant needs. He had a clear conception of the kind of music the Protestant Church would need to fully emancipate itself from papal influence. If he was to appeal directly to the German people then neither the Latin language nor the Gregorian Chants were the best means of reaching the common man. To achieve his end, Luther introduced German to replace the Latin of the Catholic Service; and as a substitute for the complex Gregorian Chant, he chose music that was simpler and less pretentious, more akin to the German folk-song.

Thus we find that the leaders of Israel were in common accord with the Greeks in opposing foreign influences. State and religion were one to the Greeks and Jews. A religious innovation could endanger the State. No wonder they guarded the music in their respective temples as diligently as their sentries queried each stranger who would enter their midst.

The Patristics kept admonishing their flock to turn a deaf ear to Roman tunes which vilified true Christianity. Each move that the masses made to inject secular strains into the Service was fought by the Church from its very inception into the ensuing centuries. But the people were adamant in bringing folk-tunes into their house of worship, and the Catholic hierarchy learned to become conciliatory in accepting inevitable musical trends. The Church insisted on tradition and simplicity but even Her liturgical composers could not help vent some of their creative energy in creating new forms.

The Platonic strain which permeated early Church music was more ably championed by St. Augustine than any of the other fathers. We noted that Plato was a creative artist whose judgment of music was often harsh and puritanic. This paradoxical trait of the philosopher with a bent towards the arts comes out just as severely but more realistically in Augustine. The philosophic theories of music which Plato expressed in the *Republic, Laws* and other dialogues were not put into practice in his own times. When we come to the early centuries of Christianity, these exacting Platonic admonitions were so effectively championed by Augustine that they became a pattern of ethical principles which characterized medieval music until the rise of humanism in Western civilization some eight hundred years later.

Augustine was a teacher of rhetoric as a young man and later became a well known interpreter of poetry. Sometime before his baptism he started the treatise *De Musica,* which is highly mystical and is devoted mainly to meter, verse and theories pertaining to numbers. Toward the end of this work, which consists of six books, Augustine attempted to analyze music in a manner that we in our own day would call psychological. The tenor of the treatise is both Pythagorean in its treatment of number relationships and Platonic in its ethical platitudes. This treatise, together with his moralistic remarks pertaining to music in the *Confessions,* crystallized official Catholic thought on the function of music in the church and state.

The humanistic spirit that was brought to the Western world with the re-birth of Aristotle came to a sorrowful end musically at the Council of Trent and the papal congregation in 1564. Presumably, the Catholic dignitaries sought to clean house artistically and theologically, which meant a return to the simpler ways of the past. Aristotle would serve the Church well in matters of theology, reasoned the Council, but music must follow the voice of Plato as echoed in St. Augustine. Polyphonic music for religious devotion was retained, but its liturgical survival depended on conceptual reservations. The Church had once more compromised with what it could not help but accept artistically. Protestantism lived through the same pattern of musical blunders, reiterating rather than foregoing these Scholastic aesthetic fallacies.

The task of compiling a Protestant repertoire of liturgical music found Luther confronted with a dilemma. Although he was an undeniable revolutionary religious zealot, he never ceased admiring the rich polyphonic music of Catholicism. He appropriated melodies from the Ambrosian hymns, medieval sequences and Gregorian Chants of the Mother Church. These tunes were revamped, simplified and fitted to his majestic chorales. He took the folk-tunes of the German people and wove them into the spiritual music of the Protestant faith. Whether Luther personally composed or guided these musical activities is not known for certain, but he must have manifested a profound understanding and love of music, from what can be gleaned from his writings.

Calvin was distrustful of Luther's liberal musical concepts. Just as the church fathers warned the early Christians against pagan tunes, so Calvin fanatically set out to obliterate whatever vestige of Catholic music remained in Protestantism. He unforgivably stifled creative initiative and reduced Huguenot music to most elemental forms. In his efforts to re-capture the original Christian spirit of simplicity and rid Protestantism of ritual and ceremony, his philosophy of music became as puritanic as those fostered in Plato and St. Augustine.

CHAPTER 5

THE AESTHETICS OF MUSIC
IN THE BAROQUE ERA

SECTION I—*Opera and Greek Drama*

THE transition from one musical era to another has invariably divided those who create and those who criticize. In the year 1600 a conservative critic, musical theorist and canon of the Church named Giovanni Maria Artusi lamented the passing of traditional music in *A Dissertation about the Imperfections of Modern Music*. Two years later the composer and singer, Giulio Caccini (b. 1550), referred to his collection of madrigals and canzonets as *Nuove Musiche* and three years after that Claudio Monteverdi (1567–1643), who composed the first important opera and whose madrigals are probably the most beautiful that were ever written, wrote in his fifth book of madrigals that he did not follow the precepts of the old school but was guided by, what he called, the second practice or the new school. Monteverdi was taking issue with the critic Artusi's diatribe against the new philosophy of music. Artusi maintained, in defense of traditional music, that Monteverdi overstressed the role and significance of dissonance in his music. Monteverdi responded that the aesthetic standards of the old or first school could not be applied to the evaluation of the new or second school.[1]

The adherents of the old school, the Renaissance, and the progressives of the new musical philosophy in the Baroque era both based their aesthetic concepts on the Platonic theory that art imitates nature, however they may have disagreed in their tonal precepts. Both the Renaissance and the Baroque composers followed this ancient doctrine. They tried to create stereotyped groups of musical tones that would imitate the human passions and natural phenomena. Aristotle, in the *Politics*, and Nicholas of Cusa, in the early Renaissance, wrote of the doctrine of affections as it related to music. The Renaissance composers employed this doctrine with caution and marked simplicity but the Baroque composer went to extremes in the manner in which he expressed the entire gamut of human emotions in his application of this doctrine. The Baroque composer also tended to underline significant words in the text with dissonance and chromaticisms to a greater degree than the Renaissance composer. Instrumental ingenuity and development further gave the Baroque composer added musical means with which to embellish the written word, to stress its meaning by intensifying feeling.

In 1581, Vincenzo Galilei, the father of the illustrious scientist, published a treatise entitled *Dialogo della musica antica e della moderna* which summed up the philosophy of music of a literary group called the Camerata. This group dedicated itself to the cause of applying the aesthetic ideals of the Greek philosophers to Italian music. The Camerata, under the leadership of Count Giovanni Bardi and Count Jacopo Corsi, included, among its better known members, the poet Ottavio Rinuccini and the composers Jacopo Peri (1561–1633) and Caccini. Galilei maintained in his treatise that the art of polyphony was responsible for the degeneration of music and must be abolished. He also believed that descriptive music was unrealistic and abounded in false imitation. Galilei expressed the musical philosophy of the Camerata by maintaining that a new monodic style would have

---

[1] Manfred F. Bukofzer, *Music in the Baroque Era*, p. 1; W. W. Norton and Co., Inc., New York: 1947.

to be created if Italian music was to emulate the Platonic ideals of Greek music.

Galilei was an unschooled, but nevertheless versatile, musician. He appears, by his condemnation of the modern tendencies in music with its emphasis on polyphony, to have been the leading spirit in the outset of this movement. The Camerata attacked the treatment of words in Renaissance music with the claim that in contrapuntal music the poetry was literally "torn to pieces" because the individual voices sang different melodies simultaneously. The Camerata insisted that the sense of an entire passage, rather than that of a single word, should be imitated in music. The recitative, in which contrapuntal writing was altogether abandoned, was created so that the music could be subordinated to the words, and, as in the ideal style of the Greeks, the words would govern the musical rhythm and cadences.[2]

The members of the Camerata erroneously believed that the Greeks sang the entire text of the play and as neo-Platonists, who glorified the past, they sought to revive what they held to be the lost art of ancient Greece. The Camerata bent their creative efforts to develop an art form in which music would embellish the spoken word, music would enhance the dramatic action of the performer, the divine marriage of music and drama would be consummated to produce the Greek ideal of Platonic aesthetics. Galilei's discovery of the hymn of Mesomedes offered the Camerata the first evidence of original Greek music, but since the members of this literary group were unable to decipher the Greek notation, they could do little else but speculate about its contents. Rinuccini became the first opera librettist by carrying out the Camerata's request for a tragedy based on Greek aesthetic principles. His dramatic poem *Dafne* was set to music by Peri and was performed in the Florentine home of Count Corsi about 1594. Only the text of the original *Dafne* has been preserved, the music has unfortunately been lost. Rinuccini and Peri, imbued with the success of their first opera, produced *Eurydice*, with help for the musical setting from Caccini. This

---

[2] *Ibid.*, p. 5f.

was presented in 1600 in celebration of the marriage of Henry IV and Maria de' Medici in Florence.

The Camerata introduced the recitative in the belief "that music should imitate the delivery of an orator and his manner of moving the affections of the audience." Caccini devotedly followed the Platonic view that music was primarily speech and rhythm and lastly melody.[3] Peri also maintained that the composer should emulate the speaking person in song. Galilei and Bardi maintained that the musician should learn from the orator how to move the affections, and Peri wrote in his Preface to *Eurydice* that he was attempting to model vocal music after human speech.

Marsilio Ficino, the Platonic purist of the Florentine Academy, had originally expressed the view that the poet and orator took the musician as their model. In this instance, Ficino was more of a Renaissance product than a devout Platonist. Zarlino also defended Renaissance aesthetics but maintained that the art of poetry and music were independent modes of expression. The views of Zarlino on the art of polyphony found favor with the Camerata since he wrote that the simple music of one voice moved the heart more profoundly than did complicated counterpoint. But Zarlino differed from the Florentine Camerata in his view of the relation of music to poetry. For the Renaissance composer the recitative was basically vocal music set to a text, but to the Baroque composer the recitative was primarily speech embellished by music. Zarlino maintained that music should arouse the affections of the words, but he insisted on the fundamental difference between the method of the poet and that of the musician.[4] The musical aesthetics of Ficino and Zarlino represented the traditional views of the

[3] *Republic*, Bk. III, 398.
". . . a song or ode has three parts—the words, the melody, and the rhythm; . . . the melody and rhythm will depend upon the words."
Giovanni Battista Doni (1593-1647) wrote "The real delight in hearing a singer derives from a clear understanding of the text." Father Marin Mersenne (1588-1648), the Frenchman and friend of Descartes, whose most important work *Harmonie universelle* appeared in 1636, agreed with Doni by adding that "A singer's performance should have the effect of a well-made speech."
[4] Manfred F. Bukofzer, *Op. cit.*, p. 7.

Renaissance and the views of the members of the Camerata represented the musical philosophies of the early Baroque.

The new music drama which the Camerata had produced was neither a reproduction nor regeneration of classical tragedy. The first opera was actually a pastoral play set to music. The members of the Camerata actually believed that they had freed music from the domination of polyphony. It appears upon reflection, however, that the Camerata went from one extreme to another by producing a word-dominated art form in which the music only supported the spoken word. The result was that the Camerata operas were mainly extended recitatives which attempted to render the spoken word to instrumental accompaniment.

The traditionalists maintained that the Florentine Camerata actually were retarding the development of music by deliberately ignoring the art of Palestrina and the accepted principles of polyphony. This group of traditionalists argued that to forego the artistic effects which Palestrina had achieved through traditional polyphony could only set back the musical art, technique and creativity of the Florentines. The traditionalists concluded, with Artusi as their spokesman, that music should be written not according to theory such as set forth by these Florentines, but on precepts which were based on traditional harmonies and rhythms.

Monteverdi resolved the conflict of the traditionalists and modernists by being conservative with regard to the preservation of polyphonic music, but decidedly revolutionary in the manner in which he employed it. "Like the *Camerata*, he laid down the axiom of the dominance of the words over the harmony, but it led to a diametrically opposed result because he applied it to polyphony, not *against* it, as the Florentines did."[5]

Claudio Monteverdi, and not the Florentine Camerata, artistically revived the spirit of antique tragedy and created a music drama in Western culture. He first obtained the post of choirmaster and conductor at St. Mark's in Venice in 1612. Opera had not yet been introduced in Venice at the time of his arrival

---

[5] *Ibid.*, p. 33.

and the opening of the first public opera in Venice did not take place until 1637. Between the years of Monteverdi's arrival at St. Mark's and the beginning of opera in Venice, Monteverdi had occupied himself with his duties as musical director of the famed Cathedral and with the creation of church music. In 1630 the terrible epidemic scourge that swept the Adriatic republic left little enthusiasm for pleasure and artistic creation. Two years later Monteverdi became an ordained priest of the Church, but his retirement from the world at large was only temporary. The introduction of opera into Venetian life met with such enthusiasm that the creative urge in Monteverdi could not remain dormant.

Monteverdi portrayed, in his music, human suffering and man's inability to control his passions. His musical scores dealt with human passions, emotion, and anguish. To achieve these effects he employed rhythms and harmonies that offended the traditionalists. Artusi attacked him for these innovations; primarily, for using dissonances and not resolving them. Artusi's Platonic view of music led him to write: ". . . insofar as it introduced new rules, new modes, and new turns of phrase, these were harsh and little pleasing to the ear, nor could they be otherwise; for so long as they violate the good rules—in part founded upon experience, the mother of all things, in part observed in nature, and in part proved by demonstration—we must believe them deformations of the nature and propriety of true harmony, far removed from the object of music, . . ."[6] But Monteverdi also found in the writings of Plato a philosophic justification for his new aesthetics. "I have reflected that the principal passions or affections of our mind are three, namely, anger, moderation, and humility or supplication; so the best philosophers declare, and the very nature of our voice indicates this in having high, low, and middle registers. The art of music also points clearly to these three in its terms 'agitated,' 'soft,' and 'moderate'. . . . In all the works of former composers I have indeed found examples of the 'soft' and the 'moderate,' but never

---

[6] *Delle imperfezioni della moderna musica,* Oliver Strunk, *Source Readings in Music History,* p. 394; W. W. Norton and Co., Inc., New York: 1950.

of the 'agitated,' a genus nevertheless described by Plato in the third book of his *Rhetoric*[7] in these words: 'Take that harmony that would fittingly imitate the utterances and the accents of a brave man who is engaged in warfare.' And since I was aware that it is contraries which greatly move our mind, and that this is the purpose which all good music should have—as Boethius asserts, saying, 'Music is related to us, and either ennobles or corrupts the character'—for this reason I have applied myself with no small diligence and toil to rediscover this genus."[8]

Monteverdi used harmonies liberally to express the poetic text. He believed that harmony must imitate the concept of the text, particularly when human passions are involved. He employed chords and harmonies not as an end in themselves but to achieve an expressive relationship of tone and word. For the Florentine Camerata music became a servant of the text but Monteverdi used music to more fully bring out the meaning inherent in the text. He believed that the meaning of the words should shape the music. Characteristic of all Baroque composers, Monteverdi portrayed the concept of the text by establishing a group of musical expressions to depict specific human emotions and actions.

The doctrine of affections of the 16th century became even more prominent in the treatises on musical aesthetics in late Baroque music. While the philosophers and theorists in general concerned themselves with the empirical nature and moral function of music, the composers insisted that what mattered was simply the sound of the music and how the listener reacted to it.

The Baroque composer originally employed the doctrine of affections to intensify the word and heighten the action of a musical score. With time, the doctrine of affections became so stereotyped that composers employed standardized musical expressions to evoke various moods and to create pictorial illusions. This rational manner of creating a category of musical effects to describe love, pity, and hate, or engender a mood consistent with the action led to a distortion of the Greek balance between

---

[7] See *Republic*, Bk. III, 399a.
[8] Oliver Strunk, *Op. cit.*, p. 413.

the text and music. The insistence of the members of the Camerata that the music should be subordinated to the words in the opera exemplifies this lack of balance between text and music. Had the aesthetic theories of the Camerata been carried to extremes, pure music might have merely become a handmaid of the drama. Monteverdi was well aware of this danger and once more as a creative musician had to undo the harm brought to music by the musical aesthetes and philosophers of the Camerata.

SECTION II—*The Aesthetics of the Italian Opera*

ITALY became the center of the musical world in the Baroque era. The simple aims of the Camerata to cleanse Western music of complex polyphony by returning to the musical styles of the ancients was both a failure and a success. On the one hand, the Italian composer did not share the Camerata's enthusiasm concerning the aesthetic evils of polyphony. He, furthermore, found it difficult to gear his musical creativity to a text. On the other hand, the Camerata was successful in introducing a new musical form which began as a pastoral play set to simple monophonic music and which eventually was developed into a form which fused all the arts into one, the opera.

The operas and madrigals of Monteverdi, the tonal richness of Giovanni Gabrieli's (1557–1612) vocal and instrumental music, religious and secular, have a quiet grandeur that we find majestic in our own time. The quality of craftsmanship that exists in the scores of these two musicians, the virility of their ideas, contradicted the theories of the Camerata that salvation for the music of the future lay in seeking refuge in the past.

The Baroque composer in Italy had some definite aesthetic precepts which we are apt to miss in listening to his music. He tried to underline important words in the text with melodic emphasis. He strove to achieve the greatest affect of the text. He consciously set himself off from the Renaissance by his use of dissonance and chromaticisms. He tried to enrich his instrumental output with tonal combinations that would give him musical sounds that were unknown to the Renaissance musician.

Above all, he prized melody for its own sake. No less than two such outstanding composers as Giacomo Carissimi (1604–1674) and Luigi Rossi (1598–1653) devised a "melodical sequence" in which a melodic phrase was introduced and then repeated lower and higher in a highly repetitive fashion to stress the independence of the melody from the text.

Baroque music may sound serene and calm to us in our own century but the complaint of Artusi was that it was bombastic, strident, cacophonous, and much too bold in dissonance and chromaticisms. Artusi proved to be a false prophet in holding that music would be ruined by moderns such as Monteverdi. We are more likely to remember Artusi today as a critic who attacked a great composer than for any other reason.

The first public opera house was opened in Venice in 1637. It was originally supported and mainly attended by royalty and the rich. Later, it welcomed anyone who had the price of admission. In order to keep the opera house well attended, enterprising managers contracted the finest singers in Europe for service in Venice. With this wealth of musical talent drawn to Venice, the theatre managers assured themselves of a handsome profit on their investment at the same time that they were making Venice the center of musical activity in Italy.

Francesco Cavalli (1602–1676), the gifted student of Monteverdi, and Marc Antonio Cesti (1620–1669) took over the leadership of the Venetian opera. Monteverdi had consciously tried to keep a balanced relationship between the music and the libretti in his operas, but these two younger composers gave more consideration to the music and less to the texts of their operas. The high esteem in which Cavalli and Cesti were held in Venetian musical circles soon had its influence on the opera in that Italian city. By emphasizing the music over the libretto, Cavalli and Cesti began to slight the dramatic aspect of the Venetian opera, thus diminishing the balance between word and song that Monteverdi had so ably accomplished in contrast to the Camerata who had emphasized the text at the expense of the song.

Cesti and Cavalli began what to them appeared as opera based on independence of melody, but which eventually led to a style of virtuoso singing that all but ruined the integrity of the operatic form. Cesti must have had a fondness for vocal music. He is believed to have initiated the Bel Canto style of singing with its long sustained passages and sensuous tones as a result of the manner in which he composed his developed arias. The influence which Cesti and Cavalli exerted upon the Venetian opera spread throughout Europe.

The democratic spirit which prevailed in the Venetian opera house did more than just invite those with the price of admission to witness opera in the style of Cavalli and Cesti. The fundamental reasons why the Venetian managers opened their doors to the public is not as important as the fact that once the doors had been opened to the public it meant that the era of the opera as a court spectacle was beginning to disappear and the beginning of an era in which the opera became the foremost musical art which appealed to the masses had begun.[9]

The hopes and aspirations of the Florentine Camerata for an opera based on the aesthetics of the Greek theatre came to a lamentable end in the Venetian opera. The ideals of the Camerata were abandoned. Opera in Venice became a form of artistic compromises which catered to luxury and amusement. Libretti were not constructed around personalities but around types. The Venetians called their music drama serious opera, but this was a misnomer since the opera was rarely tragic and the public demanded a happy ending. The three unities of the Greek theatre also went by the board in the Venetian opera since many of their operas were too short for professional use and theatre directors began to insert "fillins" to stretch the evening's entertainment. The melodies were highly ornamental

[9] Olin Downes, *The New York Times*, June 26, 1952. "Florence, Italy, June 25—One remains, even the morning after, under the spell of the noble opera 'Didone', by Francesco Cavalli, produced in Venice in 1641 and revived here three centuries later as one of the crowning events of the Florence May festival. . . . The characters are many, and each one at various lengths speaks for himself or herself. Aside from certain grand and pathetic choruses of dramatic commentary, there are no ensemble passages. All is dialogue and incipient aria or arioso style to the end. But if anybody has been misled by certain of our learned musicologists into the belief that only Monteverde knew how to write impassioned recitative, let him listen to this text and music and be moved out of himself."

and only the idolized castrati could master melodic lines that would tax an instrumental virtuoso.

The religious music of Venice was as revolutionary as the secular music in the theatre. Composers tended to write in the same vein for both religious and secular music. It was not uncommon to find a liturgical text set to the tune of an operatic aria being performed at a religious Service. The Churchmen did not take kindly to this intrusion of the secular aria into the religious Service and the introduction of elaborate instrumental music into the Church. But Rome, too, became imbued with this spirit of innovation.[10] Her composers created Masses reflecting the splendor of the Baroque. Girolamo Frescobaldi (1583–1643), the brilliant organist at St. Peter's in Rome, had originally alternated the organ and the choir. Now great bodies of singers were joined and supported by an orchestra, playing independently or with voices, to enhance the religious Service. The Roman composers also acquired an eminent position in the operatic world, but the spirit of St. Augustine was soon to manifest itself through Pope Innocent XII (Pope from 1691–1700), a stern reformer, who opposed the depraving character of the theatre and ordered the opera house in the papal city to be razed.

Toward the end of the 17th century, Naples began to loom as the center of the musical world. In this era of Neapolitan supremacy, music fared both well and badly. The Neapolitans glorified the human voice. Virtuoso singing was the aim. The libretto suffered and the entire opera of the late Baroque was concerned with masterful singing and pure tone production. Singers paid little heed to musical scores and freely substituted

---

[10] Manfred F. Bukofzer, *Op. cit.*, p. 68.

"The followers of the Roman school . . . took over the polychoral style of the Venetian school, but expanded it to unprecedented dimensions in compositions for four, six, and sometimes even twelve and more choruses that have justly been called the 'colossal baroque' in analogy with the architecture of the time. . . . The profusion of vocal and instrumental means, the innumerable echos, solos, and tuttis, reflected the pomp of the church ritual in the counter-reformation, ... It is symbolic for the subordination of the liturgy to the display of glamour that the chorus no longer had its traditional place near the altar, but was distributed in the lofts and balconies that baroque church architecture supplied in abundance."

arias of their own, which would show them at their best vocally, for arias of which they did not approve. Their emphasis on virtuoso singing and technical perfection was mainly responsible for the degeneration of the opera into a bizarre artistic form. If a singer liked a particular aria he often used the same music for different words. The importance of the singer overshadowed the composer and conductor. Those who created and those who conducted were at his beck and call. His whims were granted, his interpretations were followed. He could modify the score as he wished and embellish at will. It was in this field of vocal virtuosity that the castrati were in their fullest glory. Their vocal registers were so phenomenal that the women who ordinarily sang soprano leads were compelled to take parts in the lower register or suffer in pride at their inability to excel or emulate the vocal acrobatics of the castrati. By the second half of the 18th century the role of the castrati began to wane in the opera houses.

Naples could boast of such talented musicians as Alessandro Scarlatti (1659–1725), who was the father of Domenico Scarlatti (1685–1757), and who dedicated his more than one hundred operas to the beauty of melody and the art of singing. Their musical philosophies were in sharp contrast to those of the Florentine Camerata who at the close of the 16th century had created a music drama which they thought was in the style of the Greeks. The Camerata had subordinated the music to the text so that the spoken word would be unmistakenly clear, and had avoided the complex polyphonic practices of their day so that their operas would, they believed, be in the true spirit of the Greeks. In the early 17th century Monteverdi had discarded the austere aesthetics of the Camerata by giving more prominence to the music and the intensification of the dramatic action. Alessandro Scarlatti was more concerned with the music than the text or the dramatic action. His operas, which became the opera seria in the following century, were made up of legendary plots, shallow libretti and numerous disconnected arias which were sung by accomplished castrati; all of which delighted the Italians. Practically every foreign composer who came to Naples carried away some of the Scarlatti influence so that in the 18th century the Scarlatti opera was the model of European composers.

What Scarlatti achieved for opera seria, Giovanni Battista Pergolesi (1710–1736) equalled for the opera buffa. Both operatic forms developed simultaneously. The folk-like character and humorous dialogue of the opera buffa did not stop at the level of pure amusement, but became an instrument of effective musical satire.

SECTION III—*The Music of France, England and Germany*

IN 17th century France, a spirit strikingly similar to that of the Florentine Camerata of the previous century prevailed. Poets and musicians were attempting to revive the Greek drama. They philosophized on the fine distinctions that would bring about a proper aesthetic balance between word and text and they introduced the dance as the third element in the theatre in the hope of recapturing the true flavor of Greek antiquity. Molière (1622–1673), who satirized the social life of his day, shared in the spirit of the times aesthetically. He introduced a new musical element into the spoken comedy by uniting comedy with music and then adding the dance.

As a collaborator of Molière, the composer Jean Baptiste Lully (1632–1687) followed the Platonic thesis that music should be subordinate to poetry. He composed music for the written text with such fanaticism that the melodic line depended on the inflection of the word, the rhyme, and meter of the text. This pedantic faithfulness to the text may have exalted the spoken word but it also diminished the power of the melody. Lully was as demanding of his performers as he was of himself. He imposed stringent rules on his vocalists and instrumentalists, just as rigidly as he disciplined his own creative activity according to his aesthetic concepts. He would not allow his soloists to take arbitrary tempos or to whimsically indulge in ornamentations and cadenzas of their own invention simply to display their technical virtuosity. Lully's insistence on a faithful rendition of the musical score helped counteract the effect that the vanity of the Italian performer had upon the French theatre.

His demands for a faithful rendition of the score may well have kept the French theatre from degenerating to the vaudeville-like character of the Italian opera house.

Philosophic rationalism in France was also having its effect on music. The ever present background of Platonic thought in French rationalism led to the Greek concept of the imitation of nature which was applied to art in general and to music in particular. The Camerata had emphasized the role which music must play in making the word meaningful and in heightening the drama and, in France, the aesthetics of music also became highly intellectualized. The French rationalists did not employ music simply as a handmaid of the text, even if they did place pure instrumental music on a lower level than vocal music; but they did judge music in the manner of the Greeks, by logically deducing that since music provokes the emotions, it is on a lower scale of philosophic value than the rational thoughts of man which are expressed in words.

The philosophic rationalists believed that instrumental music was inferior to vocal music because instrumental music by itself could not express the affections fully or adequately. The German scholar and musician, Johann Mattheson (1681–1764), differed with this view by including the use of instruments in his employment of the doctrine of affections. In his work *Das neu-eröffnete Orchestre* (1713) he dispelled archaic musical notions by maintaining that a melody should be an expression of an emotion, not an imitation of the divine, and he made man himself the judge of good and bad in music. He sounds like the Aristoxenus of his day as he appealed for a judgment on music in terms of reason and sense, namely hearing. "Numbers in music," he wrote, "do not govern but merely instruct; the Hearing is the only channel through which their force is communicated to the inner soul of the attentive listener . . . the true aim of music is not its appeal to the eye nor yet altogether to the so-called 'reason' but only to the Hearing."[11]

He could see little sense in the efforts of those philosophers in his day who seemed to think that the proper way to judge

[11] Jacques Barzun, *Berlioz and the Romantic Century*, Vol. I, p. 460; Little Brown and Co., Boston: 1950.

the value of music was to compare it tonally and rhythmically to the kinds of musical examples Plato and Aristotle espoused in their own writings on music. Mattheson had just as little sympathy for technically minded musical craftsmen who were more interested in acoustical science, in the same manner as the Pythagoreans were, than in the art of music itself. Truly in the spirit of a musical humanist, Mattheson believed that an educated musical listener could form a discerning judgment of what he heard which would be based on a technical understanding of the music coupled with the ability to form his taste by being able to distinguish between what was good and what was bad in music. Mattheson foresaw a new era in music that would come through enlightenment and education.

The English philosopher, and contemporary of Mattheson, Francis Hutcheson (1694–1747), declared that "Musick hath two ends, first to please the sense, . . . and secondly to move ye affections or excite passion." The English opera indeed pleased the senses and only vicariously excited passion for it was primarily a romantic play with incidental music.

Joseph Addison (1672–1719) also ruled out a priori judgments concerning musical aesthetics in his writings in the *Spectator*: "Musick, Architecture and Painting, as well as Poetry and Oratory, are to deduce their Laws and Rules from the general Sense and Taste of Mankind, and not from the Principles of those Arts themselves; or in other words, the Taste is not to conform to the Art, but the Art to the Taste."

John Dryden (1631–1700), poet laureate of England (1679) and collaborator with Henry Purcell (c. 1658–1695) had written in his Preface to *Albion and Albanius* that "An opera is a Poetical Tale, or Fiction, represented by Vocal and Instrumental Musick, adorn'd with Scenes, Machines and Dancing. The Suppos'd Persons of this Musical Drama are generally Supernatural, as Gods, and Goddesses, and Heroes . . ."

Purcell and his teacher John Blow (1648|49–1708) injected some of the animated qualities of Italian and French music into the solemn English church scores but were only called irreverent for their efforts. Purcell incorporated the strains of the Italians and the aesthetic influences of the French into his *Dido and Aeneas* to give England her first, and to date, outstanding opera. But for every empirically minded philosopher and creative musician there were a half dozen stalwarts of Platonic tradition, as late as the 17th and 18th centuries, who defended the music of the glorious past as though reverence for the ancients was the noblest virtue of the musical purist.[12]

Toward the close of the Baroque period, the English upper class brought George Frederic Handel (1685–1759) to England to produce opera for them in the Italian style. But Italian opera did not fare well in England despite the efforts and genius of a Handel. Addison wrote in the *Spectator*: "There is no Question but our great Grand-children will be very curious to know the Reason why their Forefathers used to sit together like an audience of foreigners in their own Country, and to hear whole Plays acted before them in a Tongue which they did not understand. . . . There is nothing that has more startled our English Audience, than the Italian Recitative at its first Entrance upon the Stage. People were wonderfully surprised to hear

[12] The physician and essayist, Sir Thomas Browne (1605-1682), wrote in a true Pythagorean vein: "For there is a music where ever there is a harmony, order, or proportion: and thus far we may maintain the music of the Spheres; for those well-ordered motions, and regular paces, though they give no sound unto the ear, yet to the understanding they strike a note most full of harmony. Whosoever is harmonically composed delights in harmony; which makes me much distrust the symmetry of those heads which declaim against all Church-Music. For myself, not only from my obedience, but my particular Genius, I do embrace it: for even that vulgar and Tavern-Music, which makes one man merry, another mad, strikes in me a deep fit of devotion, and a profound contemplation of the First Composer. There is something in it of Divinity more than the ear discovers: it is an Hieroglyphical and shadowed lesson of the whole World, and creatures of God; such a melody to the ear, as the whole World, well understood, would afford the understanding. In brief, it is a sensible fit of that harmony which intellectually sounds in the ears of God. I will not say, with Plato, the soul is an harmony, but harmonical, and hath its nearest sympathy unto Music: thus some, whose temper of body agrees, and humours the constitution of their souls, are born Poets, though indeed all are naturally inclined unto Rhythm." *Of Harmony, Religio Medici*.

The English poet and satirist, Alexander Pope (1688-1744), reminds us of Aristophanes.

"Chromatic tortures soon
shall drive them hence,
Break all their nerves and
fritter all their sense."

Generals singing the Word of Command, and Ladies delivering Messages in Musick. Our Countrymen could not forbear laughing when they heard a Lover chanting out a Billet-doux, and even the Superscription of a Letter set to a Tune. . . ."[13] Addison granted that an opera may be lavish in its decorations since its function is to gratify the senses and hold the attention of the audience. He disapproved of the theatrical artificiality and stage mechanisms which were used in the opera that practically turned the English theatre into a Roman circus.

In 1728, John Gay (1685–1732) and John Christopher Pepusch (1667–1752) produced the *Beggar's Opera* as a satire on Italian opera. It is an irreverent but delightful creation which, beside satirizing the Italian opera, poked fun at the social and political trends of the time. This opera achieved such sensational success that it hastened the downfall of Italian opera in England. The *Beggar's Opera*, with its simple songs, dance tunes of popular origin, and music interspersed with animated spoken dialogues, was a sharp contrast to the Italian opera seria. The simplicity and familiarity of this music, text, and song, overwhelmingly appealed to the English. Handel was so severely affected by this phase of English sentiment for a musical art form that was not alien to their culture and understanding that he gave up the opera and turned to the oratorio.

Handel applied the Italian style of dramatic aria to the text in the oratorio. With this musical form, he related the religious history and humanistic advancement of man and used the church proper for his stage. The oratorio subsequently became for the English what the opera was for the Italians.

In Germany, early Baroque opera was supported by the ruling princes who imported Italians to produce opera for the enjoyment of their courts. The German people, by contrast, wearied and embittered by religious wars, found their solace in religious music. When Italian opera was finally made available to the German people, in the Catholic south, it might have appeared that the musical tastes of the Venetians, Neapolitans, and Romans would have infectiously spread among them. But

---

[13] Paul H. Lang, *Music in Western Civilization*, p. 521; W. W. Norton and Co., Inc., New York: 1941.

the Italian language did not convey the sense of the text to the German people, the melodic freedom in the Italian opera was altogether new to the Germans, and the unreality of the Italian opera appeared, to the German mentality, as a mockery of the theatrical trinity of unity, plot and action. The art of the Italians turned out to be as foreign to the Germans as it was to the Britons and therefore was doomed to an early failure.

The aesthetic effects of Italian operatic music may have left the German people dismayed, but the music of the Italians fascinated the German composers of the Protestant north as much as those of the Catholic south and influenced their musical ideas and styles. Heinrich Schütz tried to blend Italian melodies with sacred music. The composers Hans Leo Hassler (1564–1612), Michael Praetorius (1571–1621), Johann Kuhnau (1660–1722), Reinhard Keiser (1673–1739) and Georg Philipp Telemann (1681–1767) wrote for the Germans with an eye on the Italians.

German Baroque music historically had its beginning with Heinrich Schütz (1585–1672) and ended with Johann Sebastian Bach (1685–1750). Schütz romantically envisioned the spoken word as a subject to be conquered by the spirit of music. It was his aesthetic credo that the significant meaning of the word could be even further enhanced with musical harmonies that were repeated in a variety of ways. He devoted his musical life to a synthesis of religious and secular music in the hope that, by introducing Italian strains into religious German music, he would be creating a more balanced art of music than had resulted from the Protestant reaction to Catholic music.

Bach also was possessed with the desire to introduce the secular strains of the Italians into the religious music of his time. He shared the same views that Schütz had expressed almost a century earlier, that German Protestant music was aesthetically lacking in balance and, if anything, was on the side of the monotonous. Bach also shared the same fate that befell Schütz. The religious authorities questioned his aesthetic motives and were suspicious of his musical actions. Bach's sons were just as neglectful of his music as his contemporaries were since neither understood his musical aesthetics. In the end, Bach died, as

Schütz had before him, bitter, lonely, and depressed over his lack of recognition.

Bach was a pious Christian who believed that both a knowledge of theology and a devout religious faith were necessary prerequisites for a composer of sacred music. He reasoned that the study of theory and composition were not sufficient in themselves to create sacred music. Artistic training disciplined the intellect and made one a deft craftsman but only a fervent religious faith, added to musical technique, could enable a composer to create Protestant music that would bring the Christian into closer relationship with his Divine Maker. Bach personally felt that he needed to undergo a thorough grounding in theology in order to express the greatest degree of spirituality through music. Yet, his own generation, and several after that, found his music artistically cold, highly intellectual, and mathematical; anything but warm and fervently religious.

Bach devoted his life to reforming Protestant music. "It is my end purpose to reorganize church music", he wrote. He further hoped that through his music he could help man become a better Christian. His chief instrument of musical expression was the organ. The musical form in which he excelled was the fugue. Through the cantata, mainly, and the chorales, he brought to the Protestant Service aesthetic ideas which became the principles for a long needed reorganization of Protestant church music.

Bach's zeal for artistic reform of Protestant music met with little sympathy, for the official church record reads that his style of organ playing and music "confused the congregation with many peculiar and foreign tunes." When he became cantor at St. Thomas in Leipzig in 1722, his contract stipulated that his music must conform to the Service; that his playing must not be so long as to be out of desirable proportion to the Service; that he must not introduce Italian operatic music into the Service; and that he must always be mindful that the function of a Church organist is to foster prayer through music and not to detract from worship with vain exhibitionism while performing at the organ during the religious Service. During the Baroque age, a musician's contract stipulated that he must stay within the city and leave it only by permission. Such restrictions on his physical freedom and curbs on his musical liberties, coupled with his lack of recognition, made his last years the darkest of his life.

The Baroque era began with the introduction of Greek aesthetics into Italian music and ended with the death of Bach in Germany. In the less than two centuries which separated the meetings of the Florentine Camerata and the death of the German master, several systems of musical aesthetics came and went. The art of opera was created in Italy on an erroneous understanding of the Greek practice of dramatic art. Monteverdi corrected the misconceptions of the Camerata with a more balanced relationship of text and music and gave the orchestra a more significant role. Somewhat later, Francesco Provenzale (d. 1704) and the elder Scarlatti made the opera, with all its aesthetic shortcomings, an art of song and melody. Arcangelo Corelli (1653–1713) wrote for the violin and harpsichord in a lucid manner and simple form. The extraordinary Antonio Vivaldi (1680–1743) colored the instrumental music of the late Italian Baroque with a brilliance which retains its emotional appeal for us in our own century. In France, Lully restored some of the Platonic influence to the opera and at the same time curbed the vain practices of the operatic leads. In England, Purcell incorporated Italian music into his operatic form and religious music as well. The creative initiative passed from Italy to Germany, but Schütz and Bach still kept turning to the Italian music, which was being performed in southern Germany, for melodic suggestions with which to enrich the scores of the Lutherans in north Germany.

The early Baroque opera was philosophically and stylistically opposed to counterpoint on the one hand and required exaggerated emphasis of the spoken word, on the other hand. While the theorists, like Artusi, complained against the use of dissonance, the creative composers, like Monteverdi, kept enriching Western music with new tonalities. The harmonic system, as we have come to know it, was as yet undeveloped and had to wait for the coming of Bach and Rameau. The vague tonalities of earlier music were regulated into chordal progressions which gave music a harmonic continuity and allowed for more sustained musical forms of longer duration. The art of polyphony, which was discarded by the Camerata as being contrary to Platonic precepts, became in the scores of Johann Sebastian Bach, the formal architecture for a music of harmonic stature and melodic grandeur.

CHAPTER 6

RATIONALISM, ENLIGHTENMENT AND THE CLASSICAL ERA IN MUSIC

SECTION I—*From Descartes to Kant*

PHILOSOPHY and music do not always reflect the spirit of the times. Musical innovations which have been vindictively berated in their own times have often been the accepted styles and patterns of later periods. So, too, the philosophy of yesterday has become the science of today and much of our present philosophic speculation may well be the science of tomorrow. Philosophers and artists are indeed the prophets of the future. But the philosopher and the artist rarely share the same outlook in expressing the spirit of the times and often mistrust each others' views.

Plato is the most notable of the philosophers who held a fanatical mistrust of the artist. Yet, the aesthetics of music in Western culture stems from the writings of Plato. His evaluation of music, which for the most part can be found in the *Republic* and *Laws,* was primarily moralistic. The Scholastics appropriated the greater part of the Platonic theories on music and applied them in a thoroughly practical fashion to a Christian way of life and worship. The leaders of the Reformation followed their medieval predecessors in a similar and often more

puritanical fashion by utilizing the emotional qualities in music
to further the Protestant cause. Throughout these centuries
music had played a varied role in the systems of Western
philosophers who, with rare exception, did not possess the
necessary technical understanding or theoretical background
to evaluate music as an aesthetic expression. Consequently, music
was accorded a low status in the hierarchy of the arts up until
the close of the 18th century. Even at this late date, philosophers
treated music gingerly and evaluated it in the manner of the
ancients, in purely metaphysical, mathematical, or moral terms,
but not as an independent art justifying its own existence.

With the advent of a scientific era in Europe, during the
17th century, we still find Johann Kepler (1571–1630) cor-
relating musical tones and intervals with the movements of the
planets in a manner similar to that which Plato used in describing the Pythagorean theory of the harmony of the spheres.
René Descartes (1596–1650) retained the Platonic notion that
music was essentially mathematical and should be used as a discipline in preparation for the study of philosophy. Like the
founders of the Academy and Lyceum he also spoke of musical
affections and attributed moral values to rhythms since they
had a direct effect upon the human soul. Descartes therefore
suggested the desirability of rhythms which do not enervate or
overexcite the passions, such as rhythms which are simple, and
not complex, or, rhythms that are temperate. He stressed the
use of simple ratios for tonal intervals and, in echoing a Platonic
complaint, he decried the incongruity of musical tonalities which
the composers of his day were employing in contrapuntal techniques. In keeping with ancient doctrine, Descartes subordinated
feeling to reason so that the soul would not be led astray by
the sense of hearing or the mind perverted by the fanciful
flights of the imagination.[1] Benedict de Spinoza's (1632–1677)
interest in music began and ended with the observation that
"Music is good to the melancholy, bad to those who mourn,
and neither good nor bad to the deaf."

Gottfried Wilhelm Leibniz (1646–1716) also described music

---

[1] Katherine E. Gilbert and Helmut Kuhn, *A History of Esthetics*, pp. 206–
208; The Macmillan Co., New York: 1939.

as a manifestation of the universal rhythm whose very essence consists of number and relation. "Just as wellnigh nothing is pleasanter to the senses of man than harmony in music", he stated, "so nothing is pleasanter than the wonderful harmony of nature, of which music is only a foretaste and small evidence."[2] However music may charm us, added Leibniz, "its beauty only consists in the harmony of numbers, . . ."[3] Music, then, in the Leibnizian system is an unconscious counting or a felt relationship of numbers arranged in pleasing intervals and tonal patterns. He was primarily intent on pointing out that music is a counterpart of the rhythm pervading the universe and that the soul reacts to its effects inadvertently. Music mirrors the order and variety of the universe and through its pulsating rhythms and pleasing harmonies we intuitively become aware that God created the world according to the best possible plan; a world so begotten that it unites the greatest possible variety with the greatest possible order. It was such a world, Leibniz believed, that the great composers depicted in the discord and harmony of their music.[4]

Addison saw the 18th century in with an aesthetics of music that had its roots in the Pythagorean marriage of mathematics and sound.[5] The joy we derive from music or the delight which musical tonalities can give through stirring the imagination, Addison maintained, are indeed sensuous. But, he concluded, when we intuit the beautiful, it is one of God's means of making His handiwork known to us. Music itself then is a sensuous medium of expression which contains moral overtones that bring on religious reflection.

François Marie Arouet de Voltaire (1694–1778) and Addison had a common dislike of the Italian opera of their day. Addison wrote of it as an incongruous art and Voltaire found it some-

---

[2] *Ibid.*, p. 228.

[3] *Principles of Nature and of Grace, Founded on Reason*, p. 30; (Translated by Mary Morris) Everyman's Library, E. P. Dutton and Co., Inc., New York: 1934.

[4] *On the Ultimate Origination of Things*, p. 39; (Translated by Mary Morris) Everyman's Library, E. P. Dutton and Co., Inc., New York: 1934.

[5] *The Works of Joseph Addison*, Vol. II, pp. 34-35; Harper and Brothers, New York: 1859.

what ridiculous to listen to the hero singing an extended aria "while a city is sacked". And "what can be more absurd", he wrote, "than to terminate every scene with one of those detached airs, which . . . destroy the interest of the drama, in order to afford an opportunity to an effeminate throat to shine in trills and divisions, at the expense of the poetry and good sense?"[6] It may well be that he had such operatic activities in mind when he remarked that what is too stupid to be said is sung. But the one gem which stands out from among his witticisms is his comparison of the metaphysical philosopher to dancers of the minuet "who, most elegantly adorned, bow a few times, mince daintily across the room exhibiting all their charms, move without progressing a single step, and end up on the very spot whence they started."[7]

Lord Chesterfield (1694–1773) believed that although music was called a liberal art it was inferior to sculpture and painting and that the supremacy of music in Italy offered proof of the decline of that country. "Sculpture and painting", he wrote, "are very justly called liberal arts; a lively and strong imagination, together with a just observation being absolutely necessary to excel in either, which, in my opinion, is by no means the case of music, though called a liberal art. . . . The former are connected with history and poetry; the latter, with nothing that I know of, but bad company."[8]

Denis Diderot (1713–1784) envisioned music as an imitation of the universal harmony. Just as nature herself was never incorrect, in his estimation, so the beautiful in music consisted of proper relationships. He credited Pythagoras with founding the science of music by deducing the precise mathematical proportions and ratios from nature, thus begetting the first acoustical system. Yet in his own day, he objected to the metaphysical aesthetics of Rameau who maintained that harmony was the self-evident principle through which the philosopher and musi-

[6] Warren D. Allen, *Philosophies of Music History*, p. 222; American Book Co., New York: 1939.

[7] Curt Sachs, *The Commonwealth of Art*, p. 212; W. W. Norton and Co., Inc., New York: 1946.

[8] Jacques Barzun, *Berlioz and the Romantic Century*, Vol. I, p. 10; Little Brown and Co., Boston: 1950.

cian could arrive at an understanding of the ultimate in nature and music. He further tried to convince Rameau that music was more than a science of acoustics based on geometric calculations. The beautiful in music not only consists of proper relationships, argued Diderot, but poetry and music are inseparable. Melody and harmony must be created according to the needs of the text.

Jean Philippe Rameau (1683–1764), the founder of our system of modern harmony, evolved an aesthetics of music based on Cartesian philosophy. The application of the geometric method to metaphysics for the purpose of making it an exact science was the outstanding problem for Descartes. Rameau maintained with Descartes that music was essentially based on mathematics. "Music is a science," he wrote in his *Traité de l'harmonie*, "which ought to have certain rules; these rules ought to be derived from a self-evident principle; and this principle can scarcely be known to us without the help of mathematics."[9]

Rameau believed that the fine arts possess a relationship which is governed by the same principle, namely harmony. Nature has favored music over all the arts for it is in music that harmony is most eloquently exhibited. He calls up echoes of Aristoxenus in the passage: "We may judge of music only through the intervention of hearing, and reason has authority in it only in so far as it agrees with the ear; at the same time, nothing can be more convincing to us than their union in our judgments. Our nature is satisfied by the ear, our mind by reason; let us then judge of nothing except through their cooperation."[10] Rameau also retained the doctrine of affections: "It is certain that harmony can arouse in us different passions, depending on the particular harmonies that are employed. There are harmonies that are sad, languishing, tender, agreeable, gay, and striking; there are also certain successions of harmonies for the expression of these passions."[11] Carl Philipp Emanuel Bach (1714–1788),

---

[9] Oliver Strunk, *Source Readings in Music History*, p. 566; W. W. Norton and Co., Inc., New York: 1950.

[10] *Ibid.*, p. 567.

[11] *Ibid.*, pp. 572-573.

the son of Johann Sebastian Bach, further added, that: ". . . since a musician cannot otherwise move people, but he be moved himself, so he must necessarily be able to induce in himself all those affects which he would arouse in his auditors; he conveys his feelings to them, and thus most readily moves them to sympathetic emotions."[12]

The Greek concept of mimesis, that art is an imitation of nature, gained much prominence in the 18th century treatises on philosophy. It was an era which called for a return to nature and a turning away from urban civilization. The creative musician did not reflect this movement altogether in his compositions, for music is not always a direct expression of the spirit of the times. But the philosophers nevertheless kept reiterating the Greek theme that since art is an imitation of nature, it logically follows that music is a copy of the universal rhythm pervading the universe. If man were therefore exposed to the proper musical rhythms, he could learn to live in accordance with natural law and become one with nature.

Jean Jacques Rousseau (1712–1778) agreed with Diderot that music is an imitation of nature. His reforming spirit led him to denounce the use of the French language for vocal music because of his dubious theory that French did not lend itself to musical declamation as well as Italian. "It is the accent of languages that determines the melody of each nation;" wrote Rousseau, "it is the accent that makes people speak while singing, . . ."[13] In contrast to Addison and Voltaire, Rousseau believed that Italian music expressed the passions and feelings of its people. The French language was so ponderous and coldly intellectual, he asserted, that French vocal music would always suffer aesthetically because of the nature of the language difficulties. ". . . there is neither measure nor melody in French music, because the language is not capable of them; that French singing is a continual squalling, insupportable to an unprejudiced

---

[12] Susanne K. Langer, *Philosophy in a New Key*, p. 174; Mentor Books, New York: 1949.

[13] Alfred Einstein, *Music in the Romantic Era*, p. 339; W. W. Norton and Co., Inc., New York: 1947.

ear; that its harmony is crude and devoid of expression and suggests only the padding of a pupil; that French 'airs' are not airs; that French recitative is not recitative. From this I conclude that the French have no music and cannot have any; or that if they ever have, it will be so much the worse for them."[14]

Like most of the philosophers of antiquity, the Middle Ages, and the Reformation, he, too, was disdainful of composers who wrote music without words. Instrumental music held a secondary place in his aesthetics. "If music is able to depict only by melody, and draws from it all its power, it follows that all non-vocal music, however harmonious it may be, is only an imitative kind of music and can neither move nor depict with its beautiful harmonies, and soon leaves the ears, and always the heart cold."[15] Pointing a finger expressly at Rameau he caustically added that in the music of the defender of the great French opera the human voice merely served "as the accompaniment of the accompaniment." Again, like the ancients, and many a medieval theorist, he decried the use of contrapuntal writing. Rousseau did not deny that two melodies being rendered, at one time in agreement and at another in contrast, could be beautiful, but he preferred simplicity to complexity, for in his philosophic estimation nature herself was essentially simple.

Rousseau played the dual role of a philosopher of the Enlightenment, who called for a return to nature as a panacea for all social evil, and a musician who developed a rationalistic aesthetics of music based on metaphysical principles. He had no compunction about expressing authoritative statements, either as a philosopher or a musician. But he wrote in his *Lettre sur la musique française* (1753): ". . . I admit that I should have a poor opinion of a people who attached a ridiculous importance to their songs, who made more of their musicians than of their philosophers, and among whom one needed to speak more circumspectly of music than of the gravest questions of morality."[16] And again: ". . . it is the office of the poet to write

---

[14] Oliver Strunk, *Op. cit.*, p. 654.
[15] Alfred Einstein, *Op. cit.*, 339.
[16] Oliver Strunk, *Op. cit.*, pp. 636-637.

poetry and that of the musician to compose music, but it is the province only of the philosopher to discuss the one and the other well."[17]

Rousseau was overwhelmingly impressed with an Italian opera troupe that brought Pergolesi's delightful *La Serva Padrona* to Paris in 1752. The enthusiasm with which it was received rivaled that of the *Beggar's Opera* in England. The devotees of opera seria, however, could see only blasphemy in this highly spirited creation. In characteristic French style, the music lovers of France divided into two camps on this issue: the admirers of *La Serva Padrona* were called the "buffonists" and the stalwarts of the opera seria were called the "antibuffonists". The philosopher Rousseau came to the defense of the "buffonists" in his writings and in his own musical activity. Although he was not technically trained in music, that did not deter him from composing a comic opera on a French text, *Le Devin du Village* (1752), in which he attempted to follow the principles of the Italian opera buffa.

Rousseau maintained that melody was the essence of music. Rameau had derived his melody from harmonic progressions, but Rousseau insisted that harmony had no significance of its own apart from melody. Rousseau was more philosopher than musician in his rationalistic defiance of polyphony. "Whatever harmony several parts, each perfectly melodious, may be capable of producing together, the effect of these beautiful melodies disappears as soon as they are heard simultaneously, and there is heard only a chord succession, which one may say is always lifeless when not animated by melody; so that the more one heaps up inappropriate melodies, the less the music is pleasing and melodious, because it is impossible for the ear to follow several melodies at once, and as one effaces the impression of another, the sum total is only noise and confusion. For a piece of music to become interesting, for it to convey to the soul the sentiments which it is intended to arouse, all the parts must concur in reinforcing the impression of the subject: the harmony must serve only to make it more energetic; the accompaniment must embellish it without covering it up or disfiguring

[17] *Ibid.,* p. 637.

it; the bass, by a uniform and simple progression, must somehow guide the singer and the listener without either's perceiving it; in a word, the entire ensemble must at one time convey only one melody to the ear and only one idea to the mind."[18] Somewhat further in this letter on French music he added: ". . . to make the violins play by themselves on one side, the flutes on another, the bassoons on a third, each with a special motive and almost without any mutual relation, and to call all this chaos music is to insult alike the ear and the judgment of the hearers."[19]

Twenty years after Rousseau had written *Lettre sur la musique française* he recanted his attack on French music. The philosophic polemic and musical diatribe which he carried on against the music of his native France nevertheless paved the way for the coming of Hegelian philosophy and the Wagnerian drama in Germany. Rousseau laid the groundwork for nationalism in his social theory which found philosophic justification in Hegelian idealism. Rousseau held that a national opera was inseparable from the language of the people and, in line with this reasoning, Wagner later glorified Germanic myth in his opera for the edification of German culture. But just as Rousseau influenced the theologian Herder, the philosopher Hegel, and the musician Wagner, so he borrowed from those who came before him. He accepted the traditional Platonic view that words and music should not be separated. The Italian Bel Canto style of singing gave him good cause to favor the singing voice which he felt could move his hearers more than the finest instrumental music. He quarreled with Rameau for overemphasizing the importance of instrumental music. It was his belief that pure instrumental music produced vague generalized feelings. He maintained, with Plato, that it was the function of instruments to intensify the text and he railed against counterpoint as Plato had done in his evaluation of two part Greek music.

Christoph Willibald von Gluck (1714–1787) developed an aesthetics of music which was more acceptable to the philosophers of the Enlightenment than that of Rameau. Gluck wrote

---

[18] *Ibid.*, pp. 642-643.
[19] *Ibid.*, p. 645.

in the Foreword of his opera *Alceste*: "When I undertook to write the music for *Alceste*, I resolved to divest it entirely of all those abuses, introduced into it either by the mistaken vanity of singers or by the too great complaisance of composers, which have so long disfigured Italian opera and made of the most splendid and most beautiful of spectacles the most ridiculous and wearisome. I have striven to restrict music to its true office of serving poetry by means of expression and by following the situations of the story, without interrupting the action or stifling it with a useless superfluity of ornaments, . . . I believed that my greatest labor should be devoted to seeking a beautiful simplicity, and I have avoided making displays of difficulty at the expense of clearness, . . ."[20] Elsewhere in a letter he added: "Whatever the talent of the composer, he will never compose any but mediocre music if the poet does not arouse in him that enthusiasm without which the production of all the arts are feeble and languid; the imitation of nature is by general agreement their common object. It is this which I seek to attain. Always simple and natural, so far as is within my power, my music is directed only to the greatest expression and to the reinforcement of the declamation of the poetry."[21] Gluck thus stated the basis of his aesthetics, which he credited to his librettist, Ranieri de' Calzabigi (1714–1795), by holding that poetry was primary and that it was the function of music to illustrate and emphasize the poetic line. He defied the conventions of Italian opera seria and created a new operatic style based on a greater degree of dramatic realism.

Gluck was imbued with the philosophic spirit of his time. His desire for a return to naturalness in music promptly brought Rousseau to his side to welcome him as an advocate of the "back to nature" movement. Gluck was intent on reforming the French opera by freeing it from the absurdities and artistic deficiencies of the Italian opera. But the defenders of the Italian opera soon rose up against this attempt to deprive them of their traditional opera forms just as they did when they voiced their displeasure with *La Serva Padrona*. These opponents of reform

---

[20] *Ibid.*, pp. 673-674.
[21] Letter to the editor of the *Mercure de France, Ibid.*, pp. 681-682.

set up Niccola Piccinni (1728–1800) in opposition to Gluck and Rousseau. Piccinni represented the tradition of Italian opera and Gluck represented the reform that began in Paris with Pergolesi's opera and Rousseau's *Le Devin du Village*.

The Greek concept of imitation is prominently borne out in the aesthetics of Gluck who believed that nature and natural phenomena should be realistically represented by art and that music could serve this purpose as well as any of the other arts. In this respect, Gluck shared the aesthetic views of his century: namely, that the spheres of the arts were interchangeable and that what could be expressed by one art form could be expressed by another. He concluded, in the light of this logic, that music could give a faithful portrayal of reality by embellishing the spoken word to assure its true meaning. Rousseau, more the theoretician than musician, pondered over the aesthetic limitations of transmuting language into song and music into speech; but Gluck, more musician than theorist, based his reform on the subordination of the music to the text. It was his way of correcting the Italian evil which allowed the castrati to use words at will or change a vowel to add tonal color. Gluck believed that only a faithful rendition of the text could assure the naturalness of the music. In 1777, he modified his aesthetic position that poetry is primary and that it is the function of music to illustrate and emphasize the spoken line. He wrote that music and poetry should stand in equal position, neither dominating the other.

By the time Immanuel Kant (1724–1804) had completed the *Critique of Judgement* (1790) Bach, Handel and Gluck were dead. Haydn and Mozart were in their prime musically. A new musical world had come into being but Immanuel Kant still wrote of music in a manner befitting the ancients. He wrote that although music "speaks by means of mere sensations without concepts, and so does not, like poetry, leave anything over for reflection, it yet moves the mind in a greater variety of ways and more intensely, although only transitorily."[22] In Kantian aesthetics, poetry is the art which most appeals to reason since

<hr>

[22] *Critique of Judgement,* p. 217; (Translated by J. H. Bernard), Macmillan and Co., Ltd., London: 1914.

words are the natural medium of expression for concepts and ideas. Reason and expression, are for Kant most happily consummated in poetry. Next to poetry he ranked sculpture and painting, reserving the lowest stratum of his aesthetic system for music. Why? Music for Kant was "rather enjoyment than culture . . . and in the judgement of Reason it has less worth than any other of the beautiful arts. Hence, like all enjoyment, it desires constant change, and does not bear frequent repetition without producing weariness."[23]

Music had a strong physiological effect upon the listener for, like wit and fanciful play, it gratified because it promoted a feeling of health. Not only do we have music serving as a healthful exhilarant but since music can move its hearer with great intensity, Kant agreed with Plato that music had the power to seep into the innermost parts of the soul so that through music "we can reach the body through the soul and use the latter as the physician of the former."

Plato and Aristotle were concerned with the physiological effects which music could have upon behavior and the moulding of character. "Rhythm and melody," Aristotle wrote in the *Politics*, "supply imitations of anger and gentleness, and also of courage and temperance, and of all the qualities contrary to these, and of the other qualities of character, which hardly fall short of the actual affections, as we know from our own experience, for in listening to such strains our souls undergo a change."[24] This Greek theory of affections was retained with modifications in the musical philosophies of the Romans. The Christian philosophers reiterated it in the ensuing centuries and the creative musicians in the Gothic and Renaissance eras applied the doctrine of affections to their music as a stereotyped set of musical figures with which to evoke particular emotions in the listener. Descartes repeated this theme in the 17th century and Leibniz, Diderot and Rousseau in the 18th century, so that it is not surprising to find Kant referring to this concept of affections

---

[23] *Loc. cit.*

[24] *The Basic Works of Aristotle*, Bk. VIII, Chap. V, (Translated by Benjamin Jowett), Random House, New York: 1941.

in his own evaluation of music. "Thus as modulation is as it were a universal language of sensations intelligible to every man, the art of tone employs it by itself alone in its full force, viz. as a language of the affections, and thus communicates universally according to the laws of association the aesthetical Ideas naturally combined therewith."[25]

There is still another view in the musical aesthetics of Kant which has been traditionally stressed in the philosophies of the past, mainly a mistrust of wordless music. Plato and Aristotle were displeased with any innovation that separated the word from the tune. St. Augustine, Luther and Calvin emphasized the important role that desirable tunes and rhythms could have in acquainting the average churchgoer with Holy Writ. Kant considered music as "a beautiful (as distinct from merely pleasant) art only because it served as a vehicle for poetry."[26] He referred to music without a well-established theme, "and in fact all music without words" as sheer phantasies.[27] Pure instrumental music had little value for Kant for it was free and fanciful and did not express a definite concept.

Kant's contemporary, Johann Gottfried von Herder (1744–1803), fostered a humanistic philosophy of music, in contrast to the austere musical views of the Königsberg sage. Herder advocated a theory that music and the other arts were progressively developing from a lower to a higher order. This view was also present in Leibniz, before him, and was more fully developed in Hegel after him. Herder originally began his aesthetics of music with a Rousseau-like notion that in the folk-songs of the various speaking groups throughout the world could be found the "true voices of the peoples". Herder and his adherents then promptly set out to compile the folk-music "of the peoples", primitive and civilized. Their fascination with folk-lore, poetry, and music eventually culminated in a romantic view. This view called for a union of the arts, an aesthetic position contrary to Gotthold Ephraim Lessing's (1729–1781)

---

[25] Immanuel Kant, *Op. cit.*, p. 218.
[26] Alfred Einstein, *Op. cit.*, p. 338.
[27] Immanuel Kant, *Op. cit.*, p. 81.

distinction of the arts in the *Laocoon*,[28] but which nevertheless became an artistic reality, toward the end of the 19th century, in Wagner's operas. Herder agreed with Rousseau on the need for opera reform. Rousseau thought that he had detected a defiance of the natural order in polyphonic music. Herder found no such discrepancy or, for that matter, parallel between the songs of man and the eternal order. He probably reflected that elementary polyphony is as old as song itself and, that in the history of music, polyphony grew from a primitive to a highly developed form in the 18th century.

SECTION II—*Haydn, Mozart and Beethoven*

GERMANY was in the throes of a religious conflict and devastating war in the 17th century. Music born of such an atmosphere of strife and death could only reflect the background in which it was created. What Germany did produce musically was primarily religious in character and was usually written for the instrument of the Church, the organ. While the northern part of Germany accepted Luther as its spiritual and musical guide, the southern part of Germany, which had remained Catholic, imported Italian music and musicians for its entertainment. The Protestants, Schütz and Bach, envied their southern neighbors, musically, and what is more, tried to incorporate the aesthetic ideas of the Italian Catholics into their Protestant compositions.

Italy had become the musical center of Europe with the discovery of monody, a solo song with accompaniment, which the Camerata employed as a reaction against the complex poly-

---

[28] Lessing believed that modes of procedure peculiar to one art were inadmissible in another. "Herder, however, who had a good knowledge of music, looked forward to a combination of the arts in which the maximum of expression would be achieved with the minimum of contest between the individual idiosyncracies of each; it was to be an ideal union, between a *new* poetry and a *new* music; that is, he saw the error of Gluck . . . in supposing that music could be artistically united to words of every kind. In Herder's ideal combination, each art was to adapt itself to the other; poetry, in fact, was to 'stand truly in the middle, between painting and music.'"

Ernest Newman, *Gluck and the Opera*, pp. 285-286; Bertram Dobell, London: 1895.

phonic singing of the 16th century. The monodic style of singing had made the opera most acceptable to the Italians and had
spread this new musical form and style of singing throughout
Europe. Voltaire tells us that Cardinal Mazarin in 1646 and
1654 had Italian operas performed by singers who were brought
from Italy especially for the events. The French, however, did
not take readily to Italian opera, which had been invented in
Florence, for the simple reason, concluded Voltaire, that "There
still remained in France a remnant of ancient barbarism which
was opposed to the introduction of these arts."[29] The French
may not have taken to the Italian opera but they had no objection to operas composed by an Italian, if his work complied
with French taste. This is precisely what an Italian composer
did. The Florentine Lully created the form of the French opera,
in contrast to the Italian, which served as a model for French
composers for the next hundred years.

In the 18th century Rousseau made the art of music a facet
of his philosophic system. A return to nature called for naturalism in music. "If opera proposes to bring the language of
everyday life to the theatre", said Rousseau, "it is clear that
the language is not to be found in the grandiloquent, affected
and conventional speech of the actors of the 17th and 18th
centuries." With *Le Devin du Village* he expressed his philosophy in music and caught the spirit of French enthusiasm. His
philosophy of music guided the master composer Gluck and
influenced the young genius Mozart.

In the early 18th century, Italy and France were still musically

---

[29] *The Age of Louis XIV*, p. 258; (Translated by Martyn P. Pollack),
Everyman's Library, J. M. Dent and Sons, Ltd., London.

"The arts which do not solely depend upon the intellect had made but little
progress in France before the period which is known as the age of Louis XIV.
Music was in its infancy; a few languishing songs, some airs for the violin,
the guitar and the lute, . . . were all that we possessed. Lulli's style and technique were astonishing. He was the first in France to write bass counterpoint,
middle parts and figures. At first some difficulty was experienced in playing
his compositions, which now seem so easy and simple. At the present day
there are a thousand people who know music, for one who knew it in the
time of Louis XIII; and the art has been perfected by this spread of knowledge.
To-day, there is no great town which has not its public concerts: yet at that
time Paris itself had none; the king's twenty-four violins comprised the sum
total of French music." p. 372.

supreme in Europe, but by the middle of the century, Germany became the most creative country in the Western world. Toward the halfway mark of the century, the creative power of the Italian composer decidedly slackened. Standard music was repeated and little was produced musically which was of equal artistic attainment or quality with the music of the earlier Baroque period. Prior to the middle of the 18th century, all Europe was enriched by Italian music; after that date, Italy as well as most of Europe appeared to enter a period of artistic sterility. Only one country, Germany, showed artistic activity. While Italy settled down to enjoy her musical past, a new era in music began in Germany with Haydn, Mozart and Beethoven, all of whom were influenced in some measure by the musical aesthetics of Johann Sebastian Bach's two sons, Carl Philipp Emanuel and Johann Christian (1735–1782).

In 1745, the Prince of Mannheim engaged a brilliant violinist by the name of Johann Anton Stamitz (1717–1757) who shortly after being hired became the conductor of the court orchestra. Under the guidance of this violin virtuoso, the Mannheim orchestra became the most outstanding instrumental group of musicians in Europe. They displayed new instrumental techniques and disciplines under the direction of Stamitz. They produced rhythmic and dynamic effects which were new to European ears. They used the crescendo and decrescendo with striking success. The Baroque composer had originally added groups of instruments or voices if he wanted a climax and withdrew these instruments or voices for a diminuendo. The Mannheim School of musicians produced effects that the Baroque instrumentalists were not only unable to produce, but were unaware of.

The effects of the Mannheim School did not end with the aesthetic. The men who surrounded Stamitz became the forerunners of the storm and stress era in German art and letters. The men of the Mannheim School opposed the traditional aesthetic practices and sociological position of the artist in their day, a position which the past centuries had taken as a matter of course. This rebellious spirit showed itself in the innovative character of their music and techniques and, by their overt behaviour, they demanded a respect for their social position as musicians. Through their music and social philosophy they paved the way for the coming of a period in Western civilization which was to bring a new and more humane relationship between the middle class musician and the nobleman.

The social philosophy and musical aesthetics of the Mannheim School had their influence on Franz Joseph Haydn (1732–1809). He performed their music at the court of his Prince and joined their revolt by mildly complaining that his Prince wrongfully considered him to be nothing more than a commissioned servant at the court who was at the beck and call of his patron. Haydn did not think it proper that he should be kept in comparative isolation at the court simply to create for the pleasures of the aristocratic few. He desired to have his music extended beyond the life of the court so that "the weary and worn, or the man burdened with affairs, may enjoy a few moments of solace and refreshment," in listening to his music.

Haydn spanned the entire epoch of classical music in his life time. He initiated the classic style in music through the instrumental quartet and symphony. In the quartet, he gave each movement an independence of its own through form and contrast. He developed the concept of thinking in terms of musical themes and elaborated on the logical construction of the musical thought by drawing on the melody. He expressed these musical thoughts in motifs and he improved on the Baroque composer by distributing the importance of the melody in more parts than one. Haydn conceived of the melody as a musical thought. He retained this concept throughout his quartets and thus gave them continuity, in contrast to the less flowing calibre of Baroque music. Each voice sang the melody in its turn; through counterpoint Haydn achieved an even balance in his compositions between the four instruments.

The symphony enabled Haydn to expand his aesthetic theories even more fully. But throughout the years of his musical development, he never deliberately imposed a style which he thought was appropriate for one musical form on another. He believed that each musical form had a life of its own and that each composition must be treated as an entity in itself and written for in that way.

Haydn also composed opera for his patron. He struggled for many years to write operas equal to his quartets and symphonies and actually believed that they were superior to his instrumental forms. But his operas never reached the level of the past Baroque operas or aesthetically approached the level of his instrumental work. The philosopher Schiller did not think highly of his oratorio the *Creation*. He criticized it as a hodgepodge without character and described Haydn as a clever artist who lacked inspiration.

Wolfgang Amadeus Mozart (1756–1791) fared better at the hands of the philosopher than the elder Haydn did. The music loving Kierkegaard eulogized him as an immortal and praised his *Don Giovanni* as the creation of a divinely inspired musician. In the mystical writings of this Danish philosopher is an ever present reverence for his beloved idol, Mozart, who deepened the rhythmic and tonal expression of whatever traditional form he used to express his feelings and ideas. As a youth of twelve Mozart composed a Singspiel, *Bastien und Bastienne*, in which a spoken dialogue is used between musical numbers, patterned after Rousseau's highly popular *Le Devin du Village*. As a mature composer he showed the influence which the fatherly Haydn's *Russian Quartets* had upon him and, so that the world might know it, he dedicated some of his own quartets to the Viennese master to acknowledge his musical debt to Haydn. Mozart also reflected the reforms which Gluck had brought to the French opera but he held that poetry ought to be the obedient child of music rather than the other way round as Gluck had originally maintained. Mozart learned from Gluck that it was an aesthetic necessity to portray the dramatic action realistically, but he also was intrigued by the flowing melodies of the Italians.

In *The Marriage of Figaro* he exploited Beaumarchais' theme on the moral decadence of the aristocracy and supposedly helped pave the way for the French revolution. There is a serious undertone in Mozart's opera buffa, especially in the character

Figaro who stands for the whole conflict in which Mozart found himself and of which he had always been the victim. *The Marriage of Figaro* may seem to be of a playful nature but behind it is a serious political and satirical tone expressive of Mozart's social philosophy of the need for a new order.

Although Mozart was a devout Catholic in faith he joined the Freemasons in protest against the social inequities which the State produced and the Church permitted to exist. He rejoiced when the death of the "atheist" Voltaire was announced but, when he died himself, it was difficult to find a priest who would bury him because of his Freemasonry.

Mozart produced a music drama in which the music and the text are strikingly well balanced. He increased the number of ensembles in his operas over those of his predecessors in the belief that an ensemble offered a more dramatic effect theatrically than a lone singer. He further illustrated his theatrical ability by giving his principals a definite style throughout the opera. He intensified his characters, in ways that were not traditional, by holding a buffa atmosphere against a serious background. This operatic innovation, unfortunately, met with failure in Italy. The Italians, steeped in their own tradition by this time, had an aversion to any mixture of opera seria and opera buffa. They were accustomed to and expected opera in one style only, either buffa or seria.

The music of Ludwig van Beethoven (1770–1827) harkens to the harmony of the spheres which the philosopher Plato confirmed, wrote Victor Hugo. Beethoven's music is truly a copy of the celestial harmonies repeated Hector Berlioz in praise of his idol. The music of Beethoven is the embodiment of the universal will, the expression of the Schopenhauerian philosophy of music, wrote Wagner. Such were some of the comparisons which were made between Beethoven's music and the metaphysics of eminent philosophers.

Beethoven's musical aesthetics became the gospel of the romanticists and his success in bending the aristocracy to his will brought the social philosophy of the Mannheim School to a crowning fulfillment. He became the embodiment of the unfettered composer who wrote neither for Church nor patron, but for himself. He composed not by dictate but as he pleased and as the spirit moved him. He represented all that the classic composer looked forward to and the romantic composer looked back at with admiration and awe.

In the music of Haydn, Mozart and Beethoven the melody predominates. Beethoven's music with few exceptions remained instrumental. What little he did produce for the voice does not measure up to his instrumental music. The vocal ranges which he imposes on his singers are often taxing and unnatural. This is quite understandable if we are to take his remark seriously that "I always hear my music on instruments, never on voices." Where he does add the voice, as in the *Ninth Symphony*, his music is not enriched by it. Yet, in his lone opera *Fidelio*, the choral parts do have an extraordinary musical quality which belies the theory that he could not write for the voice as well as instruments.

CHAPTER 7

POST-KANTIAN PHILOSOPHY AND ROMANTICISM IN MUSIC

SECTION I—*The Musical Philosophies of Hegel, Schopenhauer and Nietzsche*

GEORG Wilhelm Friedrich Hegel (1770–1831) described music as the art of feeling and mood which was most conducive to provoking infinite shades of feeling and varying moods. He considered it "The second art which goes to realize the romantic type, along with and in contrast to painting, . . ."[1] Like Aristotle, he tells us that tones were much more expressive than color, hearing more ideal than seeing,[2] for "In musical tones the whole scale of our feelings and passions, not yet defined in their object, can echo and reverberate."[3] The plastic and pictorial arts had an independent existence in space, painting less so than sculpture, which we view as something outside of us. But music had no such objectivity in space for its very essence was rhythm itself. ". . . since this external objectivity disappears in music,

---

[1] E. F. Carritt, *Philosophies of Beauty*, p. 173; Oxford University Press, London: 1931.

[2] *Philosophy of Fine Art*, Vol. III, p. 341; (Translated by F. P. B. Osmaston), G. Bell & Sons, Ltd., London: 1920. *Problems* XIX, 27, 919b.

[3] E. F. Carritt, *Op. cit.*, p. 174.

the separation of the work of art from its beholder disappears also. The musical work penetrates, therefore, into the very core of the soul and is one with its subjectivity."[4] This rhythmic quality in music, added Hegel in true Platonic fashion, had such unique influence upon the soul that it more directly affected human emotions than any of the other arts. It then became the function of poetry to impose words upon sound, ideas upon feelings, concepts upon spiritual affinities, so that what was vague and indefinite in music would become more articulate and definite through the language of the poet.

The romantic trinity of the arts in the Hegelian system are painting, music and the more ideal form, poetry. Hegel also expressed a traditional preference for vocal music to that of instrumental music, for to him the latter could only be indefinite and therefore suggestive. A musical melody without words might well awaken ideas in us, but they could only be ideas that we personally have read into it. Vocal music, music with a text, reasoned Hegel, was therefore superior to instrumental music which was "only a subjective, play of forms." By adding language as an expression of reason to the formal movement which rhythm gave to melody, music became meaningful rather than fanciful, definite instead of vague, rational not purely emotional.

Hegel's delight with Italian opera, particularly that of Rossini, was surpassed only by Schopenhauer "who declared that he now understood the elemental powers of music" after listening to the works of this great composer. Hegel, after hearing a performance of the *St. Matthew Passion*, also enthusiastically took up the cause of reviving Bach's music. In his lectures on aesthetics, a course Mendelssohn himself had taken, Hegel noted the genius of Bach which had been neglected and "which we have only recently learned again to appreciate at its full value."[5]

Johann Friedrich Herbart (1776–1841) disagreed with the philosophic idealism and musical romanticism of Hegel. He did not think that it was the function of the philosopher to construct the universe, but to accept it as it was, and to explain it

[4] Walter T. Stace, *The Philosophy of Hegel*, p. 475; Macmillan Co., New York: 1924.

[5] *The Bach Reader*, Edited by David and Mendel, p. 370; W. W. Norton & Co., Inc., New York: 1945.

realistically. He also refused to view music as a facet of a general system of metaphysics. "Works of art are expected to have a meaning", he wrote, ". . . and the artists are glad to oblige. . . . But music is *music* and to be beautiful need mean nothing. . . . Even good musicians still repeat the maxim that music should express feelings; as though the feelings aroused by it, to express which it *may* accordingly be used, were the basis of those rules of double and single counterpoint in which its true essence lies. What did the old masters mean to *express* who developed the possible forms of the fugue, or those still older whose industry differentiated the possible orders of column? Nothing. Their thoughts did not travel beyond their arts but penetrated deeply into their essence. . . ."[6]

In the philosophy of Arthur Schopenhauer (1788–1860) music was considered "as *direct* an objectification and copy of the whole *will* as the world itself, nay, even as the Ideas, whose multiplied manifestation constitutes the world of individual things." Music was for Schopenhauer "by no means like the other arts," the copy of Platonic Ideas, "but the *copy of the will itself*, whose objectivity the Ideas are. This is why the effect of music is so much more powerful and penetrating than that of the other arts," he added, "for they speak only of shadows, but it speaks of the thing itself."[7] Architecture, sculpture and painting expressed respective stages of the unfolding of human desire and attainment but music was the crowning achievement for it was the sum total of all artistic expression, the voice of the complete will of man and nature. Nature revealed her inner secrets, her motives and aspirations to us through music in a manner which evaded reason but was grasped by feeling. Schopenhauer took Leibniz to task for coldly explaining music away as unconscious counting of numbers and, in the manner of Socrates in the *Phaedo*, he revised the Leibnizian epigram into his own belief that music was not unconscious counting of numbers but was the blind practice of metaphysics—unconscious philosophizing.[8]

Schopenhauer agreed with Kant and Hegel that music was an

---

[6] E. F. Carritt, *Op. cit.*, p. 156.
[7] *The World as Idea*, p. 201; The Modern Library, New York: 1928.
[8] *Ibid., pp.* 199, 211;—*Phaedo*, 61.

art of indefinite expression. He tells us that music does not "express this or that particular and definite joy, this or that sorrow, or pain, or horror, or delight, or merriment, or peace of mind; but joy, sorrow, pain, horror, delight, merriment, peace of mind *themselves*, to a certain extent in the abstract, their essential nature, without accessories, and therefore without their motives. Yet we completely understand them in this extracted quintessence."[9]

Music was a copy of the will and the musical voices had a kinship with some phase of progressive nature. The lowest harmonic voice, the bass, was like crude unorganized nature upon which all rested and from which everything originated and developed. The four voices corresponded to the mineral, vegetable and animal kingdoms, the melody being "the highest grade of the objectification of will, the intellectual life and effort of man."[10] A melody had a significant intentional connection from beginning to end and so had its counterpart in man who reflected on his past, and anticipated the future in a rational longing for continuity and wholeness.

Eighteenth century aesthetics looked with disfavor on instrumental music in contrast to the 19th century which exalted pure instrumental music over the spoken word. E. T. A. Hoffmann (1776–1822), the poet of romanticism, in his critique of Beethoven's *Fifth Symphony* wrote: "When one speaks of music as an autonomous art, one should always think only of instrumental music, . . ."[11] Felix Mendelssohn (1809–1847), the musician of romanticism, expressed his aesthetics in a letter which said "that the thoughts which good compositions express are not too vague to be contained in words, but too definite." He believed that good music "does not become more significant or intelligible through 'poetic' interpretations; instead, it becomes less significant, less clear."[12]

Schopenhauer's philosophy bears out the Romantic era in

[9] *Ibid.*, p. 206.
[10] *Ibid.*, p. 203;—*On the Metaphysics of Music*, Chap. XXXIX.
[11] Alfred Einstein, *Music in the Romantic Era*, pp. 32-33; W. W. Norton & Co., Inc., New York: 1947.
[12] *Ibid.*, p. 6.

music. He tells us that "if music is too closely united to the words, and tries to form itself according to the events, it is striving to speak a language which is not its own. No one has kept so free from this mistake as Rossini; therefore his music speaks *its own language* so distinctly and purely that it requires no words, and produces its full effect when rendered by instruments alone."[13] Words are then only of secondary value, at times even alien to a sustained melody or coloratura passage. In his chapter, *On The Metaphysics of Music*, he added: "As surely as music, far from being a mere accessory of poetry, is an independent art, nay, the most powerful of all the arts, and therefore attains its ends entirely with means of its own, so surely does it not stand in need of the words of the song or the action of an opera. . . . The words are and remain for the music a foreign addition, of subordinate value, for the effect of the tones is incomparably more powerful, more infallible, and quicker than that of the words. Therefore, if words become incorporated in music, they must yet assume an entirely subordinate position, and adapt themselves completely to it."[14] Schopenhauer thereby concluded that music was certainly able with the means at its own disposal "to express every movement of the will, every feeling; but by the addition of words we receive besides this the objects of these feelings, the motives which occasion them."[15] Just as the universal may be illustrated by an object which embodies it, philosophically speaking, so the vague musical content of any tone may be fused with the concrete meaning of a word like feeling.

Richard Wagner (1813–1883) gave lip service to this philosophy of music but it is naive to think that Wagner, who attempted a merging of the arts by marrying the text to the melody and then pitted them both against an oversized orchestra, took the prince of pessimism seriously. The essence of Schopenhauer's musical philosophy is that melody has a right to exist by

---

[13] *The World As Idea*, p. 207; The Modern Library, New York: 1928.

[14] *The World as Will and Idea*, Vol. III, Chap. XXXIX, pp. 232, 233; (Translated by Haldane and Kemp), Kegan Paul Trench, Trubner & Co., Ltd., London:

[15] *Ibid.*, p. 234.

itself, independent of text and of the action on the stage. Wagner took strong exception to this philosophy as the Italians practiced it, but inconsistently accepted it in Schopenhauer.

The philosopher who readily saw this contradiction in Wagner was Friedrich Nietzsche (1844–1900). But Nietzsche himself was guilty of a glaring ambiguity in denouncing romanticism as decadent when actually his own musical aesthetics was as much in keeping with the Romantic era in music as that of Schopenhauer's. Like his predecessor he exalted the melody over the spoken word and somewhat reminiscent of Herder he wrote: "we must conceive the folk-song as the musical mirror of the world, as the original melody, now seeking for itself a parallel dream-phenomenon and expressing it in poetry. *Melody is therefore primary and universal,* and so may admit of several objectifications in several texts."[16] "Our whole discussion", he continued, "insists that lyric poetry is dependent on the spirit of music just as music itself in its absolute sovereignty does not need the picture and the concept, but merely *endures* them as accompaniments. The poems of the lyrist can express nothing which did not already lie hidden in the vast universality and absoluteness of the music which compelled him to figurative speech. Language can never adequately render the cosmic symbolism of music, because music stands in symbolic relation to the primordial contradiction and primordial pain in the heart of the Primal Unity, and therefore symbolizes a sphere which is beyond and before all phenomena. Rather are all phenomena, compared with it, merely symbols: hence *Language,* as the organ and symbol of phenomena, can never, by any means, disclose the innermost heart of music; language, in its attempt to imitate it, can only be in superficial contact with music; while the deepest significance of the latter cannot with all the eloquence of lyric poetry be brought one step nearer to us."[17]

The Dionysian and Apollonian concepts in Nietzsche bear a striking similarity to Schopenhauer's original distinction between music and the representative arts. A passage in *The Birth of*

[16] *The Birth of Tragedy,* p. 198; (Translated by Clifton P. Fadiman), The Modern Library, New York: 1937.

[17] *Ibid.,* p. 202.

Tragedy warrants this analogy even if Nietzsche only alluded to Schopenhauer without naming him.[18] Nietzsche viewed music as a means through which man could revalue his values, and transform this crude world into a more highly imaginative and better place to live, at least temporarily; for, to him, music was preeminently the art of emotion, Dionysian. It was the artist, particularly the musician, who could partially redeem corrupt society. The musician could transport us to more rarefied heights by enhancing his art with the imaginative realization of our cravings and desires in a formal framework, and so help bring into our chaotic lives harmony and order.

Wagner again erred, in the judgment of Nietzsche, by trying to redeem mankind with an insipidly naive Parsifal who had neither loved nor sinned. Bizet's Carmen had at least loved and lost. Wagner resorted to romantic phantasy and Christian ideology, lamented Nietzsche, when it was obvious that the last Christian had died on the Cross and Christianity as a way of life was based on false values. Bizet, on the other hand, brought life realistically to his audience. One composer finally turned his back on life, the other faced it. Wagner came to be the false artist who dealt with sham and illusion by first exalting the will in Tristan and then annihilating it in ascetic Parsifal. Bizet, by contrast, was the true artist whose characters stood up to life, striving for self-realization in a chaotic world.

In the end, Nietzsche concluded with Plato that "many lies are told by the poets" and accused all artists of seeking refuge in authority for "they were at all times the servants of a moral system, a philosophy or religion." Only the superman was capable of actually transvaluating the values by which we live, argued the already embittered Nietzsche; thus, refuting his original thesis that art was essentially "affirmation, benediction, deification of existence." He agreed with Schopenhauer, that music offered escape, and interludes of peace. But whereas music fostered a transition from will to vision, from desire to contemplation in Schopenhauer, music in Nietzsche enables us to rise above our crude and chaotic world into a transfigured one expressive of our desires and hopes.

18 *Ibid.*, p. 271.

SECTION II—*Wagner and Hanslick*

WAGNER was influenced by the philosopher Ludwig Feuerbach (1804–1872) in the early stages of his career. Feuerbach attacked the orthodox theology of his day with the claim that Christianity was of human origin and that philosophy was little more than disguised theology. This naturalistic interpretation of Christianity which envisioned God merely as a changing ideal which man created and perpetuated to fulfill an aesthetic and religious need fitted in with the mid-nineteenth century revolt in Germany against the social status quo, traditional religion, and archaic art forms. Wagner's *Art Work of the Future* (1850) "owes its very title to Feuerbach's *Principles of the Philosophy of the Future* (1843), and in its original edition as a separate monograph it was introduced by a letter from Wagner to Feuerbach, beginning: 'To no one but you, my dear sir, can I dedicate this work, for with it I give you back your own property.' "[19]

Shortly after, Nietzsche introduced Wagner to the aesthetic significance of Schopenhauer and Wagner promptly forsook Feuerbach's dialectics for the Schopenhauerian concept of the Will. But with time, Wagner again changed his philosophy of art by relinquishing the Will for Christian resignation. *Tristan* was representative of Will and attainment but *Götterdämmerung* and *Parsifal*[20] were the doom and resignation that came in the final phases of Schopenhauer's philosophy, and were represented by Wagner as the destruction of lust and greed and the triumph of Christian morality through innocence and compassion. Nietzsche, who had earlier turned Wagner from Feuerbach to Schopenhauer, and himself was an exponent of the Will, tauntingly asked Wagner in *The Genealogy of Morals* is Parsifal "An apostasy and reversion to the morbid Christian and obscurantist

---

[19] Oliver Strunk, *Source Readings in Music History*, p. 874; W. W. Norton & Co., Inc., New York: 1950.

[20] Alfred Einstein, *Music in the Romantic Era*, p. 231; W. W. Norton & Co., Inc., New York: 1947.

In *Tannhäuser* (1845) "the hero is led from sensual enjoyment to 'redeeming' contrition" and "the valiant heroine is replaced by a 'saint'. This opera was the first Wagnerian fusion of lust and piety, the utilization of religious ecstasy for theatrical effect, which returned later in *Parsifal* in more sublimated form."

ideals?" Then he turned to Wagner, the perpetuator of the romantic, the traditionalist in religion, who originally sided with Feuerbach on the Christian myth: "And finally a self-negation and self-elimination on the part of an artist, who till then had devoted all the strength of his will to the contrary, namely, the *highest* artistic expression of soul and body. And not only his art; of his life as well. Just remember with what enthusiasm Wagner followed in the footsteps of Feuerbach. Feuerbach's motto of 'healthy sensuality' rang in the ears of Wagner during the thirties and forties of the century, as it did in the ears of many Germans. . . . like the word of redemption. Did he eventually *change his mind* on the subject? For it seems at any rate that he eventually wished to *change his teaching* on that subject . . . and not only is that the case with the Parsifal trumpets on the stage: in the melancholy, cramped, and embarrassed lucubrations of his later years, there are a hundred places in which there are manifestations of a secret wish and will, a despondent, uncertain, unavowed will to preach actual retrogression, conversion, Christianity, mediaevalism, and to say to his disciples, 'All is vanity! Seek salvation elsewhere!' Even the 'blood of the Redeemer' is once invoked."[21]

Eduard Hanslick (1825–1904) opposed the Wagnerian fusion of the arts and the romantic concept of uniting music and poetry. He agreed with Herbart that music did not convey meaning but was composed of tonal patterns which were thematically developed in a prescribed form and that it was not the function of music to serve as a means of representation, or to relate a story or to express states of emotion. The romantic composer sought to represent the whole gamut of human feelings in his music as an antithesis to the cold intellectualism of 17th century rationalism, but to purists such as the philosopher Herbart and the critic Hanslick, emotive meanings in music were an anathema.

"If we wish to decide the question whether music possesses the character of definiteness, what its nature and properties are, and what its limits and tendencies," wrote Hanslick in *The*

[21] p. 98; (Translated by Horace B. Samuel), The Modern Library, New York: 1937.

Beautiful in Music, "no other than instrumental music can be taken into consideration. What *instrumental music* is unable to achieve, lies also beyond the pale of *music proper;* for it alone is pure and self-subsistent music . . . the term 'music', in its true meaning, must exclude compositions in which words are set to music . . . music must leave out even compositions with inscriptions, or so-called programme-music. Its union with poetry, though enhancing the power of music, does not widen its limits."[22] Somewhat later Hanslick added: "The reason why people have failed to discover the beauties in which pure music abounds, is, in great measure, to be found in the *under-rating,* by the older systems of aesthetics, of the *sensuous element,* and in its subordination to morality and feeling—in Hegel to the 'idea'."[23]

Hanslick considered music a self-contained art which had no reference to anything outside of pure tone and rhythm. Music was not able to depict personalities or physical objects or explain philosophical systems. Music was limited to the sphere of sound. He reasoned that if moving patterns of sound thematically developed were the content of music then form and content in music were identical, for music had no content beyond its purely musical patterns. His contention was that the ideas which a composer represented were purely musical ideas. A melody came to his mind which was purely a melody in itself and represented nothing but itself. A musical idea was a tonal one, not a logical one which must first be translated into tones. The aesthetics of music was not concerned with the personal life of the composer or his loves and hates, it was concerned with his work solely for what the music itself had to say.

Like all purists, Hanslick was an objectivist in his aesthetics. He maintained that a musical work was good or bad because of its intrinsic qualities. The work of art was independent in its own right and should not be left to the subjective evaluation of the listener who judged music according to his mood. An aesthetic experience required intellectual activity. Hanslick rejected the thesis of the romantic musician that music was primarily an expression of feeling. The artistic worth of music could not be determined by the effect which it had upon the feelings, argued Hanslick, but by the spiritual and the intellectual in man. Music offered no aesthetic experience to the man who used it as a background for his own day-dreaming, but served only as an opiate. The waltzes of Strauss ceased to be music as soon as people danced to them.

Gluck gave poetry precedence over music and Mozart believed poetry ought to be the obedient child of music. The romantic composers spoke of a "language of music" which united poetry and song. Wagner believed that he had achieved a merger of the arts which reached its full consummation in the music-drama. To all these views, Hanslick replied: Music is an autonomous art.

"Robert Schumann", wrote Hanslick, "has done a great deal of mischief by his proposition:—'The aesthetic principles of one art are those of the others, the material alone being different.' Grillparzer expresses a very different opinion and takes the right view when he says:—'Probably no worse service has ever been rendered to the arts than when German writers included them all in the collective name of art. Many points they undoubtedly have in common, yet they widely diverge not only in the means they employ, but also in their fundamental principles. The essential difference between music and poetry might be brought into strong relief by showing that music primarily affects the senses and, after rousing the emotions, reaches the intellect last of all. Poetry, on the other hand, first raises up an idea which in its turn excites the emotions, while it affects the senses only as an extreme result of its highest or lowest form. They, therefore, pursue an exactly opposite course, for one spiritualises the material, whereas the other materialises the spiritual.' "[24]

The critic, Hanslick, never lost sight of the fact that the aesthetic experience is basically an emotional experience, but he categorically rejected the view that the "ultimate worth of the beautiful will always rest upon the evidence of the feelings." The essential features of Schopenhauerian aesthetics is more to

[24] *Ibid.*, pp. 16-17.

be found in this Viennese critic than in the producer of the Bayreuth festival. Hanslick agreed with Schopenhauer that pure instrumental music was superior to music that was conceptualized by a text. He also echoed Schopenhauer in repeating that music of itself could not represent or express definite feelings or depict love, hope, anger, hate, jealousy, or despair. He concluded with Schopenhauer that instrumental music developed according to prescribed musical laws and was not the unfolding of the composer's state of feelings or emotions, as the romantics believed.

Hanslick discarded the Platonic notion that music was an imitation of nature. He viewed our musical scale as a man made product and pointed out that natural sounds do not fit the diatonic scale. He rightly asked: "Who ever heard a triad or a dominant seventh chord in nature?" He again followed Schopenhauer in observing that music was not a copy of the universal will, or in more Platonic terms, an imitation of the universe, but the expression of the will itself, the universe manifesting its spirit in and through music. Music for Schopenhauer, as it was for Hanslick, had a life of its own, a world of its own, in which chaos was brought into order and a melody was similar to the completeness of a human life.

Hanslick favored a definite separation of the arts. Program music, in which natural sounds have been musically imitated, as in Haydn's *Seasons* and in Beethoven's *Pastoral Symphony* have value as imitation or as thematic material, but not as both. Imitation of natural phenomena introduced a pictorial element into music. Pure music ceases to be pure when it leaves the realm of presenting musical ideas and begins to depict natural phenomena or portray states of feeling with all the realism that the tonal system will permit.

SECTION III—*The Composer in The Romantic Era*

THE aesthetics of romanticism envisioned beauty as subservient to nothing but itself. Poet, philosopher and musician, with few exceptions, embraced the romantic ideal in art as a forerunner of a better world made real through art. The poet Novalis

(1772–1801) proclaimed that "In music mathematics appears as a revelation as creative idealism". E. T. A. Hoffmann offered the pantheistic view that "The spirit of music pervades all nature", and then, applying his poetic metaphysics to Beethoven's *C Minor Symphony*, added that music is the most romantic if not the sole purely romantic art. The philosophers were no less mystical. Friedrich Schelling (1775–1854) attributed spiritual qualities to music and Rudolph Lotze (1817–1881) divined in music, the movements of the cosmos and the unfolding of the universal drama. Hegel had originally separated the Classic from the Romantic era with the simple explanation that in classicism the subject dominates the form and in romanticism the subject matter is absorbed into form.

The romantic composer thought of himself as a revolutionary, as a prophet heralding a new era in art with which he might well reform the life of man. His aesthetics could become a substitute for religion and his art could replace the slavish morality of tradition. In this milieu, music rose to a position among the arts which it had never had before. The art of music, the art which Schopenhauer called an expression of the universal will, not a mere copy, dominated all the art forms. Poet and painter tried to inject musical elements into their respective mediums. Walter Pater (1839–1894) summed up the essence of romantic aesthetics with the view that all the arts should conspire to the conditions of music in which matter is most completely absorbed into form.

In the 18th century, the composer had been regarded as a craftsman who served the cause of religion or a patron. In the 19th century, the composer discarded his artisan status. He wrote his music with a personal freedom that few artists had ever known before. He developed the symphony, broadened the opera into a magnificent spectacle and poured his loneliness into intimate Lieder and Chansons. It is the purpose of this section to show how the creative composers in the Romantic era expressed themselves through music. We shall therefore present them according to aesthetic interests and nationalities.

Romantic opera in Germany began with Carl Maria von Weber's (1786–1826) folk-opera *Der Freischütz*, (1821). Hoff-

mann's *Undine* and Louis Spohr's (1784–1859) *Faust* preceded *Der Freischütz* but neither of these two operas can rightly be called musically romantic. Two years later Weber produced *Euryanthe* which he called "a great heroic-romantic opera in three acts". Weber's aesthetic ideal, which reached its fulfillment in the music-drama of Richard Wagner, was to make the opera a fusion of music, poetry and acting.

Franz Schubert (1797–1828), the most romantic of the romanticists and the creator of the German Lied, surpassed even Beethoven in the creation of beautiful melodies. His warm colorful, free-flowing melodies enhance all the more many of Germany's great poetic masterpieces. His veneration for Goethe inspired him to set much of his poetry to music. Goethe, however, did not share a similar esteem for Schubert's genius. For Schubert the melody reigned supreme over the spoken word. Goethe, on the other hand, believed that in the Lied, music should be subordinate to the text.

The simple classic vein in Felix Mendelssohn's music was in direct contrast to that of his contemporaries Berlioz, Liszt and Wagner. While these last three composers were striving for new musical effects and kept enlarging the orchestra, Mendelssohn, who remained a devoted follower of Mozart throughout his life, continued to write with a simple classicism. His worship of melody and his personal sense of perfectionism give his music a free-flowing lyricism that at times equals the charm of Schubert. Like Schubert, he was primarily a child of the romantic. When he was asked for words to his *Songs Without Words*, he replied that words were inadequate for his music. Words could not express his music. "A word does not mean the same thing to one person that it does to another;" he wrote, "only a piece of music can awaken the same mood."

Robert Schumann (1810–1856) was the successor to Schubert in the creation of German Lieder. Schumann originally maintained that instrumental music was capable of expressing the ineffable and baring the innermost feelings of mankind. He argued, in a typically romantic fashion, that words and texts conceptualized, and so rationalized, these feelings. Words were the fetters that held the feelings in bounds. It was these musical sentiments that Schumann kept expressing in his compositions for the first thirty years of his life. He then turned to the art of Schubert and the poetry of Heine and produced an abundance of Lieder of pure romanticism.

Franz Liszt (1811–1886), the social humanist, musical progressive and ecclesiastic, referred to Bach as the St. Thomas of music. St. Thomas had synthesized faith and reason and Liszt believed that Bach had brought feeling and reason to its final consummation in the art of music. Liszt spent his own life trying to achieve a more intimate union of music and poetry. He thought of poetry as the stimulus for musical creation, but believed that once the union between word and song, reason and feeling had been achieved, the music must be free to exalt the union, to carry it to heights of romantic ecstasy. The mysteries of the universe, the logic of the philosopher, are fused by the composer in his music. The intellectualism of the rationalists and ecstasy of the mystics, Liszt mused, are reflected in the divine art of music.

Liszt possessed a dual nature. The solitude which he longed for and later found in the sanctuary of the Church is in contrast to his creative personality as a composer. His music is brilliant, rhapsodic and abounds in folk material. He performed his scores before the public with an attitude of benevolence and at the same time indulged in displays of virtuosity at the piano that bordered on exhibitionism. He furthered the cause of music and liberal government with his generous help to the struggling composer and his efforts in the cause of social progress.

Robert Franz (1815–1892) wrote Lieder in the manner of Schubert and Schumann. His songs are less bold, more dreamy and range from folk-songs to a Lied set to a Heine text.

Anton Bruckner's (1824–1896) music is oftentimes an expression of his zealous Catholic faith. Because he passed as a disciple of Wagner, the critic Hanslick found him no equal for his own champion, Brahms. What Hanslick failed to see was that in the music of this ardent religionist the poetic and programmatic elements of the romanticists had been discarded for the thematic development of musical ideas, born of religious feelings to be sure, but presented as pure music.

Johann Strauss (1825–1899) musically portrayed in his waltzes the pseudo light-heartedness of a not-so-gay Vienna in the closing years of the 19th century.

Johannes Brahms (1833–1897) looked for his inspiration in the polyphonic scores of Bach, the symphonies of Beethoven, the songs of Schubert and the aesthetics of Schumann. His use of traditional forms and his reverence of the past kept him closer to the philosophy of the classicists than to that of the romanticists who tried to make a complete break with the past. But in the manner of the romantics, Brahms used folk material over and over again. The romantics were ardent nationalists and in this respect Brahms, too, was one of them. He flaunted his German nationalism with numerous vocal arrangements of folksongs. He enriched the thematic veins of his symphonies and concerti with the songs of the field and the street. No mortal ever wrote such sensuous musical strains into orchestral scores. Perhaps few writers equal his gracious way of writing for the human voice.

In the music of the late romanticist, Gustav Mahler (1860–1911), is to be found melodic strains from Mozart and Schubert and deep sonorous tonalities that provoke a feeling of religiosity, reminiscent of Bruckner. But he paid little heed to classic form if it impeded his flow of musical ideas. He had a tendency to become overly sentimental, at times, in pouring out his emotions in a musical autobiography. His scores are lengthy and express moods that range from dejection to exultation. His themes are as restless as his spirit, for a profound reflective mysticism permeates his work. He queries the wonders of nature in his music and asks, What is the lot of man?

While many of the poems which Franz had set to music were hardly worth preserving through song, in the Lieder of Hugo Wolf (1860–1903) the poems are of impeccable literary taste. Wolf enriched his chosen texts with intense musical feeling through a masterful display of vocal writing and piano accompaniment. Wolf began his career as a Wagner enthusiast but reacted against the aesthetics of the music-drama "with its lugubrious specter of a Schopenhauerian philosopher in the wings", as he wrote in a letter in 1890 which is quoted by Romain Rolland. But to the anti-Wagnerians, Wolf himself was guilty of Wagnerian traits. They pointed to his complex harmonies and novel chromaticisms. For Wolf, harmony and chromaticisms were simply a means to achieve a new effect, an unusual color, but the followers of Brahms saw in his work disordered harmony, melodic diffuseness and lack of rhythm. Wolf had only brought romanticism to its fullest development by broadening the musical powers of expression to depict feeling. His musical aesthetics became a link that bound the music of Tristan with the Viennese school of atonality in the 20th century.

We must now go back historically more than a half century before the birth of Hugo Wolf and consider the composer in another part of the world if we are to trace aesthetic trends in music among different nationalistic groups in the Romantic era. Mendelssohn had introduced Bach and Baroque polyphony to the romantics but to the French composer and critic, Hector Berlioz (1803–1869), Bach and his intricate counterpoint were remnants of a pedantic musical past. Berlioz was preoccupied mainly with melody; pure extended melodic passages that soared to heights of grandeur and were enriched by varied instrumental ensembles which produced musical color and brilliance never heard in an orchestra before. "I always take care to lavish melody upon my compositions", he wrote. The spoken word held a secondary place in the aesthetics of Berlioz. His romantic spirit found in the orchestra a medium of expression which sang strains of sublime lyricism that brought to its listener powerful evocative tonalities and deeply moved the emotions.

Frédéric Chopin (1810–1849) was a chronically unhappy and sickly person who converted his chaotic existence into musical forms of sheer sensitive beauty. He was the supreme master of the romantic instrument, the piano; and into this instrument he poured his hurt feelings with music of marked originality which is both eloquent and intimate, brilliant and solemn. His moods of depression and elation found expression in colorful harmonies, sharp dissonances and varied modulations. His music was a panorama of his feelings. His tonal combinations and intricate rhythms allied him with Hugo Wolf as a neo-romantic who was unknowingly paving the way for the music of the following century.

The Belgian, César Franck (1822–1890), and his Austrian contemporary Bruckner were the outstanding religious composers of the Romantic era. But if Bruckner fared badly at the hands of Hanslick, Franck was shamefully ignored by his contemporaries. Gounod called his symphony an "affirmation of incompetence pushed to dogmatic lengths". Franck died, as he lived, a lonely composer. He had much to say that had to wait for a new generation to appreciate.

In the music of Camille Saint-Saëns (1835–1921), whose life reached into the first quarter of the 20th century, romanticism is expressed by the purest of tones in his symphonies. His symphonic poems, woven around literary ideas, are traditional in form and his operas are composed to Biblical and classical texts. Saint-Saëns, poet, scholar and musician, wrote for practically every branch of music. While a new musical world had already come into being, this Parisian composed music at the dawning of the 20th century in the manner of the 19th century.

Paris was the cultural center of the world and, to her, composers from the world over came for inspiration, others for political refuge, and still others, to perform their music. From the salons, concert halls and operatic stages of this cosmopolitan city emanated music that enriched the cultural life of Western civilization. Here in Paris, Giacomo Meyerbeer (1791–1864) produced grand opera and with his premiere of *Robert le Diable* (1831) brought the romantic opera to France. The people of Paris were delighted with this German who wrote more beautiful arias and passionate duets than the Italians themselves. Parisians marvelled at his adeptness in assimilating the tastes of the French and incorporating them into his opera. Even more, he developed the operatic orchestra and introduced new staging devices to heighten the dramatic interest.

Another composer who came to Paris and stayed to become its idol was the composer of the romantic operetta, Jacques Offenbach (1819–1880). He set out to reform the French opera-comique which he declared had lost its original light-hearted gaiety and charm by trying to ape the success of the serious grand opera. He restored mirth, brevity, simple libretti and dynamic action to the operetta. He objected to the sentimentality and unnaturalness of Meyerbeer's operas and became equally critical of the Wagnerian music-drama. Offenbach parodied romantic operas which used libretti based on classical antiquity and he satirized the political and social life of the times in his operettas. The philosopher Nietzsche hailed him as a Classicist in a Romantic era, a composer of enchanting melodies who did not ignore the text.

Gasparo Spontini (1774–1851), Jacques François Halévy (1799–1862), and Meyerbeer composed their operas around a heroic figure in the style of the Italians. Charles François Gounod (1818–1893) and Georges Bizet (1838–1875) replaced the heroic concept with a more humanistic libretto and placed a greater emphasis on the text than the Italians did. The operas of Jules Massenet (1842–1912) and Gustave Charpentier (1860) have a suave melodiousness, even when Charpentier is depicting conflicting human emotions. In *Pélléas et Mélisande*, Claude Achille Debussy (1862–1918) makes the music subservient to the text and reverts to the principle of Gluck, advocating the importance of the dramatic and poetic side of opera.

In England, the Irishman Sir Arthur S. Sullivan (1842–1900), proved himself to be the successor to Offenbach by his spirit of social reform and by his musical style in writing for the operetta. His productions contain political and social satire and a parody of grand opera. The military and class distinction in 19th century England were boldly characterized and ridiculed for what they were in the Gilbert and Sullivan scores. Sullivan used quick changes which would range from highly romantic sentimentality to merriment. His melodies were usually composed with simplicity but when he wished to write in a more serious and grandiose manner, he was equal to that task too.

During the years that Gilbert and Sullivan were producing delightful operettas for a creatively impoverished England, the philosopher, Herbert Spencer (1820–1903), was championing the Romantic era in his country with a polemic against his countryman, Charles Burney (1726–1814). This highly respected

English man of letters and musical historian, Burney, had among his other resounding judgments on music, declared that it was a sensualistic art of low aesthetic value. In defense of the value of music, Spencer ranked music as the highest of the fine arts in his own synthetic philosophy "as the one which, more than any other, ministers to human welfare."

In Italy, Gioacchino Antonio Rossini (1792–1868), Vincenzo Bellini (1801–1835) and Gaetano Donizetti (1797–1848) were writing operas with an eye on beautiful melody and sustained Bel Canto singing. Their libretti were decidedly subordinated to the production of dramatic scenes which would allow the leads in the opera to display their vocal talents. Giuseppe Verdi (1813–1901) followed in the same vein as these composers, but in his late productions, he went beyond his predecessors. He created operas of a more profound nature and sustained artistic character. Verdi truly brought the Italian opera to a level of aesthetic value which belied the Wagnerian thesis that Italian opera was not good theatre.

Verdi devoted his art and his very life to the establishment of a unified Italy. The songs of the people and the spirit of revolution were brought into his work. Opera was his medium of communication with the Italian people. The human voice, the "golden" tones of the tenor, the thrilling cadenzas of the soprano, the warm notes of the contralto, and the sonorous rumblings of the bass were his tools for forging nationalism and reaching the hearts of the Italian audiences. His orchestra only supplemented the voices, the melody reigned supreme. Verdi, however, was more concerned with his libretti than his predecessors. Shakespeare was his poetic inspiration, Beethoven was his musical guide, and he was the embodiment of romantic song itself.

At the end of the 19th century, Pietro Mascagni (1863) and Ruggiero Leoncavallo (1858–1919) initiated a school of operatic realism which depicted human tragedy set to a dramatically musical score. Giacomo Puccini (1858–1924), by contrast, romanticized the tragic element. His melodic gift and instinctive theatrical sense gave his operas a balance between song and text, singer and orchestra, all of which Wagner strove for and never attained in his stupendous music-dramas.

In 1860, Bohemia acquired her long sought independence from Austria. Bedřich Smetana (1824–1884), the active Bohemian revolutionist, expressed his fervent nationalism with a cycle of tone poems glorifying his native land. In his operas, of which *The Bartered Bride* is the best known, the customs and music of his people are preserved. He used the symphonic poem, which his teacher Liszt used so fruitfully, and the string quartet as his chief instrumental forms. It was during and through the approaching years of his deafness that Smetana, like Beethoven, created his greatest music. "I do not wish to write a quartet in a formal style", he wrote, "but wish to paint my life in music." His most profound creations were created out of his anxiety and remorse, his love of country and joy; and, these feelings he expressed through instrumental music which, as the romanticists held, is more definite than words.

Antonin Dvořák (1841–1904), the second of the great Czech composers, wrote music which was not dependent on a poetic concept. His music was composed as an end in itself with imaginative thematic developments, vivacious rhythms, and sonorous tonalities. It is mainly of an absolute character which does not profess to be a personal confession, as in Smetana, but is music in the traditionally romantic sense, an end in itself.

In the north lived another ardent Republican, Edvard Grieg (1843–1907), who made his own life an example of his beliefs, and his music, a song of conviction. His harmonies are sensitive, his melodies are simple and the sentimentality of the north permeates his music. The beauty of the Norwegian countryside moved him to create, and in these creations, the injustice and strife of the outside world were resolved into lyrical tones of contemplative beauty.

In the 18th century, Russia was dominated by Italian music and musicians. In the 19th century, the Slavs had become not only nationalistic in their music but produced a group of native composers who brought new tonalities and rhythmic innovations to music such as Europe had never known. The Slavic philosophy of music was based on a concept of aesthetic realism and as such was a reaction against the romanticism of German and Italian composers. Michael Ivanovich Glinka (1804–1857) was the first of the native composers to break away from the dominant Italian tradition with the productions of his patriotic *A Life for the Czar* (1836) and the legendary *Russlan and Ludmilla* (1842). These two operas gave the initial impetus to nationalism in Russian music. The lyricism of the Italian vocal style is still present in his music, but his harmonies and melodies are Russian to the core, and his orchestral color is effusively rich and radiant.

Alexander Sergeyevich Dargomijsky (1813–1869) became the successor to Glinka in fostering Russian nationalism in music. His operas were built around a declamatory style of writing or speech-song in which musical tones were used to intensify the expression of the Russian word. Russia need no longer be dependent on foreign tongues or alien music for her artistic life. The famous group of Five, who met at the home of Dargomijsky, beginning in 1859, were imbued with this spirit of artistic nationalism, and worked toward the development of a Russian school of music. This group of Five consisted of Balakirev, Cui, Borodin, Moussorgsky and Rimsky-Korsakov. Besides fostering a new Russian music, this group counteracted the German influence which Anton Rubinstein (1829–1894) had brought to Russia with the formation of his musical society and conservatory which he staffed with German instructors. German music meant Wagnerian music and however this nationalistic group tried to shut out the Wagnerian nemesis, their music does not wholly escape his influence.

The Russian Five differed with Wagner on the role of the orchestra and the relation of the word to the text. They held with Glinka and Dargomijsky that the word took precedence over the music. If the Russian was to know what was going on in the opera, he must know what was being said. Since he was musically illiterate, it was necessary to stress the means of communication that was common to all Russians, namely the language itself. The orchestra must intensify the word.

Alexander II (1818–1881) liberated the Russian serfs and brought a breath of relative freedom to all phases of the arts. Expression in general became more liberalized. The poet and musician began to write and sing of the splendors of their own homeland rather than of lands far away. Mili Alekseyevich Bala-kirev (1837–1910), a disciple of Glinka, and the only profes-sional composer of the Five, worked assiduously for a Russian school of music until he withdrew into a sanctuary of religious mysticism. César Antonovich Cui (1835–1918) furthered the artistic revolution, as a member of the Five, through his music and literature. He had little patience with those musical or literary figures who had an exaggerated reverence for tradition in the arts. The fame of Alexander Porfirevich Borodin (1834–1887) rests on his posthumous opera *Prince Igor*. Modest Petro-vich Moussorgsky (1839–1881) was the most original composer of the Five and the most effective, after Glinka, in the creation of a Russian school of nationalistic music. His audacious rhythms, changing harmonies and sharp dissonances depicted the Russian world about him. His style was a personal one which was for him a formalized means of realistically portraying the character and life of the Russian people. If what he saw and what he felt could not always be expressed in traditional musical forms or tonalities, then tradition gave way to means of musical com-munication that would allow him adequate expression. His aesthetic credo was that music is a means of communication, not an end in itself.

Nikolai Andreyevich Rimsky-Korsakov (1844–1908) tells us in his autobiography that the Five held the Masters to be naive and out of date. "J. S. Bach was held to be petrified, yes, even a mere musico-mathematical, feelingless and deadly nature, com-posing like a very machine." Nevertheless, Korsakov did find it necessary in his thirties to give further study to the art of the traditional Masters so that he might more effectively use the tools of musical composition to give greater reign to his feelings. His ardent desire for self-realization as a composer ended in his becoming a master of orchestration and a tone colorist of exotic grandeur. With such mastery of composition Rimsky-Korsakov brought the musical aesthetics of the Five to its ultimate ful-fillment, a nationalistic school of music rooted in the music of the people and the land, for the glory of a greater Russia.

Peter Ilich Tchaikovsky (1840–1893), like the Five, was a fervent patriot who sang of his native land. Although he was contemptuous of the Five, since he was a pupil of Rubinstein, he nevertheless shared in the Five's lack of reverence for the Masters, particularly Bach. Bach had disciplined his emotions. Tchaikovsky was at the mercy of his. Bach had converted the chaos in his life into ordered music. Tchaikovsky vented his feelings in plaintive lyricism. Bach had mastered the forms which contained his feelings. Tchaikovsky was not always mindful of strict form when his feelings sought an outlet for expression. It is psychologically significant that his most fertile periods of creativity were when he was ailing or depressed. The melancholy lyricism, impulsive rhythms and orchestral color of his music places him among the late romantic composers. The expression of feeling, bordering on sentimentality, which he instills into his music, is the essence of his musical aesthetics.

Alexander Scriabin (1872–1915) became a disciple of a vague religious and philosophical group which began in Russia as a modernist movement at the beginning of the century. His aesthetic ideal was to unite the arts into a religious order in which beauty would express the eternal truth. The music which he composed in the latter part of his life, as a member of this occult group, displayed an effort to express his theosophical ideas.

Sergei Rachmaninoff (1873–1943) came to America after the Russian Revolution. His music is written in the form of the classicists and the lyrical subjectivism of the romanticists. Although he lived close to the mid-part of the 20th century, he showed little desire for musical reforms or new aesthetic systems since what he had to say did not possess sufficient originality to impel him to seek new means of expression.

The Russian composer and the composer of the various countries that have been mentioned in this section was, on the whole, creating his music with an aesthetic freedom that his predecessors would have envied. While the philosophers kept defining the nature and meaning of music with disciplined rationalizations, the composer in the Romantic era went on his merry way writing his music to suit his mood and need.

CHAPTER 8

MUSICAL PHILOSOPHIES OF OUR TIME

SECTION I—*Platonic Echoes in the Modern World*

THE philosopher, Alfred North Whitehead (1861–1947), said that the development of Western philosophy had been largely a matter of adding footnotes to Plato. The musical aesthetics of Western civilization has also been a variation of the original Platonic theme with Aristotelian embellishments. The musical views which Plato expressed in the *Republic* and *Laws* have persistently remained the aesthetic beliefs by which church and state have evaluated their respective philosophies of music throughout the ages in the Western world. There has been a decided similarity of musical concepts between the ancient, medieval and modern philosophies of authoritarian church and state and to a lesser degree in the democracies. In the Catholic Church, Plato's aesthetics of music prevails to this very day. The *Motu Proprio of Pope Pius X on Sacred Music* (1903)* bears this out.

The Church maintains in this well known document on the proper function of music as a complementary part of the solemn Liturgy that the principal function of sacred music is to em-

---

* *The White List of the Society of St. Gregory of America,* New York: 1951.

bellish the text, to emphasize the Holy Word of God. The principal office of sacred music "is to clothe with suitable melody the liturgical text proposed for the understanding of the faithful, its proper aim is to add greater efficacy to the text, in order that through it the faithful may be the more easily moved to devotion . . ."[1]

Sacred music should possess *sanctity*. It must have qualities proper to the Liturgy and must exclude all "profanity" both of a melodic nature and in the manner in which it is performed. Sacred music must also possess *goodness of form* if it is "to exercise on the minds of those who listen to it that efficacy which the Church aims at obtaining in admitting into her liturgy the art of musical sounds."[2] Sacred music must possess *universality*. While every nation is allowed to bring its native music into the Church, this music must be subordinated to the basic requirements of sacred music, proper to the Catholic Liturgy, so that the music of one land can be acceptable as sacred music in another.

The authors of the *Motu Proprio* added that these three qualities are fully manifest in the Gregorian Chant, which has always been regarded as the supreme model for sacred music. ". . . *the more closely a composition for church approaches in its movement, inspiration and savor the Gregorian form, the more sacred and liturgical it becomes; and the more out of harmony it is with that supreme model, the less worthy it is of the temple.*"[3] The Catholic Church desires that the traditional Gregorian Chant, the only chant which She has inherited from the ancient Fathers, be used once more in a large measure for public worship. Recent studies, reads the *Motu Proprio*, have restored the Gregorian Chant to its original integrity and purity* and now special

---

[1] *Ibid.*, p. 7.
[2] *Ibid.*, p. 8.
[3] *Loc. cit.*

* In the 16th and 17th centuries the Gregorian melodies were arranged into rigid rhythmical patterns and given organ accompaniment. This pitiful bit of editing was totally foreign to the original modal and religious character of the Chant. It was a case of music of one age being rearranged for another with each possessing a culture and philosophy wholly foreign to each other. Consequently, the Gregorian Chant became a monotonous plain-chant with organ

efforts must be made to encourage the use of this traditional Chant by the people, "so that the faithful may again take a more active part in the ecclesiastical offices, as was the case in ancient times."[4]

Classic polyphony, especially of the Roman school, which reached its greatest perfection in the 16th century in the writings of Palestrina, possesses the musical qualities which are found in the sacred Chant. "Classic Polyphony agrees admirably with Gregorian Chant, . . . and hence it has been found worthy of a place side by side with Gregorian Chant, in the more solemn functions of the Church, . . ."[5] Polyphonic music should therefore also be restored largely in Church functions to enhance the splendor of ecclesiastical ceremonies.

The *Motu Proprio* states that the Roman Church has always favored the progress of the arts and has admitted new music into the Service of religious worship ". . . with due regard to the liturgical laws." Modern music is also welcomed into the religious Service if it is in keeping with the needs of worship and fulfills the liturgical requirements. "Still, since modern music has risen mainly to serve profane uses, greater care must be taken with regard to it, in order that the musical compositions of modern style which are admitted in the Church may contain nothing profane, be free from reminiscences of motifs adopted in the theatres, and be not fashioned even in their external forms after the manner of profane pieces."[6]

It is forbidden to sing anything whatever in the vernacular in liturgical functions. The Church further insists that the liturgical text be sung as prescribed by the ecclesiastical authorities "without alteration or inversion of the words, without undue repetition, without breaking syllables, and always in a manner intelligible to the faithful who listen."[7]

Solo singing should never predominate to such an extent as to

---

accompaniment. During the reign of Pope Pius X the Gregorian melodies were partly restored to their original form, but the practice of organ accompaniment still persists.

[4] *Loc. cit.*
[5] *Loc. cit.*
[6] *Loc. cit.*
[7] *Loc. cit.*

have the greater part of the liturgical chant lose the character of choral music. Singers in Church have a liturgical office and since women cannot exercise such office, they cannot be admitted to form part of the choir. Only men of piety and good character should be admitted into the Church choir. Lest the presence of the choir cause the worshippers to be distracted from the ceremonies being performed at the altar, the choir should be hidden from sight of the congregation.

The *Motu Proprio* then goes on to consider the use of instruments in the Church. "Although the music proper to the Church is purely vocal music, music with the accompaniment of the organ is also permitted. In some special cases, within due limits and proper safeguards, other instruments may be allowed, but never without the special permission of the Ordinary, ... As the singing should always have the principal place, the organ or other instrument should merely sustain and never oppress it. It is not permitted to have the chant preceded by long preludes or to interrupt it with intermezzo pieces. The sound of the organ as an accompaniment to the chant in preludes, interludes, and the like must be not only governed by the special nature of the instrument, but must participate in all the qualities proper to sacred music as above enumerated. The employment of the piano is forbidden in church, as is also that of noisy or frivolous instruments such as drums, cymbals, bells and the like. It is strictly forbidden to have bands play in church, and only in special cases with the consent of the Ordinary will it be permissible to admit wind instruments, limited in number, judiciously used, and proportioned to the size of the place—provided the composition and accompaniment be written in grave and suitable style, and conform in all respects to that proper to the organ. In processions outside the church the Ordinary may give permission for a band, provided no profane pieces be executed."[8]

The *Motu Proprio* makes it quite clear that it is a serious abuse when the Liturgy is subordinated to musical considerations in ecclesiastical functions, for music is merely the humble handmaid of the Liturgy. This document also advises the Bishops to institute in their dioceses a Commission composed of persons versed

[8] *Ibid.*, p. 9.

in sacred music who should watch over the religious music in their Churches. "Nor are they to see merely that the music is good in itself, but also that it is adapted to the powers of the singers and be always well executed."[9]

This famous doctrine on sacred music asks that the Gregorian Chant be cultivated with diligence in seminaries of clerics and ecclesiastical institutions. That a Schola Cantorum be established among the clerics for the execution of sacred polyphony and liturgical music. Students of theology should be instructed in the principles and laws of sacred music and be made aware of the aesthetic side of sacred Catholic art.

The ancient *Scholae Cantorum* should be restored for the training of children and adults in religious music. Efforts should be made to support and promote higher schools of sacred music for "It is of the utmost importance that the Church herself provide for the instruction of her choirmasters, organists, and singers, according to the true principles of sacred art."[10]

The present Pope, Pius XII, in his encyclical *Mediator Dei* (1947), has reaffirmed the musical views of Pope Pius X with a plea for a type of sacred music that is pure and meaningful so that it will draw men together and bring them closer to God. Pope Pius XII permits some new additions to the ritual such as singing modern songs and playing modern music, but he does urge that caution be used in the choice and use of the new music for the religious Service. To be certain that new music which is introduced into the Church is in keeping with the spiritual aims of the Catholic Faith, Pope Pius XII insists that any departure from the traditional musical practices must be sanctioned by the ecclesiastical authorities.

SECTION II—*Music, The Church and The State**

IN February of 1948 the Central Committee of the Communist Party of the Soviet Union passed a resolution in protest against

[9] *Loc. cit.*

[10] *Ibid.*, p. 10.

* The content of this section is based on my paper entitled *Platonic Echoes in Soviet Musical Criticism* published in the *Journal of Aesthetics and Art Criticism*, June, 1950.

certain native composers whose artistic creations were departing from the aesthetic doctrines and ideologies of Soviet philosophy. This resolution was issued in the form of a condemnation of the opera, *Great Friendship* (music by V. Nuradeli, libretto by Mdivani) which was produced by the Bolshoi theatre of the USSR during the celebration of the 30th anniversary of the October Revolution.[11] The criticism began by denouncing this opera as unsound in its music, its subject matter, and, on the whole, as an inartistic composition. But the next few lines left no doubt that the Central Committee was taking the occasion, in passing judgment on this particular opera, to speak to all Soviet composers and critics.

The aesthetic credo laid down by the Soviets is not new, but is a philosophy of art that has followed in the wake of a number of religious and social revolutions in Western history. If we trace these aesthetic doctrines to their origin, we shall find that these very theories are part of a recurring pattern leading back from modern Communism to the Reformation, to the Medieval Church and finally to Plato himself.

The essence of Plato's philosophy of music, and one of the main points adopted by church and state, is that music as an educational and cultural discipline should be used for the attainment of a sound morality. Plato regarded music as superior to the other arts, on the premise that rhythm and melody more strongly affect the inner soul and emotional life of man. He concluded that exposure to the proper musical modes would encourage the unconscious development of discriminating habits which would allow one to distinguish good from evil.

In the *Republic* Plato expressed the conviction that the Ionian and Lydian modes should be banished from the State since they were of an effeminate, soft and relaxing character. The Dorian and Phrygian modes that were military in tone should be retained.[12] With his musical doctrines now rooted in moralistic principles he applied them in a thoroughly practical manner to rebuke bards who were cultivating a primitive form of polyphony that was coming into vogue in his day. Characterizing it

[11] *Izvestia*, February 11, 1948; Translated by B. L. Koten.
[12] *Bk.* III, 399.

as a cacophony which could only result in mental confusion Plato instructed the Greek bard to compose his musical ode so that it could be rendered "note for note" and not with a "complexity, and variation of notes" such as "when the strings give one sound and the poet or composer of the melody gives another, . . ." "concords and harmonies in which lesser and greater intervals, slow and quick, or high and low notes, are combined," and complex variations when adapted to the notes of the lyre, cautioned Plato, would surely create difficulties "for opposite principles are confusing."[13] The conclusion followed that variety, complexity of rhythm and melody should be avoided for they were apt to induce mental depression and confusion which might lead men away from the natural order of things into the realm of the irrational and folly.

Closer to our own day, Tolstoy's (1828–1910) moralistic aesthetics rests on a social and religious condemnation of society and its art. Many of his Platonic views were incorporated into the body of what are now the musical precepts of Soviet Russia. Much of what was merely aesthetic theory in Tolstoy's writings became political actuality in the Central Committee's first point of issue that the music of the opera "is muddled and inharmonious, constructed entirely of dissonances, of combinations of sounds that grate on the ear." The Central Committee is also strongly reminiscent of Plato when it continues in the same vein that: "Into individual lines and scenes having a pretense to melody, there break in, all of a sudden, dissonant noises completely alien to the normal human ear which cause a reaction of depression in the listener."[14] The conceptual similarities of this passage with those quoted from the past are striking indeed.

The Platonic echoes in Soviet music are borne out by a second similarity. Plato was of the view that lyric and tune were inseparable, but he did emphasize the moral value of the text by subordinating the musical form to poetry. He took issue with those revolutionary composers of his day who were actually creating music without words for "when there are no words,"

---

[13] *Laws, Bk.* VII, 812-813; (Translated by B. Jowett), Random House, New York: 1937.

[14] *Izvestia, Op. cit.*

he wrote, "it is very difficult to recognize the meaning of the harmony and rhythm, or to see that any worthy object is imitated by them."[15]

Calvin, writing in a vein strongly reminiscent of the well-known selection in Augustine's *Confessions*, stated "great caution is necessary, that the ears be not more attentive to the modulation of the notes, than the mind to the spiritual import of the words."

This treatment of text and music periodically makes its appearance as an aesthetic problem, and it is not surprising to find that the Soviets are concerned with it in the light of their immediate needs. "The formalist trend in Soviet music," writes the Central Committee, "has given rise to a one-sided passion for complex forms of instrumental, symphonic, textless music among a section of Soviet composers, . . ." "All this inevitably leads to the fact that the fundamentals of vocal culture and mastery of dramaturgy are being lost and that composers are forgetting how to write for the people."[16]

Our third point for consideration is the matter of musical innovation. Plato was most vitriolic in denouncing artistic innovation. It was on the basis of the conviction that artistic change would eventually lead to anarchy in the State that Plato wrote in the *Republic* that any musical innovation is full of danger to the State and ought to be prohibited, and that when modes of music change, the fundamental laws of the State change with them.[17]

St. Augustine's preference for the simple Psalms of David instead of the melismatic music that was making its way into the Liturgy of his day was not out of aesthetic consideration. He feared that the introduction of new music which was alien to Christian needs would be detrimental to Church welfare and threaten the stability of the Liturgy with constant and uncertain change.

Calvin wanted his religious music to be simple and expressive of humility. What was the Reformation, argued Calvin, but a

[15] *Laws, Op. cit., Bk.* II, 669-670.
[16] *Izvestia, Op. cit.*
[17] *Bk.* IV, 424.

denial of Roman pomp and ritual. Protestant music must, therefore, be guarded against the vain creations of men who compose
not for the glory of God, but for their own aggrandisement.
Music is not apart from but a part of the new Faith. A liturgical
composer has no right to dissipate his energy on any type of
musical creation but that which will assure the attainment and
advancement of Protestantism.

The Soviets carry this view further by maintaining that artistic
change for the sake of mere innovation is wasteful. It must be
directed toward a socially constructive end. "Many Soviet composers, in pursuit of falsely-conceived innovation," states the
Central Committee, "have lost contact in their music with the
demands and the artistic taste of the Soviet people, have shut
themselves off in a narrow circle of specialists and musical gourmands, have lowered the high social role of music and narrowed
its meaning, limiting it to a satisfaction of the distorted tastes of
aesthetic individualists . . ." "In the field of symphonic and
operatic composition matters are especially bad. We are speaking of composers who confine themselves to the formalist anti-
public trend. This trend has found its fullest manifestation in
the works of such composers as Comrades D. Shostakovich,
S. Prokofiev, A. Khachaturian, V. Shebalin, G. Popov, N. Myas-
kovsky and others, . . . Characteristic of such music are the
negation of the basic principles of classical music; a sermon for
atonality, dissonance and disharmony, as if this were an expression of 'Progress' and 'innovation' in the growth of musical
forms; a rejection of such important fundamentals of musical
composition as melody; a passion for confused, neuropathic
combinations which transform music into cacophony, into a
chaotic piling up of sounds."[18]

By way of summary, Plato maintained that only strictly tempered musical modes and tunes that were emotionally effective
because of their direct simplicity were beneficial. The proper
kind of music could help man to rhythmically attune his finite
soul with the infinite. Raucous cacophony might cause the soul
to clash with the ideal order of things. Bards who composed

---

[18] *Izvestia, Op. cit.*

music incongruous with the natural order must be cast out of society for they were the destroyers of souls and the forerunners of social doom.

These philosophical views took on religious significance in the labors of those early ecclesiastical composers who were imbued with a monastic mission to create music for the Glory of God and Church. It was incumbent upon them that they forego their personal feelings and musical tendencies to fulfill the needs of the Church.

Luther, like his Catholic predecessors, thought it essential to make use of every means possible to win over the emotional and psychological forces in man. As a composer in his own right and the leader of the Reformation he evolved an aesthetics of music, Augustinian in flavor to be sure, but realistic to the point of reducing art to an instrument of religious expediency. To help achieve his end, Luther introduced German to replace the Latin of the Catholic Service; and as a substitute for the complex Gregorian Chant he chose music that was simpler and less pretentious, more akin to the German folk-song.[19]

Calvin thought Luther's musical concepts to be much too liberal. In the same manner that Augustine warned the early Christians to shut their ears to the pagan strains that emanated from the Roman theatre so Calvin sought to keep Protestantism pure by obliterating whatever vestige of colorful Catholic music Luther had retained. He did agree with Luther that the Service should be understood by all and so the Liturgy of Calvin was in the vernacular.

Some three hundred years later in Czarist Russia, Tolstoy sought to achieve social and artistic reforms based on Christian principles. One brief passage from *What is Art?* synthesizes the musical aesthetics of Plato, Augustine, Luther and Calvin. As this passage effectively summarized the moralistic aesthetic views of the past so, too, was it prophetic of the musical aesthetics of the Russia of today. "The art of the future," he wrote, "will thus be completely distinct, both in subject-matter and in form, from what is now called art. The only subject-matter of the

[19] Hugo Leichtentritt, *Music, History and Ideas*, p. 105; Harvard University Press, Cambridge: 1946.

art of the future will be either feelings drawing men toward union, or such as already unite them; and the forms of art will be such as will be open to everyone. And therefore, the ideal of excellence in the future will not be the exclusiveness of feeling, accessible only to some, but, on the contrary, its universality. And not bulkiness, obscurity, and complexity of form, as is now esteemed, but, on the contrary, brevity, clearness, and simplicity of expression. Only when art has attained to that, will art neither divert nor deprave men as it does now, . . ." Elsewhere he added: ". . . the melodies of the modern composers are amazingly empty and insignificant. And to strengthen the impression produced by these empty melodies, the new musicians pile complex modulations on to each trivial melody, not only in their own national manner, but also in the way characteristic of their own exclusive circle and particular musical school. Melody—every melody—is free, and may be understood of all men; but as soon as it is bound up with a particular harmony, it ceases to be accessible except to people trained to such harmony, and it becomes strange, not only to common men of another nationality, but to all who do not belong to the circle whose members have accustomed themselves to certain forms of harmonization. So that music, like poetry, travels in a vicious circle. Trivial and exclusive melodies, in order to make them attractive, are laden with harmonic, rhythmic, and orchestral complications, and thus become yet more exclusive; and far from being universal, are not even national, i.e., they are not comprehensible to the whole people but only to some people."[20]

The Central Committee is in full accord with Tolstoy on these aesthetic principles. They, too, insist that music must be realistic and not abstract or detached from the people and needs of Soviet life. This function of music was lost, writes the Central Committee, because "The composer" of *Great Friendship* "did not utilize the wealth of folk melodies, songs, tunes and dance motifs in which the creative art of the peoples of the USSR is so rich." But the nub of their argument is that "The breaking away of some Soviet musicians from the people has reached such a point

[20] Leo Tolstoy, *What is Art?*, pp. 173; 148; (Translated by Aylmer Maude), Thomas Y. Crowell and Co., New York: 1899.

that a corrupt 'theory' has spread among them, according to which the fact that the music of many contemporary Soviet composers is incomprehensible to the people, is explained by the fact that the people, seemingly, have not as yet 'grown up' to an understanding of their complex music, that they will understand it in a hundred years and that it is not worthwhile becoming upset if some musical compositions find no listeners. This thoroughly individualistic theory," continues the Central Committee, "anti-public to the core, has made it possible for some composers and musicologists to fence themselves off from the people, from the criticism of Soviet society, to an even greater degree and to shut themselves up in their shells."[21]

A year after *Izvestia* carried the resolutions of the Central Committee, Dimitri Shostakovich (1906) delivered a speech in New York which bore out the effectiveness of these resolutions. He compared the musical philosophies of the Western composers with the aesthetic realism of his own music and that of Prokofiev. He accused Igor Stravinsky, as a representative of the Western composers, of a decadent formalism which can only lead to the degeneration of music.

Shostakovich first pointed out that Stravinsky had great promise as a composer until he broke with the traditions of the Russian national school and joined the camp of the "reactionary modernistic musicians". Shostakovich then accused Stravinsky of ignoring the musical needs of the masses. He quoted Stravinsky's statements: "The 'mass', in relation to art, is a quantitative term which has never once entered into my considerations." . . . "The broad mass adds nothing to the art, it cannot raise the level, and the artist who aims consciously at 'mass appeal' can do so only by lowering his own level, the soul of each individual who listens to my music is important to me, and not the mass feeling of a group." Shostakovich then asked how such subjectivism bettered the life of the people? How can such "decadent" music promote a political idea? Stravinsky answers these questions eloquently, continued Shostakovich, with the simple statements: "My music does not express anything realistic" . . . "My music has nothing to narrate." In this proclamation which stresses the

---

[21] *Izvestia, Op. cit.*

meaningless and absence of content in music, warned Shostakovich, is to be found the philosophy of decadence which char-
acterizes the music of Stravinsky and prevails in the musical
aesthetics of the capitalistic nations.

Shostakovich then proceeds to explain what the Soviets mean
by realism in music by making a distinction between naturalism
and realism. Naturalistic imitation in music is the imitation of
the cuckoo in Beethoven's *Pastoral Symphony* and the bleatings
of the lambs in Strauss's *Don Quixote*. Shostakovich notes that
this type of musical imitation has been carried to extremes by
composers who imitate the roar of locomotives and the clatter
of industrial machinery. Composers who adhere to the philosophy of art for art's sake confuse the meaning of naturalistic
imitation and realism in music. The formalistic composers have
learned how to depict all kinds of noises in music but, laments
Shostakovich, they have forgotten how to accurately convey
and depict the emotions, feelings and experiences of humanity.
Because of this detachment from the life of the masses, continues
Shostakovich, the formalistic composers have lost the art of
describing the feelings and experiences of the people. Realism
in music means to "generalize upon the great experience of living, and at the same time to single out that which is most
important in the process of living. It is a question of the artist
as a progressive element of human society, as a teacher and
educator, who reaffirms in his works moral and aesthetic values.
It is a question that music must cease being a diversion and a toy
in the hands of sophisticates, gourmands, aesthetes, and become
once again a great social force serving humanity in its struggle
for progress and the triumph of Reason."

Shostakovich illustrates the Soviet principle of realism in music
with such works as Prokofiev's (1891–1953) cantatas *Alexander
Nevsky* and *Zdravitsa* and the opera *War and Peace*. Shostakovich attributes his own success as a Soviet composer to the
fact that in the past he managed to establish intimate contact
with the Russian people through his music. "I strove to find a
language whose meaning could be understood. Conversely, in
those of my works—especially those after the post-war years—
in which I departed from big themes and contemporary images,

I lost my contact with the people—and I failed. My work found response only among the narrow strata of sophisticated musicians —but they failed to meet with approval among the broad masses of listeners."

SECTION III—*Music as Expression*

THE philosopher, John Stuart Mill (1806–1873), had written "I was seriously tormented by the thought of the exhaustibility of musical combinations. The octave consists only of five tones and two semitones, which can be put together in only a limited number of ways of which but a small proportion are beautiful: most of these, it seemed to me, must have been already discovered, and there could not be room for a long succession of Mozarts and Webers to strike out, as these have done, entirely new surpassing rich veins of musical beauty."[22] Mill's fears were grounded in a closed harmonic system which could be exhausted, since he considered the concept of the beautiful in music in terms of traditional values. But the composers of the second half of the 19th century had already gone beyond considering the beautiful in music in terms of using the five whole tones and two semitones of the octave in a limited number of ways.

Wagner deliberately used harmonic dissonance to embellish expression. The beautiful in music for him was expression, consonance and dissonance were simply emotionally effective contrasts and at best academic distinctions. Debussy accepted this phase of Wagnerian aesthetics for he too was intent on enlarging the imaginative world through music. He extended harmonic relationships, employed dissonance without preparation or resolution and used notes foreign to the chord. Debussy injected oriental and modal coloring into his music and modulated with complete enharmonic freedom. He was preoccupied with conveying a mood and all the notes of the scale, major and minor chords, were used and diffused to beget the impression he wished to convey. Between the German romanticist, Wagner, and the French impressionist, Debussy, the aesthetic and technical char-

[22] Nicolas Slonimsky, *Thesaurus of Scales and Melodic Patterns*, p. vi; Coleman-Ross Co., Inc., New York: 1947.

acter of music was ingeniously revolutionized. The aesthetics of modern music in the 20th century stems from the creativity of these two composers who belied the fears of the philosopher that music is a closed system with limited possibilities of producing beautiful tones. In dealing with the music of our time we shall show, in a limited fashion, how the creative composers in various countries expressed themselves.

Erik Satie (1866–1925) was the spiritual father of Les Six in Paris after the First World War. His span of musical ideas extend from deliberate buffoonery to contemplative philosophy. He took selections from Plato's dialogues and set them to music in his most ambitious work, the symphonic drama, *Socrate*. Satie has become the esoteric idol of the musical avant-garde element and philosophic existentialists who credit him with the culmination of the anti-Wagnerian trend in French music and with the use of daring harmonies before Debussy and Ravel (1875–1937).

Each age in music seeks a muse. The romantics made Beethoven their inspiring idol and the German, Max Reger (1873–1916), turned to Bach to recapture the spirit of polyphony. Reger thought he found in Bach a pristine example of classic detachment which would serve as an antidote to the gushing emotions of the romanticists. He was concerned with technical values of tone and form and, because of his zeal for purism, misinterpreted his idol Bach by emphasizing the musical symbol rather than the emotion which the symbol represents.

Richard Strauss (1864–1949) did not share the aesthetic purism of his countryman Reger. Like Reger, he was a master technician, but unlike Reger he used his technique to exploit the possibilities of instruments and form to convey his feelings and thoughts in the most highly descriptive musical manner. His music is eclectic and pictorially realistic and at times soars to melodic climaxes that make the neo-romantic scores of Wagner seem mild by comparison. With Wagner and Mahler he shared the inability for brevity. He is lengthy and verbose.

The Italian-German composer, pianist and theorist, Ferruccio Busoni (1866–1924), like Reger, protested against 19th century romanticism and asked for a return to the clarity and logic of

18th century classicism in music. Reger became an avowed disciple of Bach and Busoni turned to Mozart whom he considered the greatest musical stylist. The return of Reger and Busoni to the formalism of classicism and away from emotional romanticism brought to the 20th century an aesthetics of music that culminated in the neo-classicism of Hindemith and Stravinsky.

Busoni's *Sketch On A New Esthetic of Music* (1907) is an aphoristic defence of his reverence for pure form and clear style. He disagreed with the ancients' belief that music is an imitation of nature and he scoffed at the romantic concept that music is an imitation of life. Music for Busoni was a stylized way of expressing mood and emotion. Wagnerian aesthetics was as much an anathema to him as it was to Hanslick. In his own opera *Arlecchino* he ridicules the romantics with a satire on society, morality, war, philosophy, religion and above all the unreality of the romantic use of operatic form.

Busoni came to the conclusion that the music of the romantics had become overly descriptive. He maintained that their music (particularly the scores of Richard Strauss, for one, whose tone poems employed music for descriptive realism such as a churning wind mill or the bleating of sheep) contained elements that were alien to the true nature of music. He maintained that music must remain pure tone and form. It is not the function of music to excite the passions but to produce rationalized tonal combinations and stylized forms.

Busoni regarded romanticism as a musical aesthetics which raised the passions of men and stifled the intellect. He agreed with Hegel that classicism is the triumph of form over matter, intellect over emotion. He concurred with Goethe's observation that everything that is healthy is classic, everything that is diseased is romantic. His views were embellished in the writings of Oswald Spengler (1880–1936) who claimed that program music was a romantic concept that properly belonged to the art of painting and not music. "All romantic art is a swansong," wrote Spengler; it is "the final expression of a civilization, the rich autumn tints of decay, the writings on the wall, the flaming comet heralding the approach of anarchy and dissolution."

Busoni did not share Spengler's historical cynicism. His book on aesthetics is a testament of faith that a new musical world was in the offing. He strove both as a theorist and composer to develop the possibilities of our tonal system and favored experimentation with new instruments.

The Finnish composer, Jean Sibelius (1865), has been described by his contemporaries as a folk-composer who derives his inspiration from nature and portrays her in a romantic hue. Sibelius on his own account expressed the belief that the aesthetic principles of classicism are the way of the future. Aaron Copland wrote: "Sibelius is, by nature, a folk composer. . . . There is the constant tendency in him to fall back into a pastoral mood of folk inspiration, to repeat himself in themes and technical formulas, to put us always into the same emotional atmosphere. None of these tendencies is characteristic of the first rate composer."[23] The critic, Olin Downes, wrote: "The fact is that it is Sibelius, not Stravinsky with his fake imitations of old masters, nor Hindemith with his modern revival of old counterpoint and pure instrumental forms, who is the neo-classic master in the music of today."[24]

In the music of England's Ralph Vaughan Williams (1872) there is a definite neo-classic emphasis on the use of counterpoint and form. Imaginative feelings and poetic concepts are translated into tonal combinations which, however startling to the ear, are intended to express musical feelings and nothing else. Benjamin Britten (1913) is the promising hope of English music. He, too, expresses "an undying devotion to Bach". He also follows Bach in the view that the voice is the ultimate instrument and that the better orchestral instruments are, the more they sound like the human voice. Britten may have a preference for the voice but his greatness is also manifest in his orchestral and chamber music. His opera *Peter Grimes* is truly a realization of Weber's aesthetic aspiration of making opera a fusion of poetry, song, and action. The return to the Greek fusion of the arts has come alive in the operas of Benjamin Britten.

The state of music in our own country, if we may go back

---

[23] *Our New Music*, pp. 42-43; Whittlesey House, London: 1941.
[24] *New York Times*, December 21, 1947.

almost two centuries for a moment, was best described by
Thomas Jefferson in a letter to a correspondent in France. "If
there is a gratification, which I envy any people in this world,
it is to your country its music. This is the favorite passion of my
soul, and fortune has cast my lot in a country where it is in a
state of deplorable barbarism . . ." Even in the last century
when Europe was enjoying the great era of romanticism, the
foremost American philosopher, Ralph Waldo Emerson (1803–
1882) wrote of the creative musician: "How partial, like muti-
lated eunuchs, the musical artists appear to me in society! Politics,
bankruptcy, frost, famine, war—nothing concerns them but a
scraping on a catgut, or tooting on a bass French horn."

The beginning of an American school of music started with
the compositions of George W. Chadwick (1854–1931), Charles
Martin Loeffler (1861–1935), and Edward Alexander Mac-
Dowell (1861–1908). The influence of the Europeans strongly
showed itself in their musical ideas and use of form, try as they
might to paint the American scene with native color. The music
of Charles Ives (1874–1954) which followed, shows more originality of ideas and boldness of expression. America has since come
of age musically. She has offered refuge to those composers who
fled the Russian Revolution and Nazi scourge and who have
stayed to enrich our land with their music, both as composers
and teachers. America has, since the beginning of the century,
become less dependent on European composers as models. Roy
Harris (1898), Roger Sessions (1896), Walter Piston (1894),
Virgil Thomson (1896), Randall Thompson (1899) and Aaron
Copland (1900) as composers, teachers and critics were the
initiators of a musical renaissance in this country which was
accelerated by the influx of foreign musicians and the advance-
ments of a scientific age. America owes much to these men, even
if they themselves owe a debt to Europe. They possess a virility
of ideas that bring a freshness of originality to the art of music.
They create their music with a hymn-like directness and classic
simplicity.

The succeeding generation of composers do not allow any
musical bounds to fetter their ideas and will for expression.
Marc Blitzstein (1905), William Schuman (1910), Samuel

Barber (1910), Paul Bowles (1911) and Leonard Bernstein (1918) consider tone and form as a medium and pattern of communication which must change with the needs of expression. They retain the aesthetic contention that if the artist says old things then he should say them in a new way. If he possesses the ability to say something new then he must not necessarily say it with the forms of the past but should say what he has to in whatever way it can be said in music.

The cry of many contemporary critics and philosophers that modern music is cacophonous and degenerate is hardly new in the history of the arts. The transition from one musical era to another has always been marked with ridicule and scorn on the part of both the conservative and progressive. Voltaire said that it takes a whole generation for the human ear to grow familiar with a new musical style. This is somewhat of an exaggeration, but is in the main true. It is also said that because our contemporary composers prefer an objective and impersonal style of music they thereby eschew all semblance of feeling in their art. This is equally as absurd as the charge that our music is degenerate. The contemporary composer says what he has to in his own way. The manner in which he expresses himself is different from that of the past. We would no more expect a contemporary poet to write in the speech and style of an Elizabethan bard than we would have a composer in our day express himself in the form and style of a Baroque master.

The modern composer creates according to a pragmatic scale of musical values. He says what he wishes or must in whatever way that he can for his music to be affective. The critic who hears this music for the first time and tries to evaluate this novel expression of feeling is not to be envied. He must bear in mind that not all that is novel is good; that not all change is progress. He must also be aware that if he evaluates new music with traditional standards, he may become the Artusi of his century.

SECTION IV—*A New Aesthetics of Music*

ARNOLD Schönberg (1874–1951) became aware, around the turn of the century, that for over a course of approximately

75 years the diatonic system with its major and minor modality had begun to disintegrate. The aesthetics of Western music which is based on the principle of tonality was giving way. The tonal order so essential to the Western concept of a musically logical structure, which the diatonic system provided, was being disrupted by the chromaticisms of late 19th century music Schönberg therefore evolved a twelve tone system as a substitute for the disintegrating diatonic system by establishing and maintaining a new set of relationships (the tone row) in which each of the twelve tones have equal standing, instead of the primacy of the tonic and dominant in the diatonic system. The concept of tonality was not abandoned by this system, as its critics argued, only a new type of tonality was brought forth.

The music of Schönberg and his school is a reaction against the romanticism of the 19th century. It was the contention of the Viennese school that the harmonic and melodic idiom of the diatonic scale, as that system progressively lost its musical integrity, began more and more to rely on non-musical material. As music gradually lost its ability to project a purely musical idea because of the near exhaustion of its logical structure, it came to rely more and more on the literal and programmatic devices which are so essentially non-musical to the purist. Schönberg maintained that the musical aesthetics of the 19th century made necessary first, a new vocabulary (harmonic, rhythmic, and tonal) and second, a new understanding of the problems of projecting a sound musical logic. The aesthetics of Schönberg rests on the thesis that music must strive toward one goal which supersedes any secondary goals it might have: to project a clear musical logic which will be significant to the audience by virtue of the beauty and clarity of this logic. Contemporary music, in general, is rooted in this thesis.

"The method of composing with twelve tones grew out of a necessity", Schönberg wrote. "In the last hundred years, the concept of harmony has changed tremendously through the development of chromaticism. The idea that one basic tone, the root, dominated the construction of chords and regulated their succession—the concept of *tonality*—had to develop first into the concept of *extended tonality*. Very soon it became doubtful whether such a root still remained the center to which every harmony and harmonic succession must be referred. Furthermore, it became doubtful whether a tonic appearing at the beginning, at the end, or at any other point really had a constructive meaning. Richard Wagner's harmony had promoted a change in the logic and constructive power of harmony. One of its consequences was the so-called *impressionistic* use of harmonies, especially practised by Debussy. His harmonies, without constructive meaning, often served the coloristic purpose of expressing moods and pictures. Moods and pictures, though extramusical, thus became constructive elements, incorporated in the musical functions; they produced a sort of emotional comprehensibility. In this way, tonality was already dethroned in practise, if not in theory. This alone would perhaps not have caused a radical change in compositional technique. However, such a change became necessary when there occurred simultaneously a development which ended in what I call the *emancipation of the dissonance*."

"The ear had gradually become acquainted with a great number of dissonances, and so had lost the fear of their 'sense-interrupting' effect. One no longer expected preparations of Wagner's dissonances or resolutions of Strauss' discords; one was not disturbed by Debussy's non-functional harmonies, or by the harsh counterpoint of later composers. This state of affairs led to a freer use of dissonances comparable to classic composers' treatment of diminished seventh chords, which could precede and follow any other harmony, consonant or dissonant, as if there were no dissonant at all."

"What distinguishes dissonances from consonances is not a greater or lesser degree of beauty, but a greater or lesser degree of comprehensibility."[25]

Alban Berg (1885–1935) was the most gifted of the Viennese composers who were drawn to Schönberg's musical aesthetics. His outstanding achievement is the opera *Wozzeck* which is based on the almost forgotten novel of Georg Buechner who died more than a hundred years ago at the age of 24. The cynicism of youth, the futility of existence, the despair of man, are

[25] *Style and Idea*, pp. 103-4; Philosophical Library, New York: 1950.

all expressed here vocally and instrumentally with a passion and drama that brings the tragic in life close to the sublime in art

The tonal aesthetics of Schönberg, the dramatic effectiveness of Wagner, the haunting melodic quality of Mahler, depict the crazed mind of Wozzeck, which can only find surcease from life in death. The music is decidedly novel, effective and intensely dramatic, but for all that, the opera *Wozzeck* may be recorded in musical history as the last of the romantic operas in the 20th century. The libretto deals with the sickly, the crazed and the dead. It is a weird, frenzied, if not fantastic opera of romantic decadence which brings forth the warning of Goethe, the observation of Spengler: the romantic is all that is sick, the romantic is the dying echoes of Western culture. But whatever may be said about the decadent and psychological probing into the inner recesses of the mind in the Berg opera, there is much aesthetic significance in the score of *Wozzeck* and the unfinished opera *Lulu* that will unfold itself to a music listener with patience and time. Berg, first of all, was a humanist who employed his artistic powers to depict the evil and ugly as it exists in society. The term romanticism needs semantic clarification when applied to his music, for he did not offer his listeners an escape from reality through his music but he brought them face to face with human lust and greed. He said what he had to say with the additional tonal innovations that his teacher Schönberg created. He expressed his feelings with polytonalities and polyrhythms. In his operas *Wozzeck* and *Lulu* the fundamental structure of the twelve tone scale takes on aesthetic significance. Berg, more than Schönberg, proved that the traditional reverence of the tonic-dominant relationship could be replaced by a scale in which each tone or note is as important as any other note or tone in the scale, thus making the entire musical scale of equal importance. He furthermore saw no reason why a composer could not begin his music on any note of the scale that he wished and finish on any note that he chose.

To those of us who have been brought up on the *Well-Tempered Clavier* and have prided ourselves on hearing in Wagner what our elders were unable to, the music of Berg is fresh, startling, tonally vibrant, and tensely rhythmic. Many of us, on he other hand, are as musically conditioned in our way as our grandparents were in theirs and thus we continue to evaluate the music of Berg with the music of Beethoven. We hear complaints that Berg's strident dissonances are pure cacophony, that his vocal lines are unsingable. We do not realize how monotonous this historical charge must sound to the Muse of song. Berg is no more cacophonous today than Monteverdi was in his day and in *Wozzeck* and *Lulu* he actually reverts to the musical aesthetics of Monteverdi by emphasizing the spoken word in the play through the use of the speech-song idea which Schönberg had tried to use with less success in *Pierrot Lunaire*.

Igor Stravinsky (1882) agrees with Schönberg that the diatonic scale has outlived its usefulness; he originally showed interest in the twelve tone technique, but instead of substituting a new system, such as Schönberg had done with a rigid twelve tone system, Stravinsky uses multiple tonalities to produce new harmonies and musical effects. Stravinsky is altogether opposed to Schönberg's overly systematized use of the twelve musical tones as a solution for a new aesthetics. He believes that each score is unique in itself and possesses a logic of its own that makes it different from all other scores. He further holds that Wagner not only applied a stereotyped musical logic to all his compositions, but failed to recognize what Schopenhauer well knew and he himself maintained in his Harvard lectures: that music is an autonomous art which must not give up its independence for a fusion of the arts.

In the opera, *Oedipus Rex*, Stravinsky gave a practical demonstration of his aesthetic belief that the words should have value purely as sounds and should not detract from the music itself. Stravinsky is not concerned with the conceptual meaning of the text. He simply wants his listener to be aware of the sounds and rhythms of the vocal parts. Ernst Křenek (1900) does the same thing and Schönberg maintained that in "all music composed to poetry, the exactitude of the reproduction of the events is as irrelevant to the artistic value as is the resemblance of a portrait to its model".

Igor Stravinsky has had a greater and more far reaching effect on the musicians of two generations than either Wagner or

Debussy. From the very beginning of his career his music has possessed an exoticism which has its source in liberally borrowed melodies from Russian folk-songs. He has no hesitancy in using the themes of other composers either. He has a remarkable ability to work borrowed material into his own scores in a thoroughly personalized fashion and the dynamic quality of his music, which is derived chiefly from his forceful rhythms, is quite often of jazz origin. It seems like a paradox that a composer who borrows so freely from others could still be so original and influential. The answer probably is that other composers spend most of their energy disguising what they borrow and Stravinsky uses most of his energy to do with the music of other composers what they were unable to do with it themselves from a point of rhythmic and melodic development.

Few instances in the history of music equalled the furor which greeted the early works of Stravinsky. His multiple tonalities, bold dissonances and primitive rhythms confounded his listeners. For Stravinsky, as for Wagner and Debussy, dissonance was no longer a harmonic value which bridged one chord with another or facilitated a modulation from one key to another. Dissonance to these three composers meant the use of any chord in any possible way to get a desired musical effect. Rhythm was not a strict tempo but a beating pulse that was never constant and was always changing in rate. Stravinsky was only doing in a modified way, in his own century, what many a creative composer had done in the past centuries to express his musical feelings. Philosopher and critic, as usual, were not too quick in recognizing this. The Thomistic philosopher, Jacques Maritain, wrote after some years of reflection: "I regret having thus spoken of Stravinsky. All I had heard was *Le Sacre du Printemps*, and I should have perceived then that Stravinsky was turning his back on everything we find distasteful in Wagner. Since then he has shown that genius conserves and increases its strength by renewing it in light. Exuberant with truth, his admirably disciplined work teaches the best lesson of any to-day of grandeur and creative energy, and best answers the strict classical 'austerity' here in question. His purity, his authenticity, his glorious spiritual strength, are to the gigantism of Parsifal and the Tetralogy as a miracle of Moses to the enchantments of the Egyptians."[26]

For Béla Bartók (1881–1945), as for Stravinsky, each score was a unique work in itself, with a definite aesthetic concept of its own. Bartók did not compose according to any set system either of his own or others. The development of a musical idea and the aesthetic treatment of the development of that idea were the two necessary conditions in Bartók's philosophy of music. But Bartók, perhaps even more than Stravinsky, was unpredictable in how he might decide to develop a musical idea or what aesthetic concept he might devise to embody the idea within the context of the score, or in the treatment of the entire score itself. One thing is certain, each piece of music he created has a uniqueness that is all its own and is not an obvious carry over or a variation of a thematic idea or a reshaping of an aesthetic concept of something he had done before. Only a composer with an endless source of virile ideas, as Bartók was, could create in such a fashion. The clarity and distinctness of his entire output displays a disciplined musical mentality that gives forceful direction to his ideas and feelings.

The music of Bartók is a magnificently logical structure, each work in itself aesthetically creative, to be sure; but beyond its technical merits, which of itself offers the purist aesthetic enjoyment, it contains a powerful appeal to emotion. For Bartók and Stravinsky, the logical and structural unity of the work is as important as the emotional result is for the listener. It is a mistake, however, to think that either composer ever loses sight of the fundamental fact that music is primarily emotional in its appeal. Bartók tried to affect his listeners emotionally in the same way that he was affected himself, for example, by the folk-music of Hungary, Rumania and their neighbors. He was not interested in the sociological implications that the philosopher Herder read into such folk-music or in its literal connotations. Bartók was simply interested in these folk-tunes as musical expression and he tried to convey, in his own music, a musical

[26] *Art and Scholasticism*, p. 47; (Translated by J. F. Scanlan), Charles Scribner's Sons, New York: 1946.

idea, born of emotion to appeal to emotion, with a clarity and directness which is classic in spirit.

Paul Hindemith (1895) was one of the leading figures in a German movement known as Gebrauchsmusik in his early years as a composer. The term Gebrauchsmusik or "utility music" denoted a type of music which was written for general participation in contrast to music written "for its own sake". The adherents of the former viewpoint considered the musical needs of the masses while those with the latter viewpoint held the highly personalized credo of the earlier German romanticists. The leaders of the Gebrauchsmusik movement therefore emphasized the anti-romantic element in their music and by their own example helped to remove the musical virtuoso from the pedestal which he had mounted in the 19th century. The members of this movement tried to bring a type of music to the masses which they could understand and perform so that music would become a practical art to enhance the daily lives of the people. Gebrauchsmusik was characterized by forms of moderate length, a simplicity and clarity of style, small ensembles, and avoidance of technical difficulties so that it would be suitable for use by groups without professional training.

The Gebrauchsmusik movement was both a social and aesthetic reaction against romanticism. Because of the socialistic tendencies of the German Government after the First World War the reaction of the Gebrauchsmusik movement against the exaggerated individualism of late romanticism was received with favor. The Bach revival among the neo-classicists in the early part of the century also held an attraction for the vanguard element of Gebrauchsmusik. Not only did they try to acquire Bach's manner of musical directness, but they spoke of him as one of the early exponents of Gebrauchsmusik who labored to fulfill the musical needs of the people. The members of the Gebrauchsmusik movement pointed out that Bach did not write for an élite group, or a selected few, but for the entire congregation, the general public. He did not create at his own pleasure, if and when the spirit moved him, but labored from day to day, as any other craftsman, to fulfill his obligation to his society and church.

The Gebrauchsmusik movement eventually failed but Hindemith retained the aesthetic concepts of this movement in his later writings. Music has remained a craft for him, not a divinely inspired art.[27] Writing music is a constructive work; music is made, not drawn purely from inspiration, Hindemith would say, but he is quick to add that the creation of music begins with the emotions and its end function is to evoke the emotions.

Hindemith was at one time in the past also interested in the aesthetic views of Schönberg but he has since given up the twelve tone technique and has come to write music with decided tonality in the traditional sense. He is also the most outstanding of the 20th century composers in his interest in the pre-Bach composers and, more often than not, the complicated polyphony in his music is an emulation of the art of counterpoint in the 16th century, when music was a craft and not an art, when music was for the many and not the few.

---

[27] Igor Stravinsky said in his Harvard University lectures which are recorded in his *Poetics of Music*: "I shall not forget that I occupy a chair of *poetics*. And it is no secret to any of you that the exact meaning of poetics is the study of work to be done. The verb *poiein* from which the word is derived means nothing else but *to do* or *make*. The poetics of the classical philosophers did not consist of lyrical dissertations about natural talent and about the essence of beauty. For them the single word *techné* embraced both the fine arts and the useful arts and was applied to the knowledge and study of the certain and inevitable rules of the craft. That is why Aristotle's *Poetics* constantly suggest ideas regarding personal work, arrangement of materials, and structure. The poetics of music is exactly what I am going to talk to you about; that is to say, I shall talk about *making* in the field of music. Suffice it to say that we shall not use music as a pretext for pleasant fancies." p. 4; (Translated by Arthur Knodel and Ingolf Dahl), Harvard University Press, Cambridge: 1947.

Stravinsky classifies himself, in the Aristotelian sense, as one who makes or a maker. Stravinsky further develops the Aristotelian view that the means whereby he is able to convey his musical ideas into an art form has its roots in what Aristotle would call "wisdom" and "excellence" or technique.

CHAPTER 9

CRITERIA FOR AN AESTHETICS OF MUSIC

SECTION 1—*The Philosopher and the Musician*

THE philosophers have claimed, with rare exception, that the value of music lies in its effects. They have further reasoned that if the value of music lies in the effect which it produces upon the listener, then the proper function of music is not to convey pleasing sounds and rhythms which merely charm the senses, but to produce certain reactions in the listener that will mould him into a "good" man. The philosophers have maintained that if music offers us no more than fleeting pleasures and does not move us to do "good" deeds and become "better" men, then music is simply an idle pleasure; and so, therefore, wasteful of human effort that could well be spent in more virtuous ways. The philosophers have concluded that music should lead to "right action" otherwise it is only an opiate which enables us to flee reality and muse in a world of fancy.

The creative composer has generally shunned the ethical views of the philosopher with reference to music. The composer has lived by the aesthetic credo that the value of music does not lie in producing a "good" man or a "perfect" state but that the value of music is to be found in the sensuous tones and moving rhythms which please the senses and evoke emotions. The musician has always claimed that the proper function of music is to appeal to emotion; the philosopher has always been disdainful of music because it does not primarily appeal to reason. Thus the philosopher and the musician both agree that music primarily appeals to the emotions. The musician is only concerned in evoking the emotions for a pleasurable end. The philosopher insists that the emotion which music provokes should be of such a nature that it can be guided toward a good end, the moulding of character. The musician is interested in creating an aesthetic experience. The philosopher is concerned with an ethical result.

The composer has always striven by his music to produce in other minds the tonal sounds and impressions of the world about him. He is like Romain Rolland's Jean Christophe who translated his every experience into music. The composer does not primarily create music to appeal to the intellect; he does not write music to appeal to the moral sense; nor does he write music to instruct and edify. The composer creates his music to awaken the emotions.

Ben Jonson once said that "Art hath an enemy called ignorance." This wise observation has applied, and still does, to music more than to any other of man's creative activities in the fine arts. The sensual pleasure that we derive from musical tones and the physiological effect which musical rhythms have upon us have caused the philosopher, theologian and statesman to view music with misgiving and suspicion. They have shown contempt and awe for the creators of music. They have envied them their powers of expression throughout the ages and have condemned them in their fear and ignorance of what the powers of music might and might not do to the mind and body.

It often comes about that musicians who stood in their youth for the new ideas of their time, clung so tenaciously to these original ideas that they were unable to welcome succeeding ideas and became, in their later years, hardened reactionaries. There is no brushing aside of this factor, the history of music bears it out. But the philosophers, with few exceptions, as the history of philosophy shows, have engaged in what Whitehead referred to as adding variations to the original Platonic theme. This is undoubtedly more true of aesthetics, particularly with reference to music, than of any other phase of philosophic inquiry. The philosophers have not even bothered to be creative, even in their youth, in developing an aesthetics of music. They have simply spent their entire lives defending what Plato said about music.

The role which the philosopher has played in the history and development of music as an art is more to be condemned than praised. His logic chopping tendencies have impeded musical progress on the one hand; and on the other, his persistent questioning of musical values has influenced the aesthetic principles of the musicians themselves. The harm which the philosopher has done to music through the ages unfortunately outweighs the good; but he has many compatriots, in this respect, among the theologians and state guardians. These men of pure reason, faith and political action have, for the most part, kept music as a handmaid of a system, a religion or a state. The creative musician has been more free in certain cultures than he has been in others but Nietzsche, for all his bitterness, clearly saw that the musician has always been a slave of morality and religion. There have been few musicians in the past, and for that matter in the present, who could escape this condemnation.

Music of all the arts has been the most neglected and the least well defined in the writings of the philosophers. Various systematic schools of philosophy have nevertheless influenced musical thought; and new musical values have, in turn, anticipated philosophical trends. Music has been regarded by philosophers as a key to the understanding of the nature of the universe and as a mathematical preparation for the study of philosophy. The Platonists have described music as an imitation of reality and the Aristotelians have regarded the art of music as an idealization of reality. The theologians have looked upon music as a means of bringing man closer to God through the musical embellishment of the Holy Text. Music has been regarded by the theologian and philosopher alike as a means of improving or corrupting morals. The philosophers have considered music as either a mere sensual pleasure or great spiritual force, and as a therapeutic for the body and soul of man.

We have seen that our earliest knowledge of music in Western civilization stems from the writings of the Greek philosophers. We have also been made aware that it is in the Platonic writings particularly that we find a synthesis of the musical ideologies of East and West. Here, the ethical and psychological values of music are explained in terms of metaphysics. The rhythmic element in music is presumably fashioned after the universal rhythm. Erratic rhythms and a cacophony of dissonant tonalities cause the human soul to clash with the ideal order of things. Plato thus began to construct his musical aesthetics by attributing morality to the Greek modes. He regarded music as being superior to the other arts on the premise that rhythm and harmony more strongly affect the inner soul and emotional life of man than architecture, painting and sculpture. Music, therefore, should be utilized to temper behavior, mould character, and discipline the intellect for the noble study of philosophy. Melodic invention or separation of the lyric from the song, in the Platonic system, were manifestations of restlessness which menaced traditional values and threatened the status quo.

Aristotle retained the Platonic theories of music and Plotinus echoed them with profound admiration. Augustine began work on his *De Musica* in true Platonic fashion with a consideration of music as a discipline in preparation for philosophic study; and, the musical doctrines of Boethius, at least those that were written at the beginning of his literary career, were, like Augustine's of a Platonic nature. Descartes also retained the Platonic notion that music is essentially mathematical and should be used as a discipline in preparation for the study of philosophy. Like Plato and Aristotle, he spoke of musical affections and attributed moral values to rhythms since they have a direct effect upon the human soul. He therefore suggested the desirability of rhythms which do not enervate or overexcite the passions. He stressed the use of simple ratios for tonal intervals and, in echoing a Platonic complaint, he decried the incongruity of musical tonalities which the composers of his day were employing in contrapuntal techniques. Leibniz described music as a manifestation of the universal rhythm whose very essence consists of number and relation. However music may charm us, Leibniz held, "its beauty only consists in the harmony of numbers."

Music is an unconscious counting or felt relationship of numbers arranged in pleasing intervals and tonal patterns. Rousseau believed that since art is an imitation of nature, it logically follows that music is a copy of the universal rhythm pervading the universe. If man were therefore exposed to the proper musical rhythms he could learn to live in accordance with natural law and become one with nature.

Kant also agreed with Plato that through music "we can reach the body through the soul and use the latter as the physician of the former." His aesthetics also shows a contempt for wordless music. Purely instrumental music had little value for him, for he considered it free and fanciful and not expressive of a definite concept. In Kantian aesthetics, poetry is the art which most appeals to reason, since words are the natural medium of expression for concepts and ideas. It then becomes the function of poetry, added Hegel, in elaborating this view, to impose words upon sounds, ideas upon feelings, concepts upon spiritual affinities, so that what is musically vague and indefinite will become more articulate in the language of the poet. But Schopenhauer and Nietzsche took exception to this bit of dialectic by insisting that melody had a right to exist by itself independent of the spoken word. Nietzsche further agreed with Schopenhauer that music offers an escape, an interlude of peace. But whereas music fosters a transition from will to vision, from desire to contemplation in Schopenhauer, music in the aesthetics of Nietzsche enables us to transcend our crude and chaotic world and enter into a transfigured one expressive of our desires and hopes. Tolstoy differed with this notion of artistic escapism and formulated an aesthetics that became one with Christian ethics.

In our own century only a few philosophers have had anything to say about music. What they have written is only a gratuitous acknowledgment of the existence of music. They have shown little interest in its place and function in society. They have not even been concerned with it as a provocative form of communication between man and man. It is not that they wash their hands of the subject of music, but only that the philosophers of our day mistrust feeling more than they guard reason. Philosophers in the 20th century envy the scientist more than they do the artist. They are disdainful of aesthetic theory since they derive little satisfaction from applying positivistic methods of evaluation to the composer's work.

Of the philosophers who have written about music in the 20th century, the Frenchman, Henri Bergson (1859–1941), included music as just another member of the art family which gives man a more direct vision of reality. Music, in the aesthetics of Bergson, "has no other object than to brush aside the utilitarian symbols, the conventional and socially accepted generalities, in short, everything that veils reality from us, in order to bring us face to face with reality itself."[1] He declared in a cryptic passage in *Time and Free Will* that "If musical sounds affect us more powerfully than the sounds of nature, the reason is that nature confines itself to *expressing* feelings, whereas music *suggests* them to us."[2] Bergson's English contemporary, Gilbert K. Chesterton (1874–1936), tied the art of music to the historical struggles and evolution of man and society. He did not share Bergson's mystical notion that music could bring man closer to the true reality but regarded music as a subjective expression of feeling and emotive states.[3] The German, Oswald Spengler, considered music as a facet of our culture which he visualized as being foredoomed in our own time to decay because of the senility of Western Culture. "It is all irretrievably over with the arts of the West," he wrote. "What is practiced as art today is impotence and falsehood: a faked music, filled with artificial noisiness of massed instruments." He gloomily predicted that for the Western world there can no longer be any question of great

[1] Melvin M. Rader, *A Modern Book of Esthetics*, p. 183; Henry Holt and Co., New York: 1935.

[2] p. 15; (Translated by F. L. Pogson), George Allen and Unwin Ltd., London: 1928.

[3] G. K. Chesterton, *Heretics*, p. 90; The Bodley Head Ltd., London: 1905.

"When men were tough and raw, when they lived amid hard knocks and hard laws, when they knew what fighting really was, they had only two kinds of songs. The first was a rejoicing that the weak had conquered the strong, the second a lamentation that the strong had, for once in a way, conquered the weak. For this defiance of the *statu quo*, this constant effort to alter the existing balance, this premature challenge to the powerful, is the whole nature and inmost secret of the psychological adventure which is called man."

music for "We are today playing out a tedious game with dead forms to keep up the illusion of a living art."

The American philosopher David Wright Prall (1886–1940) would have agreed that "If a composer has no emotions to express, no vital feelings to externalize in sound, the best that he can do is to repeat more or less conventional or banal patterns, . . ."[4] But he would hardly have agreed with Spengler that the music of the Western world in the 20th century is a declining art which is beyond redeeming. Prall saw in the music of our century an art which could heighten the sensual pleasures and deepen the intellectual life of man, for, of all the arts, he wrote, "perhaps music is in the matter of emotional expressiveness the deepest and richest, of the widest range and greatest power, as well as the most flexible . . ."[5] Of the remaining American philosophers, Santayana (1863–1952) cynically lamented that "Music is essentially useless as life is: . . ." and "What most people relish is hardly music;" he wrote, "it is rather a drowsy revery relieved by nervous thrills."[6] John Dewey (1859–1952) created an intellectual universe without immutable truths or fixed beliefs of beauty and goodness and saw fit to view all musical ideals as mere hypotheses to be forever tested by individual experience.

To evaluate the role which the philosophers have played in directly or indirectly influencing the course of musical history we need only recall that what appeared as mere aesthetic theory in the Platonic writings became an artistic actuality in early

---

[4] *Aesthetic Judgment,* p. 216; The Thomas Y. Crowell Co., New York: 1929. The Italian philosopher Croce (1866-1952) would agree with Prall on this point. To a would-be composer who laments that he could move the world if he were only able to express what he feels, Croce would in turn aptly answer that he either does not feel deeply enough or the feeling is too meager to be expressed. A composer who has anything to say, according to Croce, will say it by one means or another, one form or another. Croce also says that art dies in the artist who becomes a critic. The composer Schönberg found this to be true in his own experience that in the moment when the composer writes criticisms he is not a composer for he is not musically inspired. "If he were inspired he would not describe how the piece ought to be composed, but would compose it himself."
Style and Idea, p. 3; Philosophical Library, New York: 1950.

[5] D. W. Prall, *Op. cit.,* 214.

[6] *Reason and Art,* pp. 45, 51; *The Life of Reason,* Charles Scribner's Sons, New York: 1922.

Christianity. The Church fathers ethically distinguished between sacred and secular strains, between Christian and pagan tunes. Through music the illiterate Christian could be taught the Holy Text, even if it required an aesthetic marriage between an infectious pagan tune and a Scriptural passage. The Church fathers thwarted new musical tendencies lest some Roman or Hebraic influence disturb the spiritual simplicity of Christian life and worship, and the leaders of the Reformation reiterated these musical tendencies to protect their own faith, rather than profiting from the aesthetic fallacies of the Mother Church.

Boethius was another philosopher who profoundly influenced the history of music. What he actually tried to accomplish was the reconciliation of the moralistic strain in Plato with his own interpretation of the scientific one in Aristotle. His untimely death did not permit him to complete this work, but it was carried out by the medieval musicians who created the Boethian legend which reverted to the Pythagorean theme that if music is to imitate the harmony of the spheres then musical composition must be as precise as the laws which govern the celestial bodies. Morality in music thus became dependent on science, and the science of music eventually resulted in stereotyped forms.

Rousseau was disdainful of composers who wrote music without words or employed complex polyphony. He attempted to correct both of these aesthetic shortcomings, much to the regret of those of us who are in a position to reflect upon the historical developments that followed, by abolishing the French music drama for a lyric play with music in the manner of the Italians.

Tolstoy envisioned the art of the future as rooted in feeling which would draw mankind toward a common union of understanding and action. He hoped that the ideal of excellence in the music of the future would "not be the exclusiveness of feeling, accessible only to some, but on the contrary, its universality". We need only compare these views with modern Soviet musical criticism to become aware of the impact which Tolstoy unwittingly had upon the musical philosophy of the USSR.

Aristoxenus, the pupil of Aristotle, was the first of the philosophers to formulate an aesthetics of music based on humanistic values. He tried to shy away from the moral issues and purely mathematical interpretations of music to which both Plato and Aristotle held. He believed that sense and reason, the power to hear and the ability to discriminate should enable one to judge for himself whether a given piece of music is good or not. He refused to accept the view that any preconceived systematic metaphysics, or traditional doctrine of morality, or Pythagorean reduction of musical tonalities to mathematics, are in themselves valid criteria for an evaluation of music.

The greater number of philosophers who came after Aristoxenus nevertheless defined music within their respective systems in terms of a metaphysics, moral value, or both; or again, as purely mathematical. But with the passing of time, philosophers have come to give up the picturesque analogy between the element of rhythm in music and the harmony of the spheres. They have also drawn away from viewing music simply as a structure of numbers arranged in such mathematical fashion as to produce a unique series of tonalities. Philosophers no longer attempt to explain pleasing or consonant tonalities as proper numerical ratios and dissonant tonalities as improper. They have become all too aware that consonance and dissonance are contrasts of musical sounds that are wholly relative in aesthetic value. But, of the ancient trinity of metaphysics, mathematics and ethics, the last of the three is still very much with us.

In the religious realm, the Church still differentiates in an ethical sense between good and bad music; and in the social realm, the Soviets determine the musical value of a composition on the basis of whether it is in keeping with sound political ideology. Theoretically, at least, the very nature of a Democracy such as ours would presumably exclude even the last of this trinity, ethics, as a valid criterion for an aesthetic judgment. The composer in America can be thoroughly individualistic, as the Soviets point out, live in social isolation, and create music wholly personalized so that it is meaningful only for a select few. He can, paradoxically, be the most undemocratic in a democratic state; but if he is in the service of an authoritarian church or a member of a totalitarian state, he is philosophically compelled to create for the greatest good of the greatest number, as that good is conceived by the leaders of the church or state.

SECTION II—*The Meaning and Nature of Music*

THE concept of musical meaning has a twofold significance in modern aesthetics. On the one hand, music which is produced in the democratic world is judged and evaluated in terms of formal values. On the other hand, music which is produced in those areas of the world under Soviet dominance is judged and evaluated in terms of ideological soundness. In the former, the musical work does not necessarily strive for clarity of meaning, but confines itself to the communication of a mood. In the latter, the musical work strives for clarity and simplicity; form is effective only if it intensifies a "realistic" presentation of the content. Music in the democracies is therefore limited in meaning and subjective in evaluation because of the formal treatment which the composer gives to his musical ideas or content. Music in the Soviet dominated countries, to be ideologically sound, must be clear in meaning so that it will be generally comprehensible.

The poet Longfellow called music the universal language of mankind. But what is there that is universal about music? A musical score that has cultural familiarity for one group of people will, in a general sense, produce certain effects upon that group that it cannot produce upon another. The rhythmic pulse, the tonal system, are musical patterns and sounds to which one group is conditioned and another is not. The same piece of music cannot mean the same thing to two different groups, let alone to two different people. It is true that we can enjoy the music of the East and Near East with a vicarious pleasure and that we can derive aesthetic satisfaction from such music, but only if it bears some similarity to our own music. Music which is alien to us both intellectually and culturally can hardly draw an emotional response from us. The music must have some common tones or styles which approximate our own otherwise it brings up nothing from our background of experience, demands nothing from our immediate apprehension. A new style or tonal system even in our own civilization requires, as Voltaire said, almost the passing of an entire generation before it is acceptable. But in this respect, music is not a lone art.

Walt Whitman wrote: "All music is what awakens from you when you are reminded by the instruments." Here music is not a universal language. Music is not a metaphysics. It is not an art conceived of a priori forms. It is we who give music its existence. Music remains nothing but rhythm and sound unless we endow these phenomena with psychic enrichment. The form, the rhythm, the tonal patterns, can only mean to me what I understand them to be. I can only get from a rendition of a score what I bring to it in understanding and emotional susceptibility. I may be moved emotionally even when I cannot discern the meaning of the musical symbols but my aesthetic satisfaction does not go beyond the emotional level. I may not be sufficiently tutored in music to even know whether the music is properly rendered. There is furthermore no empirical gauge by which I can even know whether I have recaptured the original mood which the composer intended me to have on hearing his music. But one thing is certain: the more I know about the music, the more appreciative can I be of its merits, the more critical of its rendition and the more profoundly affected by a stirring performance. Musical literacy does not diminish aesthetic appreciation. The understanding of a musical selection does not lessen the intensity of the emotional experience which that music can offer. To know that a musical rendition is being rendered in the spirit of the composer, that the difficult passages are being executed with consummate skill, that none of the nuances are lost, only heightens the satisfaction and intensifies the emotions. A musical knowledge will also work the other way round; enlightenment carries no guarantee of a constant state of happiness in matters of music or life.

The musical purist would scoff at the idea that music is a universal language or that music is what the instruments awaken in me. He would be more apt to take the view that music is an art which possesses inherent qualities that exist independent of my awareness of them. It is these intrinsic qualities in the music that make it a work of art for all time and in all places in his judgment. Cultural familiarity is not a necessary prerequisite to understanding the music of other cultures, he would continue. Feeling for rhythm, and sensitivity to tone are the only requirements necessary to appreciate music in our culture or any other. He would argue further that the appreciation and enjoyment of music is not a democratic activity. He would agree with Schönberg and Stravinsky that serious music is not for the masses but for the fortunate few who are sufficiently tutored and are sensitive enough to derive an aesthetic experience from such music.

What is music? Perhaps if we could say what music is not, we shall come closer to defining what it is. First, it is not an imitation of the harmony of the spheres. The Pythagoreans believed that all bodies in motion produce sounds and the heavenly bodies are no exceptions. The ancient teachers taught that these sounds were imperceptible to human ears for various reasons, but the Pythagoreans and the Jews claimed that their respective leaders alone could hear this celestial music. The scientific advances of the 20th century have, in some measure, brought the sounds of the would-be harmony of the spheres to us which the movement of the stars produce while in motion, but rather than being a celestial harmony, it sounds more like plain cacophony to modern ears.

The Pythagoreans also set forth the thesis, which Plato accepted, that the intervals between the planets and the spheres of fixed stars corresponded mathematically to the intervals between the notes of the octave. We do not have any empirical evidence to warrant this notion that the Greek modes or our own system of scales is so constructed that the relationship of one tone to another corresponds to the relationship of one planet to another. The theory of the harmony of the spheres and the theory of co-ordination remain ancient myth which cannot tell us what music is, although they attempt to tell us from whence it emanates and why it is constructed as it is.

Secondly, music is not an expression of morality or immorality. Music cannot be good or bad in an ethical sense, no more than it can be gay or sad in itself. The music may be of such a character that it conveys a gay or sad mood which the composer experienced. The manner in which the mood was musically formalized and produced may be good or bad, but good or bad not in an ethical sense, but as an aesthetic judgment. Aristotle claimed that like begets like. He was convinced that there is good and bad music in a moral sense as Plato was before him. Good music could mould the human soul just as bad music could corrupt the soul. There is no denying that certain types of music have different effects on its listeners. In that respect Aristotle cannot be refuted. But Aristotle is not justified, any more than Plato was, in attributing moral qualities to the Greek modes themselves because of the character of their construction and application. Aristotle was also not justified, to our way of thinking, in maintaining that a bad man, in a moral sense, can only beget evil music. Since Plato and he made no distinction between the ethical and the aesthetic they saw no contradiction in their position.

The sensual pleasure we derive from musical tones and the physiological effect the rhythms have upon us can instill a variety of moods in us. But it is doubtful whether Boethius was justified either in saying that a man who delights in hearing "indecent melodies, and one who listens to them frequently will be weakened thereby and lose his virility of soul". It is equally doubtful whether music has the power to make man good or bad as the poet Milton claimed in the 17th century.

We could not deny that many immoral composers have created great music which has elevated those that have come in contact with their music. We could not deny that Wagner was a detestable creature, who was a law to himself. But who could deny the genius of his powers, the wonders of his music? We must divorce the creator from his creation, whether we like it or not and as difficult as it may be in our present world. Music is good or bad only in an aesthetic sense but not in an ethical one. Music is an expression of feeling. The feeling in itself may be evaluated in ethical terms but once the feeling is expressed in music it is no longer personal but impersonal. It is no longer personal fancy but objectified art. Actions are judged in terms of ethics and art is judged in terms of aesthetics. The aesthetics of music has a direct relation to life. It is not concerned with censures that society imposes upon man but with the free expression of man. It is not interested in the social approval or disapproval of human feelings but the expression of those feelings.

Thirdly, music cannot be political or religious in itself. What is called religious music is music that is written to induce worship and therefore it has to be appropriate for the purpose for which it is created. Şuch music contains certain qualities which the church authorities insist on, such as simplicity, clarity and the embellishment of the Holy Text. What the composer may feel to be religious in character may or may not be acceptable to the religious authorities. Music for devotion is what the religious hierarchy think it ought to be. Just as the priests of religion guide us in matters of faith, so they approve or disapprove of music for worship. They believe that certain music will help intensify the religious experience and other music will detract from furthering the religious end.

When we speak of sacred and secular music, we separate a type of music which we consider suitable for religious needs from all other music. Religious music can have its origin in a number of sources. It may have been written specifically for divine worship or it may have been of a secular character originally which, in later years, was taken over into the Service of worship. Some of the most religiously moving music is based on folk-tunes that were once disapproved of by the priests of religion, Jewish, Catholic and Protestant. The stigma of immorality and banality has often fallen away from some earlier music when it was modified and applied to religious devotion. Succeeding generations came to know this music only in its sacred context so that through the centuries this music has taken on traditional meaning for us which we associate with worship and holy seasons. The "immoral" songs of earlier centuries, the "banal" tunes of a yesteryear, for the most part, remain just that, if they survive at all.

Music in itself cannot be political either, as Goethe insisted. Schumann's aphorism that the plans for a revolution could be written into the score of a symphony and the police would be none the wiser is highly romantic. Schumann was less romantic in pointing out to the Czar of Russia, who invaded Chopin's

Poland, that in the mazurkas of this Polish patriot were musical strains that would incite the people to revolt against their oppressors. We have come to associate certain musical strains with patriotism and political action. This music may be traditional or purposely written to fire the patriotism of the citizens. Chopin's music may have had such meaning for the Poles, Verdi's certainly did for the Italian revolutionists, but the music is not patriotic in itself, it only engenders and incites a mood of patriotism. It is what we associate with the music that causes us to call this type of music political and that type religious. The former may be quick in tempo, fiery in spirit, loud in brass and cymbals; the latter may be subdued and serene, or plaintive and aspiring. The music is apt to do one thing or the other to us, but only because such rhythms and tones have a cultural significance for us that moves us emotionally in one respect or the other.

Fourthly, music is not mathematics alone. It is essentially mathematical in structure but music is more than mathematics. The theoretician may reduce the composer's intuitive use of tonal combinations to mathematics but the theorist does not attempt, and, even if he tried, could not explain why the composer chose the combinations he did. The composer is consciously aware that certain groups of tones lend themselves to the expression of certain feelings, but the composer does not rationally deduce that certain mathematical relationships, in the use of tonal groups, will give him a desired effect. He either uses traditional tonal patterns, sometimes to extremes, such as the composers of the Baroque and Renaissance used in their musical affections to express feelings in a stereotyped manner, or he creates new tonal combinations for the occasion to say what he wishes or has to say. If music were mathematics and mathematics only, then music would become a science, as exacting as mathematics itself, in which the composer could express moods in precisely standardized ways rather than remain an art in which the emotions are uniquely expressed. Nevertheless, practically all the composers of the past, and present, who have had anything new to say in a non-traditional way, have been accused of reducing music to mathematics.

Fifthly, music is not an imitation of an inherent order of

musical sounds in nature. The original constructors of our musical system were of the belief that there is such an a priori order of sounds in nature and they may well have believed that they were simply imitating these natural sounds in music. Our music is based on a science of acoustics which began with the empirical investigations of the Pythagoreans, was improved on by Aristoxenus and developed centuries later by Zarlino, Rameau and Bach. All of these to a lesser or greater degree thought of their music as a copy of a prearranged order of sounds in nature and tried to explain their systems according to natural law. But there is no such order of sounds in nature. There are no dominant sevenths or minor thirds in nature as Hanslick points out. Quite often, new music to which our ears has not been conditioned and which is particularly disturbing has been and still is called unnatural as though the composer were blaspheming against a sacred tonal order in nature.

What is music, if it is not metaphysics, not mathematics, not ethics, not politics or religion—what indeed is it then? It is all of these and more. It is what the poet Whitman said the instruments awaken in you. It is the experience of everyday life but it transcends experience. It is a tonal echo of our dreams and our hopes, our strife and our sadness. It is a rhythmically compelling art which can penetrate the innermost parts of the body and rule the mind, as the ancient philosophers well knew. It is patterns of tones arranged in forms in prescribed tempos with which we associate the whole gamut of human feeling. It is precisely what we ourselves bring to tones and rhythms, what these tones and rhythms awaken in us, that enables yet another poet to say "The tune is . . . In thee!"

Music is feeling embodied in rhythmic and tonal symbols. But we must never think of these symbols as music itself, otherwise we mistake the symbol for what the symbol actually represents. Music is what the performer produces in tones and tempos on his instrument. Music is essentially melody and rhythm which stirs our emotions and kindles our imagination. Music is, above all, what we psychically endow these melodies and rhythms with from our own experience, hopes and aspirations. Music is, to our civilization, a cultural phenomenon through which one man communicates his emotions to others in a form more emotionally provocative than any other art form. Music cannot laugh or cry. Music is not sad or gay. Certain tones and rhythms awaken feelings which are akin to a mood of gaiety or sadness. The music is what it is for me, gay or sad, only if it can call up from within me such feelings. It is I who associate this mood or that mood with this rhythm or that tone. It is I who attribute human values and meaning to musical sounds and movement.

Music begins with the composer whose musical moods and ideas are conveyed to us usually by a performer. Music thus differs from most other arts for we, the listeners, are at least twice removed from the intentions and desires of the composer. We may marvel at the musical powers of our performers, but they are recreators and not creators. They are lesser artists, in their own right, who convey the composer's moods and ideas to us. In painting and sculpture, there is some empirical basis for making a judgment of a copy of an original because the pictorial and plastic arts offer tangible evidence for evaluation, but in music, only feeling can remain our guide.

SECTION III—*A Philosophy of Musical Values*

AESTHETICS is that branch of philosophy which is concerned with the study of artistic values, just as ethics is concerned with right action, metaphysics with ultimate principles, epistemology with theories of knowledge, and logic with the proper use of knowledge in reason. Each of these five divisions of philosophy is a specialized field of study, and each of these is a facet of a general system of thought. The ancient and medieval philosophers considered the beautiful and the ugly, the comic and the tragic, the pretty and the sublime, as part of their over-all philosophic position. A philosopher's conception of the beautiful is the product of his basic analysis of the nature of the universe and of the role man plays in the universe. In the idealistic explanation of the world which Plato gave, we saw that music was described as an imitation of an abstract ideal, an echo of universal harmonies. In the philosophy of Sextus Empiricus, music was more naturally defined as a form of human expression, and nothing more. Philosophic idealists and philosophic naturalists in our day are splintered into groups whose views range from the extreme right to the extreme left. However varied the shades of intellectual differences may be within the two groups, philosophers in the 20th century basically fall into one of these schools of thought or the other. In the past as in the present, whatever the philosophers have had to say about music, from the time of Plato to that of Dewey, has been based on idealism or naturalism and what they have had to say has influenced the intellectual and artistic life of man throughout the history of Western civilization.

The man who bases his aesthetic values of music on philosophical idealism is apt to extol the rational faculties over the sensory ones. He may overemphasize the importance of reason in aesthetic matters and minimize emotion. His values will rest on the idealist's premise that the world is divided into spirit and matter, soul and body, and that the natural laws which regulate the material body cannot govern the spiritual soul. He is likely to regard the composer and the metaphysician as coworkers who strive to unfold the "true" reality to man through music and philosophy. The metaphysician and musician will bring us closer to the ideal, the universal. They will guide us toward the spiritual realm with the aid of philosophy and permit us a fleeting glimpse of universal beauty through music.

Systems of musical aesthetics based on philosophic idealism have throughout Western history accounted for the origin of music in terms of metaphysics, the meaning of music in terms of teleology and the nature of music in terms of ethics. Idealists consider music to be the sensuous embodiment of an idea in musical tones and rhythms. It is not beyond them, even in the present, to maintain that music can improve or degrade the morals of men. There are some idealists who think that music is a gratuitous blessing which a beneficent God bestowed upon mankind to help him bear his earthly lot.

The idealist has an objective criterion of values. He maintains that music possesses certain qualities that make it good or bad. We may err in our evaluation of certain music. We may also come to change our minds and develop different tastes through

the years, but it is we who change in our interpretation of these values. The values themselves remain constant, insists the idealist, for beauty in music, just as truth and goodness is the third member of the eternal trinity.

The philosophic naturalist does not share the idealist's penchant for dualities. It is unlikely that a man who bases his aesthetic values on philosophic naturalism would share the idealist's enthusiastic view that music unfolds "higher truths" or enables the listener to intuitively bridge the gap between the "real" and the "unreal". He is content to regard music as an expression of human emotion rather than a sensuous embodiment of a spiritual idea. He does not believe that finite beings can achieve a state of exultation through music that will make them one with the infinite. There is little doubt that the naturalist and the idealist experience the same kind of emotions in listening to music. The difference is that both men frame their personal response to music according to the fundamental conception which they hold philosophically. Whereas the idealist mystically ascribes spiritual significance to the aesthetic experience, the naturalist empirically replies that the aesthetic experience affords us momentary release from our immediate surroundings, escape from our trials and tribulations, and gives us time to refresh ourselves or exhaust ourselves with a new experience that adds variety to our lives and more meaning to our living.

The philosophic naturalist envisions the world in terms of perpetual change. He does not accept the idealist's reasoning that the beautiful in music means that the composition contains inherent qualities that are absolute in nature and are independent of the subjective interpretation of the listener. The followers of naturalism do not explain music in terms of transcendental metaphysics or teleology or ethics. They are only too well aware that music affects human behavior, but they find no conceivable tie between the expression of human emotion in melody and rhythm, and Divine Will and universal goodness. The naturalists believe that music is one more form of expression, which man devised in his evolutionary development, through which he communicates his feelings and thoughts and that man therefore is the sole judge of the worth and merit of the music that he creates or appreciates. If, however, a man is ignorant of the elemental nature and structure of music, if the music remains varied tones and rhythms that please the senses and nothing more, then he is quite apt to make false idols of the musical connoisseurs and hold the professional music critic as the voice of the Delphic Oracle. Ignorance in music, as ignorance in a general sense, produces fear of the unknown, superstition and idolatrous worship.

It is possible to devise a system of aesthetic values that is based on certain views from both idealism and naturalism. People who find it desirable to maintain an eclectic set of musical values try to form their system out of those specific points in aesthetic idealism and aesthetic naturalism that appeal to them personally. An eclectic system of musical values may therefore evolve into little more than the equivalent of a musical potpourri but it can also develop into a self-asserting endeavor in which the listener tries to employ the most logical group of values to changing musical styles for the most aesthetically reliable measure of musical worth.

There is another type of individual who insists that he has no philosophy of life or music. A man who reacts to a completed rendition of a musical score by saying: "I like what I like and I don't care why", is expressing a philosophy of music even though he may think that he is denying one. It is not a philosophy that most of us agree with for this kind of personal reaction to music, without rational evaluation, is extremely primitive and minimizes man's rational powers of introspection and reflection. The man who is indifferent to any factors beyond the pleasure which music will afford him stifles his full capabilities as a human being.

The somewhat more sophisticated music listener who romantically says "that the ineffable sense of delight which I receive from music is verbally inexpressible" is deluding himself psychologically. Man is a rational being as well as an emotional animal. If such a listener means that the emotional intensity of the aesthetic experience cannot be conveyed to another person verbally with full justice, then he is on safe grounds. The aesthetic experience is a personal experience that cannot be imparted to another with any assurance that it will convey the same emotional impact. But if he means that the aesthetic experience is a unique affair of the emotions that must not be analyzed lest it lose its effect, then he is confining his music appreciation purely to a sensory level.

The music listener may well become enraptured with tonal beauty and rhythmic patterns of movement. Nothing but the ecstatic delight which the music provokes in him should be of value for the moment, for that is the nature of the aesthetic experience. But upon reflection, this listener ought to try to understand why he felt as he did. What was there in the structure and interpretation of the music that could bring on this state of exultation? It is absurd to reason that to analyze the aesthetic experience is to destroy it. It is fantastic to think that the more we try to learn why we react as we do to rhythm and melody the more we diminish its effect upon us. Knowledge does not curb emotion, knowledge refines emotion.

It is only because we are a musically illiterate people that the role of the music critic in our society has such an importance. The critic holds his high office because we are so woefully lacking in the rudiments of musical theory. Most of us cannot understand what the composer is saying for very few of us can read or write simple music and although many of us are amateur performers of a sort, we lack self-assurance in forming a personal judgment of a conductor's rendition of a classic score. We take refuge therefore in the authority of the critic who tells us what is being said and how it is being said.

The professional critic in our day has a cultural duty to perform. His free and often vitriolic criticisms are not only a symbol of a free society and unfettered art but his usual negativism is essential for musical progress even if he has been more wrong than right in anticipating trends and evaluating music. It is foolish to think, as some people actually do, that he could be dispensed with altogether. But it is true that as we develop greater perceptual powers to fathom the composer's music, we become more independent in our own judgment and less dependent on the decisions of the critic. His role of authority lessens as we become more enlightened.

The music critic who lives under the banner of Fascism or Communism would have only scorn for an aesthetics of music based on humanistic values. He would label it as a romanticized system of aesthetics which can only destroy itself in emphasizing individual freedom and ignoring the total needs of the citizenry. He would point out that the relation of the individual to the state in an authoritarian government cannot tolerate personal judgments or the whims of "cliques" that question social policy or deride Central Committee resolutions on matters of criticism.

The totalitarian structure of Fascism based its musical values, at least in Nazi Germany, on racial distinctions. Hitler simply decided that Mendelssohn's music must be "verboten". Mendelssohn was a Jew, ranted Hitler, and Jews cannot write music the equal of Aryans. "We Aryans are a superior race", he continued, and therefore Mendelssohn's Semitic music is inferior. Only a mad dictator could propose such logic and deduce from its false premise the musical value of a composer's output on the basis of a pseudo-racial distinction.

The more benign social philosophy of Leo Tolstoy is no less of a threat to a humanistic system of aesthetics than that of an authoritarian state or totalitarian dictator. Tolstoy's self-imposed mission to establish a society based on Christian precepts led him to evaluate all music with an evangelical spirit that equalled the ardor of the Church fathers. He excluded practically all the classic works from his ideal order on the basis that they were too complex to be universally understood and therefore lacked the infectious simplicity that would bind all men together. The little music that he did retain to aid him in fostering this brotherhood and the music which he rejected because it fell short of his fanatical mission leaves one, upon reflection, with amazement and wonder. The severity with which he decided which music is suitable to establish the Kingdom of God on earth turned him from a master of literature into a musical fool.

Tolstoy thought well of some Bach arias and certain parts from the music of Haydn, Mozart and Schubert. He viewed the music of Chopin with favor ". . . (when his melodies are not overloaded with complications and ornamentation) . . ." He liked some of Beethoven's early music, but he rejected the music of the later period as "shapeless improvizations". The *Ninth Symphony*, the posthumous quartets, which are perhaps the greatest music that any mortal has ever written, and the piano sonatas of his last period, particularly opus 101, are ridiculed as exclusive and too complex for Christian needs. The music of Wagner, Liszt, Berlioz, Brahms, and Richard Strauss are rejected completely.

The dogmatic certainty with which Tolstoy cast aside the musical scores of these composers should give us good cause to ponder over the cultural dangers that can be created by philosophers, statesmen and theologians who apply absolutist standards of evaluation to musical criticism. Just as soon as the philosopher supposes that he has found a final and comprehensive solution to the nature of the universe, the meaning of life and the validity of human values, he then ceases to be a Socratic inquirer and becomes enmeshed in apologetics or propaganda. The very moment that a music critic produces an all embracing formula which must conform to theological or political principles, then he too becomes an apologist for a faith, a propagandist for a cause.

There are no absolute truths or final judgments. Values are not eternal, they are perpetually born. There is no omniscient critic to whom we can look for an ultimate answer in musical values. It is unfortunate that so many among us wait on the word of the critic so as to know how to think about this music or that concert. It is a pity that these people choose to be led rather than enlightened and guided. Some of these same people would disagree or even become righteously indignant with the leading critic of a metropolitan newspaper on the merits of a controversial book. These very literate readers would accept the review of the music editor of the same paper without question or challenge.

There are also some among us who stand in awe of the musical intelligentsia who make a fetish of the unusual and discuss Erik Satie with existential reverence. We must pay no heed either to the claim of the self-styled intellectuals who categorically state that chamber music is the choice of the aesthetic purist and opera is the popular entertainment of the masses. A person who is deeply moved by a good performance of a Schubert Quintet can be equally affected by a Puccini aria that is well done. Only a person who is insensitive to the values of others would be scornful of popular musical forms.

We must also humor those extremists who will only listen to Renaissance madrigals or Baroque concerti and be disdainful of any music that has been written since the death of Bach. There is no harm in being particularly drawn to a certain period of music because the forms and tonal timbre of the instruments have a unique personal appeal. Such emphasis on the historical past can become misguided however if a person develops into a specialist in one period of music and remains deaf to the music of other periods. By the same token, the man who absurdly believes that the music of the past is inferior to the music of the present needs some reorientation. There is just as much aesthetic satisfaction to be gained from a Corelli violin solo as there is from the closing death scene in *Tristan and Isolde*. The simple beauty of Corelli's music offers us a serene aesthetic experience and the impassioned music which Wagner wrote for the final scene of this overpowering music-drama gives us a feeling of sensuous ecstasy. Both types of music serve their purpose. One type creates what Nietzsche called an Apollonian mood and the other a Dionysian frenzy. Both are necessary to human life.

Critics of a short while back, such as Hanslick and Busoni, and a rare philosopher like Herbart believed that music has no meaning beyond itself. These men reacted against romanticism by declaring that music was an autonomous art. We have such purists in our midst too who are intent on keeping music pristine pure, free of psychological implications, sociological trends and moral issues. They believe that the aesthetics of music should be confined to the analysis of the formal values in a score and to nothing else. Their premise is that music, as Hanslick said, is the expression of musical ideas. Music which excites the passions and ignores the intellect, only partially fulfills its function of appealing to the whole man. Music which appeals more strongly to the emotions than the intellect would, following this line of neo-Platonism, appeal to the primitive, the baser elements in man. The ideal music, aesthetically speaking, would be an arrangement and distribution of formal values in a manner so effective as to accomplish the complete task of pleasing the emotions and stimulating the intellect. No one could disagree with this aesthetic ideal. But many of us do take exception to the purist's emphasis on the intellectual and the lack of emphasis on the emotional in the aesthetic experience.

Musical analysis of the formal values in a voluminous symphonic score or a simple Lied is only a facet of aesthetics. Melody, rhythm, harmony, and form are the essential musical values. The melodic line, the thematic development, the rhythmic changes, the harmonic and formal structure of a musical composition are of primary concern to the performer and conductor. The ability to discern the formal relationships of these values to each other, the ability to appreciate the integration of these values into a composite musical form, the ability to know whether these values are being sensitively dealt with and artistically rendered, all these factors will heighten the aesthetic experience of the enlightened listener. But the aesthetics of music is a more embracing system of values than the analysis of the music itself. The aesthetics of music also has to consider the creative and affective aspects of music because the psychology of art creation and the analysis of artistic appreciation are fundamental aesthetic problems. The aesthetician must also remember that music can only be understood and evaluated in its historical context. The religious and the secular, the political trends of the time and the social beliefs of the people, are necessary for a study of the aesthetics of music.

The creation as well as the enjoyment of music is rooted in the emotions since it is a tonal and rhythmic medium of expression through which the composer conveys his feelings to others. A system of values for an aesthetics of music must therefore be similarly rooted in the emotions, but it also requires from the individual a sensitive musical ear and discerning intellect. The degree of originality and imagination with which the composer expresses himself determines the aesthetic merit of his music. We cannot derive from this music any more than we bring to it in perceptive sensitivity and analytical judgment. Music is born of the emotions to appeal to the emotions. It is received through the senses and evaluated by the intellect. It can have aesthetic value for us only when it is meaningful to us.

The aesthetic merit of a musical composition depends on two things: first, on how well the composer can convey his feelings and moods, either directly to us or through an interpreter; secondly, on the worth of those feelings and moods which are conveyed. But in order that the first feat be accomplished, the listener must be able to recreate what the composer was trying to say. A proper aesthetic reaction depends on whether the listener can recapture the spirit of the original mood. He can do this only through the hearing and intellect, as Aristoxenus maintained. Music can serve as a medium of emotive communication only when one is receptive to those moods and feelings which the composer tried to convey. In the wake of this emotive experience the recipient must then be able to form a discerning judgment on the worth of those feelings and moods in the composition. Since many new musical compositions are often beyond our degree of perceptive tolerance and understanding we can only with effort and patience, over a period of time, form a reasonable judgment of the worth of the feelings and moods in the composition as they are embodied in novel rhythmic and melodic ideas. On the other hand, certain music can have considerable appeal for us in its initial rendition, but it may soon wear thin because it fails to provide us with a stimulus for an aesthetic experience.

The formulation of a value judgment is a conceptual activity. It is a rational process of evaluating the moods and feelings of the composer as he has expressed them in a musical form. It is an intellectual appraisal of the manner in which the formal values of melody, rhythm and harmony have been integrated into a composite musical form. Melody is an expression of feeling. Rhythm animates this feeling. Rhythm is to music what the inexorable law of change in its manifold forms is to nature. Harmony is the blending of these feelings and rhythmic changes into a unified expression that might otherwise have remained individual feelings and diverse rhythms. Mood and feeling are the emotional states. The study of these moods and feelings is an intellectual activity.

In order to evaluate music, a keen perceptive ear must be acquired through training and guidance. Our initial response to music is essentially a subjective one. We bring to it a personal background of varied experiences which have been moulded by our particular religious, cultural and economic environment. If music is capable of inducing an aesthetic experience which fulfills a psychological or social need, then it has definite value as an artistic means of enhancing our daily lives. Music has value only when it is meaningful to its listener. It may have meaning for one person and not for another. The composer, Berlioz, wrote that: "What I find beautiful is beautiful for me, but it may not be so for my best friend." The philosopher, Chesterton, wrote: "Ordinary people dislike the delicate modern work not because it is good or it is bad, but it is not the thing that they asked for." The nature of musical meaning lies in the emotions which are colorfully and imaginatively embodied in rhythmic patterns and harmonic structures. A simple melody or an elaborate theme was originally raw emotion which was formally shaped and colored for the purpose of achieving artistic effectiveness. Music is the consummate blending of feeling and intellect, of content and form. A musical composition is a formal device for communicating feeling and emotion. Our present state of musical illiteracy makes a great part of our musical heritage and most of our new music meaningless to the average public. The communicative worth of music is implicit in the rhythmic and structural character of the composer's score. It can only become explicit when there are performers to interpret it, ears to hear it, and minds to evaluate what the composer was trying to say. One cannot derive from music any more than one brings to it in perceptive acuity and intellectual discernment.

But what values are we to listen for in music? Music above all must have an emotional appeal which can be either immediate or long in coming, for the enjoyment of music is primarily a unique affair of the emotions. Since music is born of the raw emotion which seeks and cannot find release in the hard world of reality, it should contain a colorful transfiguration of moods and feelings which transcend the realm of the immediate. Even when it attempts to be realistically descriptive, it should say usual things in an unusual way or make the ordinary world of tonality sound extraordinary.

The composer's skill is not measured by how well he can recreate natural sounds but how well he is able to embellish natural sounds so that what we have come to take for granted is presented to us in a novel way that will catch our fancy and affect our feelings. A composer's measure of value for us is not how well he imitates sounds and moving phenomena but how well he idealizes these sounds and movements in nature. Ottorino Respighi (1879–1936) breaks the aesthetic mood of his listeners when he stops the music in his score for a natural rendition of a chirping bird on a victrola record. Beethoven retains the musical mood of his listeners when he embellishes the warbling of a bird against a subsiding rain storm in his score. It is a problem as old as Plato who believed that the composer should give a faithful rendition of nature in his music. Aristotle responded by saying that it is not the function of the composer to simply imitate nature in his music as nature is, but to recreate nature in his music in an idealized form. It is not the external appearance of phenomena or the obvious sounds in nature that are important. What is important is the expression of the inner feelings which these sounds provoke in the composer and which he expresses in his music, not as they naturally are, but as the composer conceives them to be. He creates a world of sound more glorious than the one which served as his model.

A musical composition must lend itself to the texture and appropriate range of the voices or instruments for which it is being written. Beethoven wrote for the human voice as though it had the range and flexibility of a violin. Wagner unmercifully pitted the singer against an oversized orchestra. However great the genius of Beethoven and Wagner may be, they are less worthy composers for the voice than they respectively are for the orchestra.

Our contemporary music is often considered to be lacking in aesthetic value because it does not contain suitable melodies for the voice and sustained instrumental themes. The contemporary composer is accused of creating music in a mechanical fashion devoid of melody, and what little melody he does produce is adjudged to be less satisfying than the melodies of the past. Every age has had its traditionalists who complained that the composers of their generation were torturing the singers with unsingable airs and belaboring the instrumentalists with unplayable scores. There are however any number of vocal passages in the romantic Italian operas that are as taxing and inappropriate for the singing voice as there are in contemporary operas. Vocal music which is exhaustively demanding, which strains the normal range of the voice, and which does not consider the textural quality of the voice, is unsuitable music for the voice, whether it was written in the Romantic era or in the present era. This is just as true for instruments as it is for the singing voice. Contemporary composers do produce melodious airs for the voice and instruments which, for obvious reasons, differ from those of the past. The value of these melodies, of the past and the present, depends first, on whether they suit the range of the voice and instruments; and secondly, whether they enable the vocalist and instrumentalist to bring out all the possible musical value that the voice and the instrument are capable of producing according to their nature.

A musical composition must fulfill the purpose for which it was created and originally intended. The Central Committee of the Soviet Union, for example, ruled that the music of the opera *Great Friendship* did not fulfill the purpose for which it was created and intended. The music was complex and did not give a "realistic" representation of the folk-life and music of the region around which the opera was constructed. The composer of this opera, according to the Committee, did not give the Soviet citizen a "true" understanding of the life and culture of a neighboring locale. This opera was therefore a failure educationally and politically. Whether the composer of the opera shared the same point of view privately is questionable. He simply had to abide by the decision of the Committee, that his music had negative ideological value because it did not fulfill the artistic needs of the masses.

In the religious realm, the situation is somewhat similar. Johann Sebastian Bach believed that he was creating music of a profoundly religious tone for the Protestant Service, but his superiors thought otherwise on many occasions. Bach wrote music for the organ that he felt was suitable for a religious atmosphere, but the fact that his contract read that he should not perform music at the Service which would detract from worship, meant that his superiors considered some of his music inappropriate for meditation. As far as they were concerned, Bach's music did not always fulfill the purpose for which it was written.

Music fulfills a purpose in religion and politics according to a criterion of values which is standardized. But it would be wrong to say that only music which is associated with the religious and the political is evaluated in such an objective manner. The Soviets and we would agree that when a composer writes a march, it is expected to be military in character, simple in rhythm and melodically infectious. If a composer creates music for a ballet, the Soviets as well as we would expect the music to be intensely rhythmic and suggestive. These are formal musical requirements that must be met if soldiers are to march to music and ballets are to be performed with music. Since our soldiers march alike and our ballerinas dance alike, our required values for these activities are the same.

When a composer is required to create according to a prescribed set of musical conditions, then the problem of ascertaining whether his music has fulfilled the purpose for which it was written is a relatively simple one. Music, such as this, which is not created as an autonomous art can only be evaluated in terms of function. Music which is autonomous fulfills the purpose for which it was created and intended when it gives the listener an aesthetic experience, that and that alone. The composer fulfills his purpose artistically if his music contains an effective integration of the formal musical values which can evoke an emotional response of an aesthetic nature in the listener.

Stravinsky's *Petrouchka*, *The Fire Bird Suite* and *The Rites of Spring* were written for the ballet. These selections fulfilled the purpose for which they were written with phenomenal success. When these selections are played in the concert hall they are even more sensational as musical masterpieces. This music is of such strength and originality that it serves us well at the ballet and in the concert hall, as does the operatic music of Wagner and Debussy. But ordinarily, music which is written as accompaniment to a ballet, as a march, or as an opera, has a specific purpose to perform and should only be evaluated in those terms. If, however, this music is separated from its subordinate role and is performed as autonomous music, then the measure of the composer's successful fulfillment depends on the personal evaluation of the listener.

A jazz composer also has his scale of formal values which differ from those of a Schönberg. In our evaluation of a jazz selection and a so-called classic work, for example, we should not pit one against the other since the composer's musical intentions were dissimilar. There is good serious music and poor serious music just as there is good jazz and bad jazz. To enjoy one of these styles does not preclude the enjoyment of the other. We take what we can from one or the other to fulfill the needs which either one or both will afford us to enrich our lives. Only a fop would deign to make the distinction that one style is for the masses and the other is for the élite.

Another aesthetic factor which we must include under this consideration is that of musical adaptation and transcription. Beethoven's *Pastoral Symphony*, to cite one instance, was originally intended for and descriptively fulfilled the purpose of portraying nature in symphonic form. But if this score is subordinated to the purpose of a ballet, it no longer conveys the original moods and feelings of the composer. A Bach prelude and fugue for the organ is not the same classic work when it is transcribed for a modern orchestra. Our judgment of these respective works must concern itself with the composer's original intentions and not with the application to which his works are put by others long after the death of the composer.

Music must have an emotional appeal to be of aesthetic value. It must lend itself to the voice and instrument for which it is written. It must fulfill the purpose for which it is intended. Lastly, an advanced musical score should contain a variety of ideas and have unity and balance. A musical score which contains a variety of ideas is potentially richer in aesthetic value than a score which repeats themes monotonously. A good score must contain more than a display of virile ideas, however. These ideas must be skillfully developed and balanced within the context of the complete score. The opera which overemphasizes the solo arias to the detriment of the opera as an artistic entity, is not properly balanced. The symphony which introduces nostalgic melody repeatedly without thematic variation is of less aesthetic value than a symphony in which the melody is thematically developed with a rich variety of ideas.

A musical composition should therefore display a variety of ideas in the development of thematic material. It should be a unity in which the various developments have balance and contrast in their relationship to each other. The greater the amount of harmonic, polyphonic and rhythmic freedom the composer employs, the more adequately can he express his sentiments and feelings. Composition cannot be wholly free, however, for where there is no semblance of order, there is chaos. Freedom in music means exploiting all the tonal and rhythmic possibilities to attain the greatest amount of expression.

A composer has more musical freedom in certain forms than he has in others. He is less restricted in writing for pure music than he is for music with words, where a composer should mould his music in some degree to the rhythm and rhyme of the text. The composer who follows the conceptual meaning of the text religiously will subordinate his music to the text. A composer like Virgil Thomson who has adjusted his music to Gertrude Stein's elusive verbal lines in *Four Saints and Three Acts* and its successor *Mother of Us All*, has gone to the other extreme of ignoring the conceptual meaning of language.

The philosophers of the past, with the exception of Schopenhauer and Nietzsche, stressed the need of articulate language to make the rhythmic flow of musical emotion conceptually meaningful. The religious leaders viewed music as an expedient medium of propagating the word of God. Modern Soviet musical criticism maintains that the composer must not be given to a "one-sided passion for complex forms of instrumental, symphonic, textless music."

Poetry and music are man's two most accomplished artistic forms of communicating his feelings and ideas. Musical feeling and poetic feeling are best expressed in their respective mediums. What may be effective in one medium is apt to be lost if expressed through another medium. When a poetic line or prose sequence and melody are successfully merged so that neither one loses its individuality, but enhance each other, then the composer has achieved a rare artistic merger of provocative forms of human expression.

The composer's moods and thoughts are made known to us through the ability of the performer, the understanding of the conductor. They are the intermediaries between the few mortals who create and those of us who live in awe of the creative spirits who embellish our lives with tonal beauty. The creator and appreciator are both dependent on the performer.

A first rate performer will give us a more faithful rendition of a composer's music than a second rate performer. The former recreates the score in the spirit and style of the composer. His own sensitivity and understanding enables him to fathom the composer's moods and convey them to us. He gets out of the score what he brings to it. He has to feel the composer's music and understand how to convey the nuances and shades of feeling of the music before he can perform it effectively. He can breathe musical life into musical symbols and make the dead and the past live again in rhythm and harmony.

A less talented performer will be unable to stress the musical style of a composer or be sensitive to the subtle demands of the score. He will make little distinction between singing, playing or conducting one master or another. Whatever he will perform will sound monotonously similar. The styles and nuances of different composers will be lost on him for he is incapable of feeling himself into the life and music of the man he is attempting to recreate. Training may help him to observe the mechanical aspects of performing, but in the end he too will only be able to communicate to his listeners what he was able to get out of the music and what he brought to it in sensitivity and understanding. If the latter two faculties are undeveloped, he will remain a craftsman, a technician, but not rise to the level of a musical artist.

The musical symbols which the performer recreates for us

into tonal music is comprised of formal values. These values of rhythmic patterns and harmonic structures embody the composer's feelings and ideas. The task of the performer is to relate these musical moods to us with fidelity. This music will then take on value for us if it evokes a state of feeling of an aesthetic nature that can fulfill psychological and social needs and enhance our prosaic existence. It will afford us temporary release from our immediate surroundings and draw us into a world of fancy in which we can muse and then return refreshed to the main stream of life and action. This does not mean that we should use music solely as an opiate to indulge in personal phantasy. The aesthetic value in music lies in the extent to which we can enter into a common experience or series of experiences with the composer who is portraying the world to us as he sees and hears it. Our lives can be made richer and our existence fuller, because of the art of music.

BIBLIOGRAPHY

Allen, Warren Dwight   *Philosophies of Music History,*
     American Book Co., New York: 1939.

Apel, Willi   *Harvard Dictionary of Music,*
     Harvard University Press, Cambridge: 1945.

Aristotle   *The Basic Works of Aristotle,*
     Edited by Richard McKeon,
     Random House, New York: 1941.

Aristotle   *On the Art of Poetry,*
     With a Supplement *Aristotle on Music,*
     Translated by S. H. Butcher,
     Edited by Milton C. Nahm,
     The Liberal Arts Press, New York: 1948.

Aubry, Pierre   *Trouvères and Troubadours,*
     Translated by Claude Aveling,
     G. Schirmer, New York: 1914.

Bach   *The Bach Reader,*
     Edited by Hans T. David and Arthur Mendel,
     W. W. Norton and Co., Inc., New York: 1945.

Blom, Eric   *Mozart,*
     Pellegrini and Cudahy, New York: 1949.

Bosanquet, Bernard   *A History of Aesthetic,*
     George Allen and Unwin Ltd., London: 1922.

Brown, Calvin S.   *Music and Literature,*
     The University of Georgia Press, Athens: 1948.

Bukofzer, Manfred F.   *Music in the Baroque Era,*
     W. W. Norton and Co., Inc., New York: 1947.

Bukofzer, Manfred F.   *Studies in Medieval and Renaissance Music,*
     W. W. Norton and Co., Inc., New York: 1950.

Carritt, E. F.   *Philosophies of Beauty,*
Oxford University Press, New York: 1931.

Confucius   *The Wisdom of Confucius,*
Translated by Lin Yutang,
The Modern Library, New York: 1938.

Cooper, Lane   *The Poetics of Aristotle,*
Marshall Jones Co., Boston: 1923.

Copland, Aaron   *Music and Imagination,*
Harvard University Press, Cambridge: 1952.

Ducasse, Curt J.   *The Philosophy of Art,*
The Dial Press, New York: 1929.

Einstein, Alfred   *Mozart, His Character, His Work,*
Translated by Arthur Mendel and
Nathan Broder,
Oxford University Press, New York: 1945.

Einstein, Alfred   *Music in the Romantic Era,*
W. W. Norton and Co., Inc., New York: 1947.

Farmer, Henry George   *Historical Facts for the Arabian Musical Influence,*
William Reeves, London: 1930.

Flaccus, Louis W.   *The Spirit and Substance of Art,*
F. S. Crofts and Co., New York: 1941.

Flower, Newman   *Franz Schubert, The Man and His Circle,*
Frederick A. Stokes Co., New York: 1928.

Freeman, Kathleen   *The Pre-Socratic Philosophers,*
Basil Blackwell, Oxford: 1949.

Gilbert, Katherine E. and Kuhn, Helmut   *A History of Esthetics,*
The Macmillan Co., New York: 1939.

Gradenwitz, Peter   *The Music of Israel,*
W. W. Norton and Co., Inc., New York: 1949.

Gray, Cecil   *The History of Music,*
A. A. Knopf, New York: 1931.

Greene, Theodore M.   *The Arts and the Art of Criticism,*
Princeton University Press, Princeton: 1947.

Groves Dictionary of Music and Musicians,
The Macmillan Co., New York: 1946.

Hanslick, Eduard   *The Beautiful in Music,*
Translated by Gustav Cohen,
Novello and Co.: 1891.

Hindemith, Paul   *A Composer's World,*
                         Harvard University Press, Cambridge:
                         1952.

Hospers, John   *Meaning and Truth in the Arts,*
                         University of North Carolina Press,
                         Chapel Hill: 1946.

Idelsohn, A. Z.   *Jewish Music,*
                         Tudor Publishing Co., New York: 1944.

Jaeger, Werner   *Paideia: The Ideals of Greek Culture,*
                         Translated by Gilbert Highet,
                         Oxford University Press, New York:
                         1945.

Kant, Immanuel   *Critique of Judgement,*
                         Translated by J. H. Bernard,
                         Macmillan and Co., Ltd., London: 1914.

Lang, Paul H.   *Music in Western Civilization,*
                         W. W. Norton and Co., Inc., New York:
                         1941.

Langer, Susanne K.   *Philosophy in a New Key,*
                         Mentor Books, New York: 1942.

Langer, Susanne K.   *Feeling and Form,*
                         Charles Scribner's Sons, New York: 1953.

Leibniz   *Philosophical Writings,*
                         Translated by Mary Morris,
                         Everyman's Library,
                         J. M. Dent and Son Ltd., London: 1934.

Leichtentritt, Hugo   *Music, History, and Ideas,*
                         Harvard University Press, Cambridge:
                         1946.

Macran, Henry S.   *The Harmonics of Aristoxenus,*
                         Oxford: The Clarendon Press, London:
                         1902.

Maritain, Jacques   *Art and Scholasticism,*
                         Translated by J. F. Scanlan,
                         Charles Scribner's Sons, New York: 1946.

McKeon, Richard   *Selections from Medieval Philosophers,*
                         Charles Scribner's Sons, New York: 1929.

Mead, Hunter   *An Introduction to Aesthetics,*
                         The Ronald Press Co., New York: 1952.

Munro, Thomas   *The Arts and Their Interrelations,*
                         The Liberal Arts Press, New York: 1949.

Nahm, Milton C.   *Aesthetic Experience and Its Presuppositions,*
                         Harper and Brothers, New York: 1946.

Neiman, Walter   *Brahms,*
Translated by Catherine A. Phillips,
A. A. Knopf, New York: 1929.

Nettl, Paul   *Luther and Music,*
Translated by Frida Best and Ralph
Wood,
The Muhlenberg Press, Philadelphia:
1948.

Newman, Ernest   *Gluck and the Opera,*
Bertram Dobell, London: 1895.

Newman, Ernest   *The Life of Richard Wagner,*
A. A. Knopf, New York: 1933-46.

Newman, Ernest   *The Man Liszt,*
C. Scribner's Sons, New York: 1935.

Newman, Ernest   *Hugo Wolf,*
Methuen, London: 1907.

Nietzsche   *The Philosophy of Nietzsche,*
The Modern Library, New York: 1937.

Oates, Whitney J.   *The Stoic and Epicurean Philosophers,*
Random House, New York: 1940.

Oxford History of Music,
Oxford University Press, London: 1938.

The White List of the Society of St.
Gregory of America, Papal Documents on
Sacred Music, From the 14th to the 20th
Century,
The Society of St. Gregory of America,
New York: 1951.

Parker, DeWitt H.   *The Principles of Aesthetics,*
F. S. Crofts and Co., New York: 1946.

Pater, Walter   *The Renaissance,*
Jonathan Cape, London: 1873.

Plato   *The Dialogues of Plato,*
Translated by Benjamin Jowett,
Random House, New York: 1937.

Plutarch   *Plutarch's Miscellanies and Essays,*
Little Brown and Co., Boston: 1898.

Portnoy, Julius   *Similarities of Musical Concepts in Ancient*
and Medieval Philosophy,
The Journal of Aesthetics and Art Criticism, March, 1949.

Portnoy, Julius   *Platonic Echoes in Soviet Musical Criticism,*
The Journal of Aesthetics and Art Criti-
cism, June, 1950.

Prall, D. W.   *Aesthetic Judgment,*
The Thomas Y. Crowell Co., New York:
1929.

Pratt, Waldo Selden — *The Music of the Pilgrims,*
O. Ditson Co., Boston: 1921.

Rader, Melvin — *A Modern Book of Esthetics,*
Henry Holt and Co., New York: 1952.

Reese, Gustave — *Music in the Middle Ages,*
W. W. Norton and Co., Inc., New York: 1940.

Reese, Gustave — *Music in the Renaissance,*
W. W. Norton and Co., Inc., New York: 1954.

Rimsky-Korsakoff — *My Musical Life,*
Translated by Judah A. Joffe,
Alfred A. Knopf, New York: 1924.

Rolland, Romain — *Handel,*
Translated by A. E. Hull,
Kegan Paul, Trench, Trubner and Co., Ltd., London: 1920.

Sachs, Curt — *The Rise of Music in the Ancient World, East and West,*
W. W. Norton and Co., Inc., New York: 1943.

Sachs, Curt — *The Commonwealth of Art,*
W. W. Norton and Co., Inc., New York: 1946.

St. Augustine — *The Fathers of the Church,* Vol. 2,
Cima Publishing Co., Inc., New York: 1947.

Salazar, Adolfo — *Music in Our Time,*
Translated by Isabel Pope,
W. W. Norton and Co., Inc., New York: 1946.

Schopenhauer — *The Philosophy of Schopenhauer,*
Edited by Irwin Edman,
The Modern Library, New York: 1928.

Schrade, Leo — *Beethoven in France,*
Yale University Press, New Haven: 1942.

Schrade, Leo — *Monteverdi,*
W. W. Norton and Co., Inc., New York: 1950.

Schweitzer, Albert — *J. S. Bach,*
Translated by Ernest Newman,
A. and C. Black, Ltd., London: 1935.

Slonimsky, Nicolas — *Music Since 1900,*
Coleman-Ross Co., Inc., New York: 1949.

Stravinsky, Igor — *Poetics of Music,*
Translated by Arthur Knodel and Ingolf Dahl,

Harvard University Press, Cambridge: 1947.

Strunk, Oliver — *Source Readings in Music History*, W. W. Norton and Co., Inc., New York: 1950.

Taylor, Henry Osborn — *The Medieval Mind*, Macmillan and Co., Ltd., London: 1927.

Thompson, Oscar — *Debussy, Man and Artist*, Dodd, Mead and Co., New York: 1937.

Tolstoy, Leo — *What Is Art?* Translated by Aylmer Maude, Oxford University Press, London: 1946.

Tovey, Donald F. — *Beethoven*, Oxford University Press, London: 1945.

Wagner, Peter — *Introduction to the Gregorian Melodies*, Translated by Agner Orme and E. G. P. Wyatt, The Plainsong and Mediaeval Music Society, London: 1901.

INDEX